GN OMON

T0094504

GNOMON

ESSAYS ON CONTEMPORARY LITERATURE

HUGH KENNER

DALKEY ARCHIVE PRESS

First published by McDowell, Obolensky in 1958.

First Dalkey Archive edition, 2016

Library of Congress Cataloging-in-Publication Data

Names: Kenner, Hugh, author.
Title: Gnomon : essays on contemporary literature / by Hugh Kenner.
Description: First Dalkey Archive edition. | Victoria, TX : Dalkey Archive Press, 2016.
Identifiers: LCCN 2015040756 | ISBN 9781564784308 (pbk. : acid-free paper)
Subjects: LCSH: English literature--20th century--History and criticism. |
American literature--20th century--History and criticism. | Criticism.
Classification: LCC PR474 .K4 2016 | DDC 820.9/0091--dc23
LC record available at http://lccn.loc.gov/2015040756

Partially funded by the Illinois Arts Council, a state agency.

www.dalkeyarchive.com
Victoria, TX / McLean, IL / London / Dublin

Dalkey Archive Press publications are, in part, made possible through the support of the
University of Houston-Victoria and its program in creative writing, publishing, and
translation.

Printed on permanent/durable acid-free paper

**For
Marvin Mudrick**

Contents

GNOMON

Foreword

WHEN THE EMPEROR YAO ASKED VAINLY FOR ONE
man *"qui soigne les choses d'une manière con-
forme à leur nature,"* he was proposing, among other
things, an ideal for the critic. He also sent his astron-
omers into the four corners of the kingdom to watch
the shadows of their gnomons and so, in fixing the sea-
sons, regulate the conduct of the new epoch by the
swing of the sun and stars. The critic who would
render accessible the renovation of intellectual energies displayed by the imaginative writing of the past
fifty years can undertake no less than the astrono-
mers Hi and Houo.

This book is a report on ten years' watching of
shadows, with the results of the attendant calculations. It should not be taken for a collection of definitive estimates; nor on the other hand should conclusions be drawn from gaps in the table of contents,
which are partly accounted for by the existence of
other books, either published or in preparation.

The function of criticism is "the elucidation of
works of art"; from this follows "the correction of
taste." The foundation of criticism is exegesis. This
is generally taken to mean the fussy explication of
matters too small to invite normal attention; but in
its most helpful and perhaps least practiced form it
brings into view outlines too large to be often noticed, so aiding the reader to realize *what* he is reading. Mr. Eliot pointed out that "To His Coy Mistress"

3

has the structure of a syllogism; and the most helpful thing to be said about Shelley's "Ode to the West Wind" is that it pursues for three stanzas the methods of the magical formulae for summoning up a spirit for consultation, by means of a ritual enumeration of the spirit's attributes. Exegesis characteristically cannot be "proved," and requires only the adduction of sufficient exemplification to make clear exactly what the critic means to say. The examples, however, by readers accustomed to the canons of the research paper, are frequently thought to be intended for evidence, and clear assertion assisted by no more than a handful of examples is mistaken for arrogance. Newton is said to have performed an exegesis of the solar system with the aid of one apple; it was no doubt arrogant of him not to wait until the orbits of all the asteroids had been plotted.

The test of exegesis is that it enlightens.

Nothing is duller than someone's opinion, the least informative phase of autobiography. What is commonly called "taste" is a collection of authorized opinions; what is commonly called "criticism" is the provision of authorizations. The wish to know what one will be safe in commending fathers the demand that the critic provide what are called "value judgments." These are commonly ways of saying that Work A does (or does not), or ought to (or ought not to), evoke (in the fit reader) more complex spiritual contortions than Work B; or else they are tips on the current state of the market. Frequently they are just ways of reprimanding other critics. But if the critic's function is to help the reader see what he is reading, then he will pass beyond exegesis in two ways only: by the judgments implicit in his choice of subjects to write about, and the comparisons implicit in any discussion of a particular work's or writer's nature. The latter are best articulated by the technique of unexpected juxtaposition; Vulcan performed a critical act when he exhibited Venus and Mars in a net.

The essays in this book were without exception commissioned at various times by editors who wanted something or other discussed. But though I have not (except in accepting the commissions) altogether chosen my topics, I have chosen what to reprint here. The book concerns itself with those parts of the seminal poetry and prose of the twentieth century which seem at present in greatest need of clarification: the methods of Yeats, Pound, and Dr. Williams, the stature of Wyndham Lewis' last work, the nature of Miss Moore's uniqueness, the patient intelligence of Ford Madox Ford, and what the reader who grasps these qualities will perceive to be the irrelevance or perversity of three or four critical and pedagogical fashions.

Throughout the book there is rotated for the reader's inspection what I take to be the significant life of the mind in the past fifty years. The seminal intellectual activity of this half-century has a character as marked as that of the Augustan Age or the Romantic Movement, more clearly identifiable than that of the Victorian Age (which the Auden-Spender decade somewhat resembles), less elusive than the English Renaissance. It lacks a name; I should call

it, expanding the scope of a term of Lewis', the
Vortex: a shaped, controlled and heady circling,
centripetal and three-dimensional, around a funnel
of calm. It is dissipating at present, as all intellectual
vortices do; but the publication in its very late
phases of such works as *Paterson, Rock-Drill,* and
The Human Age draws attention to the fact that for
the first time since the death of Pope the procedures
of literary creation are again in such adjustment as
to permit the best writers of a time to do their best
work in the later years of a long life.

So spectacular a literary phenomenon has enjoyed, it goes without saying, a peculiarly fructive
relation to the past. I include an essay on Whitman
to indicate some of the bearings of Dr. Williams'
work and the Benton Cantos, and one on Pope to
indicate the nature of the continuity that has been
resumed. In a long historical perspective, the Vortex
is the third of a series of concerted attempts to deal
with certain problems of perception and action which
were presented by the Renaissance and which came
to a focus in the early eighteenth century; my forth-
coming book *The Night World* will elucidate this
statement. Literary history is generally written in
terms of the writer's relation to his readers, and the
absence of a coherent reading public is generally
made to account for the peculiar features of Eliot's
work, or Pound's, or Joyce's. But it is doubtful
whether the relation of writer to reader has ever
been as satisfactory as we like to suppose. The Age
of Pope, the Age of Wordsworth, can hardly have
been recognized as such by more than a few hun-

dred contemporaries; as for Shakespeare, the fact of his pre-eminence was for decades a coterie opinion. It is the good minor writer who suffers from the absence of an identifiable public; and it is not so much the readers that he requires (Andrew Marvell did not even publish his poems), as the confidence lent by the felt existence of diffused, coherent taste. Our century possesses figures comparable to Jonson and Milton, but none comparable to Carew or Marvell, and for that at least "the times" may be blamed.

These essays, or earlier versions of them, have previously appeared in *Shenandoah, Poetry, Hudson Review, Sewanee Review, Perspective, Yale French Studies,* and *Irish Writing,* to the editors and publishers of which I am indebted for permission to reprint and revise. I am grateful to Mr. Fred Siegel of New York City for generously placing at my disposal the results of his industriousness with the Chinese dictionary.

Hugh Kenner
Santa Barbara College,
Santa Barbara, California.

1. The Sacred Book of the Arts

The way out is via the door, how is it no one will
use this method?

—Confucius

1. Catechism

Q: In "Among School Children" we read of a "Le-
daean body." Where are we to seek information
about that?

A: Not from the mythological dictionary, but as
everybody knows, from the poem "Leda and the
Swan."

Q: And where is this poem to be discovered?

A: On the previous page.

Q: Very good. You are on the way to noticing something. Now consider the last stanza of "Among
School Children." After an apostrophe to "self-
born mockers of man's enterprise" we read:

> Labour is blossoming or dancing where
> The body is not bruised to pleasure soul,
> Nor beauty born out of its own despair,
> Nor blear-eyed wisdom out of midnight oil.
> O chestnut-tree, great-rooted blossomer,
> Are you the leaf, the blossom or the bole?
> O body swayed to music, O brightening glance,
> How can we know the dancer from the dance?

That "where" is by its placing in the line made
very emphatic. Its gesture implies a place or a
state intensely real to Yeats. Does he print lines

9

elsewhere that might be taken as descriptive of that place or state?

A: He does; in "Colonus' Praise," after invoking "immortal ladies" who "tread the ground/Dizzy with harmonious sound" (which invocation of course we are meant to connect with "O body swayed to music"), he goes on,

> And yonder in the gymnasts' garden thrives
> The self-sown, self-begotten shape that gives
> Athenian intellect its mastery . . .

the self-born no longer a mocker, body and intellect thriving in unison, neither bruised to pleasure the other; and the miraculous olive-tree that, as he goes on to tell us, symbolizes that perfection, is to be connected with the domestic "chestnut-tree, great-rooted blossomer" of the famous peroration.

Q: Excellent, excellent. And now tell me where, in relation to "Among School Children," this song in praise of Colonus is to be found?

A: On the following page.

Q: You are answering today with admirable point and economy. Now tell me: were the three poems you have mentioned as bearing upon one another written, as it were, simultaneously?

A: I find by the chronology at the back of Mr. Ellman's *Identity of Yeats* that the first was written nearly four years before the last. I notice furthermore that the arrangement of the poems in the volume we are discussing, *The Tower,* is far from chronological. "Sailing to Byzantium"

(Sept. 26, 1926), with which it begins, was written *after* "Among School Children" (June 14, 1926), which is located two-thirds of the way through the book. In between there are poems dating as far back as 1919, and the volume ends with "All Souls' Night," 1920.

Q: We should be lost without these American scholars. You would say, then, that the arrangement of poems within the volume was deliberate rather than casual or merely chronological?

A: I would indeed. But wait, I have just noticed something else. In "Sailing to Byzantium," at the beginning of the book, the speaker has abandoned the sensual land of "dying generations" and is asking the "sages standing in God's holy fire" to emerge from it and be his singing-masters. At the end, in "All Souls' Night," he announces that he has "mummy truths to tell" and would tell them to some mind that despite cannon-fire from every quarter of the world, can stay

Wound in mind's pondering
As mummies in the mummy-cloth are wound.

In the former poem he was calling forth sages to teach him; throughout "All Souls' Night" he is calling up ghosts to hear him. Pupil has become master.

Q: How often must I enjoin precision on you? It is the land of sensual *music* he has left: bird-song, love-songs. "All Souls' Night" opens, by contrast, with the formal tolling of "the great Christ

Church Bell," like the "great cathedral gong"
that dissipates "night walkers' song" in "Byzantium." Furthermore, there is a calling-up of
ghosts near the beginning of the book too, in
the poem called "The Tower," where he sum-
mons them not (as later) to instruct them but
to ask a question. What else have you noticed?

A: Why, it gets more and more deliberate as one
examines it. He began the volume by renouncing
his body; he ends it in the possession of disem-
bodied thought:

Such thought—such thought have I that hold it tight
Till meditation master all its parts . . .
Such thought, that in it bound
I need no other thing,
Wound in mind's wandering
As mummies in the mummy-cloth are wound.

Earlier he had expected to need the body of a
jeweled bird. Through that volume, *The Tower,*
runs a dramatic progression if I ever saw one.
And the presence of such a progression, once it
is discerned, modifies all the parts. Now I have
a theory . . .

Q: Stop, you grow prolix. Write it out, write it out
as an explanation that I may read at my leisure.
And please refrain from putting in many footnotes that tire the eyes.

2. Explanation

"Among School Children," to begin with that
again, is as centrifugal a major poem as exists in the

language. Whoever encounters it out of the context
Yeats carefully provided for it, for instance in an
Anthology Appointed to be Taught in Colleges, will
find himself after twenty minutes seeking out who
Leda was and what Yeats made of her, and identifying the daughter of the swan with Maude Gonne
(excursus on her biography, with anecdotes) and
determining in what official capacity, through what
accidents of a destiny sought and ironically accepted, the poet found himself doubling as school
inspector. So true is this of the majority of his major
poems, that the anthologists generally restrict themselves to his minor ones, his critics practice mostly
a bastard mode of biography, and his exegetists a
Pécuchet's industry of copying parallel passages
from *A Vision* (first and second versions), from letters and diaries, from unpublished drafts, and occasionally from other poems. Even Dr. Leavis calls his
poetry "little more than a marginal comment on the
main activities of his life." Occasionally someone
feels that Yeats' poems need to be reclaimed for the
modern critic's gallery of self-sufficient objects, and
rolling up his sleeves offers to explain "Two Songs
from a Play" without benefit of *A Vision*. This requires several thousand words of quasi-paraphrase.
The least gesture of unannounced originality on a
poet's part suffices to baffle critical presupposition
completely, and the two regnant presuppositions of
the mid-twentieth century—the old one, that poems
reflect lives and announce doctrines, the new one,
that poems are self-contained or else imperfect—
are rendered helpless by Yeats' most radical, most

casual, and most characteristic maneuver: he was an architect, not a decorator; he didn't accumulate poems, he wrote books.

It would have been surprising if he had not, preoccupied as he was with sacred writings. When he functioned as a critic, as in his essay on Shelley or his useful generalizations on Shakespeare, it was the oeuvre, not the fragment, that held his attention.

The place to look for light on any poem is in the adjacent poems, which Yeats placed adjacent to it because they belonged there. And the unit in which to inspect and discuss his development is not the poem or sequence of poems but the volume, at least from *Responsibilities* (1914) to *A Full Moon in March* (1935).[1] This principle is sometimes obvious enough; anyone can see that the six songs following "The Three Bushes" belong in its entourage, or that "The Phases of the Moon" incorporates the half-dozen poems appended to it. Such obvious instances are, however, slightly misleading; one is apt to think of the main poem as not quite completed, raveling out into lyrical loose ends, or not quite definitive in scope, making shift to appropriate, like a handful of minnows, lesser foci of energy that ought to have been brought within its sphere at the time of composition. In the Age of Eliot, the poet is supposed to gather his interests and impulses and discharge them utterly in a supreme opus every so often, and evades this responsibility at the price of being not

[1] It isn't clear how much, if any, of *Last Poems* was arranged by Yeats himself.

quite a major poet. Those weren't the terms in
which Yeats was thinking; we misread him if we
suppose either that the majority of the poems are
casual or that in each he was trying for a definitive
statement of all that, at the time of composition, he
was.

"Men Improve with the Years" looks like an attempt of this kind; it cuts off, of course, too neatly.
The poet was once young, and a lover; now he is a
monument, and no lady will love him. The quality
of the rhetoric is impeccable, but the poem, on some
acquaintance, appears to reduce itself to its mere
theme, and that theme so simple-minded as to invite
biographical eking out. The unspoken premise of
Yeats criticism is that we have to supply from elsewhere—from his life or his doctrines—a great deal
that didn't properly get into the poems: not so much
to explain the poems as to make them rich enough
to sustain the reputation. It happens, however, that
"Men Improve with the Years" has for context not
Yeats' biography but two poems about a man who
did not undergo that dubious improvement: at the
climax of "In Memory of Major Robert Gregory"
we read,

Some burn damp faggots, others may consume
The entire combustible world in one small room
As though dried straw, and if we turn about
The bare chimney is gone black out
Because the work had finished in that flare.
Soldier, scholar, horseman, he,
As 'twere all life's epitome,
What made us dream that he could comb grey hair? . . .

Dried straw, damp faggots; in "Men Improve with
the Years" we discover a "burning youth" succeeded
by water:

> A weather-worn, marble triton
> Among the streams.

Major Robert Gregory, "all life's epitome," concentrated all in an instantaneous conflagration; the
speaker of "Men Improve with the Years" has advanced serially through phases one can enumerate
to the condition of a statue. Statues, of course, have
their immortality, their nobility of arrested gesture.
Yeats isn't being picturesque in specifying the kind
of statue; tritons blow their wreathèd horns, and a
marble one would be puffing soundlessly at a marble
trumpet, like an official Poet; not even in the open
sea, but amid the fountains of Major Gregory's
mother's garden. The poem isn't a small clearing in
which Yeats sinks decoratively to rest, it is a counter-
rhetoric to the rhetorical memorial poem. It doesn't
come quite on the heels of that poem, however; between the two we hear the dry tones of the Irish
Airman ("soldier, scholar, horseman") himself:

> Those that I fight I do not hate,
> Those that I guard I do not love.

Midway between Yeats' contrasting rhetorics, Gregory ("An Irish Airman Foresees His Death") hasn't
a rhetoric but a style. He wasn't exhilarated by the
prospect of consuming "the entire combustible
world"; "a lonely impulse of delight" redeems from
calculation the decision born of an explicit disen-
chantment:

> I balanced all, brought all to mind,
> The years to come seemed waste of breath,
> A waste of breath the years behind
> In balance with this life, this death.

Those are the words from which we pass to these:

> I am worn out with dreams:
> A weather-worn, marble triton
> Among the streams.

—the traditional sonorities, the diction ("my burning youth!"), the conventional elegances of cadence evoking (while just evading) a "literary" tradition against which is poised the next poem in the volume: "The Collarbone of a Hare."

> Would I could cast a sail on the water
> Where many a king has gone
> And many a king's daughter,
> And alight at the comely trees and the lawn,
> The playing upon pipes and the dancing,
> And learn that the best thing is
> To change my loves while dancing
> And pay but a kiss for a kiss.

This live rhythm quickens a remote, folkish idiom, unsonorous and wry. "Men Improve with the Years" seems in retrospect heavier than ever. In this pastoral kingdom not only are there no marble tritons (its tone has nothing in common with that of the Land of Heart's Desire where the Princess Edain was "busied with a dance"), but the newcomer's characteristic gesture is to look back through "the collarbone of a hare" and laugh at "the old bitter world where they marry in churches" with a lunatic

peasant slyness. The symbol of trivial death proffers
a peephole or spyglass; it doesn't, as death is re-
puted to do, open vistas. You can squint with its
aid at the old world, from fairyland. Yeats is trying
out different arrangements of a poetic universe with
the blunt fact of death in it. In the next poem he
reverses the situation and rearranges the perspective. Stretched for nonchalant slumber "On great
grandfather's battered tomb," Beggar Billy sees the
dancing-world: not

>   the comely trees and the lawn,
>   The playing upon pipes and the dancing,

but

>   a dream
>   Of sun and moon that a good hour
>   Bellowed and pranced in the round tower . . .
>
>   That golden king and that wild lady
>   Sang till stars began to fade,
>   Hands gripped in hands, toes close together,
>   Hair spread on the wind they made;
>   That lady and that golden king
>   Could like a brace of blackbirds sing.

This is the celebrated music of the spheres; and
Beggar Billy decides that "great grandfather's battered tomb" that educes such noisy and energetic
visions is no place for him. So the book, having de-
graded its initial persona to beggardom (there are
curious analogies with *Lear*) and preoccupied itself
with themes and images of death until it has set
the celestial boiler shop going, takes leave of this

theme for a time and turns to quieter matters like the dead lovers Solomon and Sheba.

That initial persona now wants looking at. The volume we are examining, *The Wild Swans at Coole*, began not with the Gregory elegy—that is its second poem—but with "The Wild Swans at Coole" itself: an image of personal dejection ("And now my heart is sore") that uses the permanent glory of the swans to silhouette the transience attending human beings who must keep their feet on the ground and try to assimilate the "brilliant creatures" by counting them.

> All's changed since I, hearing at twilight
> The first time on this shore,
> The bell-beat of their wings above my head
> Trod with a lighter tread.
>
> Unwearied still, lover by lover,
> They clamber in the cold
> Companionable streams or climb the air;
> Their hearts have not grown old; . . .

"All's changed" is a mood, not a summary of presented facts; this initial poem confines itself to a wholly familiar *Angst*, a setting documented in a spare but traditional manner—

> The trees are in their autumn beauty,
> The woodland paths are dry—

a specified month and time of day, a poet who does and thinks and feels nothing unusual, verbs no more than inert copulas, and swans that are scarcely more than swans. We are in the presence of a mind reflecting nature and then reflecting Locke-wise upon

what it reflects: tantalized—not teased, but under-
going the pangs of Tantalus—because it must undergo change while nature—the swans—remains
other, "unwearied still." Though none of the great
Romantics could have written it with such economy
and directness, the poem remains within, say, the
Coleridgean orbit of experience.

It is upon experience resignedly ordered in this
plane that the brilliant death of Major Robert, the
Irish Airman, impinges; he took wing like the swans;
his heart has not grown old; he demonstrated that it
lay within human capacity to

> consume
> The entire combustible world in one small room
> As though dried straw.

This death and the contemplation of the poet's impotent middle age ferment and interact throughout
the volume, entoiling other materials, discovering
unexpected resonances in the pastoral mode ("Shepherd and Goatherd") and in the lingering end of
Mabel Beardsley ("Upon a Dying Lady"), never for
long oblivious of the piercing hypothesis that maximum human intensity coincides with human extinction. What is arrived at is an extinction not of the
person but of his natural context. At the end of the
volume October water no more mirrors a natural
sky:

> On the grey rock of Cashel the mind's eye
> Has called up the cold spirits that are born
> When the old moon has vanished from the sky
> And the new still hides her horn.

The mind's eye, no longer the Newtonian optic; and
that moon isn't nature's moon. Nor does the mind's
eye see swans that fly away, but calls up three
arresting figures—one a sphinx—observed not in
placidity but in active intensity:

> Mind moved but seemed to stop
> As 'twere a spinning-top.

> In contemplation had those three so wrought
> Upon a moment, and so stretched it out
> That they, time overthrown,
> Were dead yet flesh and bone.

The poem—and the volume—closes on a note of
triumph; Yeats tells us he "arranged"—deliberate
word—his vision in a song—

> Seeing that I, ignorant for so long
> Had been rewarded thus
> In Cormac's ruined house.

The poles of this volume are its first and last
poems, "The Wild Swans at Coole" and "The Double
Vision of Michael Robartes," as the poles of *The
Tower* are "Sailing to Byzantium" and "All Souls'
Night." Between the observation of the swans and
the vision of the sphinx passes the action of the
book. The crisis occurs when, in "Ego Dominus
Tuus" (which immediately follows the account of
the Dying Lady's heroic arrogance) "Ille" [2] determines to "set his chisel to the hardest stone" and
forget about the kind of self-fulfillment envisaged
by people who tell us that men improve with the

[2] "Willy," commented Ezra Pound.

years. Immediately a long poem devotes itself to the
moon, the faded cliché of a thousand mewling nature poets; and examining it not as they do in the
Irish sky but by way of the sort of diagram one discovers in a penny astrology book, sets the stage for
the double vision of Michael Robartes.

The Wild Swans at Coole is a book about death
and the will. A component poem like "Men Improve
with the Years" will no more pull loose from it than
the "foolish fond old man" speech will pull loose
from *King Lear*. It is a radical mistake to think of
Yeats as a casual or fragmentary poet whose writings float on a current discoverable only in his bio-
graphable life. How much time does he not spend
telling us that he has carefully rendered the mere
events of his life irrelevant!

3. Anti-Nature

Yeats' quarrel with nineteenth-century popular
Romanticism encompassed more than its empty
moons. He turned with increasing vehemence
against a tradition that either laid streams of little
poems like cod's eggs or secreted inchoate epics.
Against the poet as force of nature he placed of
course the poet as deliberate personality, and cor-
respondingly against the usual "Collected Poems"
(arranged in the order of composition) he placed
the oeuvre, the deliberated artistic Testament, a
division of that new Sacred Book of the Arts of
which, Mr. Pound has recalled, he used to talk. It

was as a process of fragmentation, into little people and little poems, that he viewed the history of European poetry, from the *Canterbury Tales* to the Collected Poems of, say, Lord Byron.

> If Chaucer's personages had disengaged themselves from Chaucer's crowd, forgot their common goal and shrine, and after sundry magnifications become each in turn the centre of some Elizabethan play, and had after split into their elements and so given birth to romantic poetry, must I reverse the cinematograph?

The *Canterbury Tales*, it should be recalled, isn't a bloated descant on some epic idea but, like *The Divine Comedy* or *The Wild Swans at Coole*—or *The Cantos*—a unity made by architecture out of separate and ascertainable components. And the cinematograph seemed indeed reversible:

> . . . a nation or an individual with great emotional intensity might follow the pilgrims as it were to some unknown shrine, and give to all those separated elements and to all that abstract love and melancholy, a symbolical, a mythological coherence.

This unity isn't substituted for the existing traditions of poetry, it unites them. Ireland, furthermore, might well be the chosen nation:

> I had begun to hope, or to half hope, that we might be the first in Europe to seek unity as deliberately as it had been sought by theologian, poet, sculptor, architect, from the eleventh to the thirteenth century.

For Ireland had her autochthonous mythology, and

"have not all races had their first unity from a mythology, that marries them to rock and hill?" [3]

It was natural that he should inspect the practice of any discoverable forerunners, and inevitable that he should see himself as standing in the same relation to Irish folklore as Wordsworth to the English folk ballads. One of his own false starts (seduced by this parallel) had been to write ballads; Wordsworth's unreconsidered false start, it must finally have seemed to Yeats, had been to marry only himself and not his race to "rock and hill." Wordsworth had undertaken his work with an insufficient sense of hieratic dedication; for him a poet was only "a man speaking to men" (though a more than usually conscious man), not the amanuensis of revelation. That is why old age overtook not only his body but his speech. *The Prelude* is a narrative of self-discovery, in which the lesson of life, muffled by the automatic grand style, is that knowledge and experience will not synchronize.

Hic: And I would find myself and not an image.
Ille: That is our modern hope, and by its light
        We have lit upon the gentle, sensitive mind
        And lost the old nonchalance of the hand;
        Whether we have chosen chisel, pen or brush,
        We are but critics, or but half create,
        Timid, entangled, empty and abashed. . . .

That is the formula of Wordsworth's decline. As Yeats moved into middle age, the sole survivor of the Rhymers' Club's "Tragic Generation," the paral-

[3] Above quotations from *The Trembling of the Veil*, Book I, Ch. 23–24.

lel between his destiny and Wordsworth's grew
more insistent; had Wordsworth not in the same
way survived for a quarter of a century Keats, Shelley, and Byron, the other members of the last great
wave of creative force? And had he not, assuming
the laureateship, turned into a "sixty year old smil-
ing public man," moving further and further from
the only time in his life when he had been alive,
and lamenting over the dead imaginative vigor of
his boyhood? That is the context of the defiant opening of "The Tower":

> Never had I more
> Excited, passionate, fantastical
> Imagination, nor an ear and eye
> That more expected the impossible—
> No, not in boyhood when with rod and fly,
> Or the humbler worm, I climbed Ben Bulben's back
> And had the livelong summer day to spend.

"Or the humbler worm" is a tip to the reader; it
isn't Yeatsian diction but a parody of Wordsworth's.
Unlike Wordsworth, Yeats the poet has passed sixty
undiminished and needs no man's indulgence.

Wordsworth had developed "naturally," moving
on the stream of nature; and streams run downhill.
For the natural man the moment of lowest vitality
is the moment of death; in the mid-eighteenth century the image of an untroubled decline into the
grave fastened itself upon the imagination of England, and "*Siste viator*" was carved on a thousand
tombstones. "Pause, traveller, whoever thou art, and
consider thy mortality; as I am, so wilt thou one day

be." The traveler came on foot, examined the inscription, and went on his way pondering, his vitality still lower than before. This was one of the odd versions of pastoral sentiment that prepared the way for Wordsworth's career of brilliance and decline; Yeats turns powerfully against it in the Goatherd's song on Major Gregory (see "Shepherd and Goatherd"), more powerfully still in the epitaph he designed for himself. The last division of his Sacred Book closes with an apocalypse, superhuman forms riding the wintry dawn, Michelangelo electrifying travelers with his Creation of Adam, painters revealing heavens that opened. The directions for his own burial are introduced with a pulsation of drums:

> Ún dér báre Bén Búl bén's héad
> In DRUMcliff churchyard . . .

The mise en scène is rural and eighteenth century —the churchyard, the ancestral rector, the local stonecutters; but the epitaph flies in the face of traditional invocations to passers-by:

> *Cast a cold eye*
> *On life, on death.*
> *Horseman, pass by.*

Much critical ingenuity has been expended on that horseman. He is simply the designated reader of the inscription, the heroic counterimage of the foot-weary wanderer who was invited to ponder a *"siste viator"*;[4] the only reader Yeats can be bothered to

---

[4] Though Swift wrote, *"Abi, Viator, et imitare si poteris . . ."* which Yeats paraphrased as "Imitate him if you dare,/World-besotted traveller."

address. And he is not to be weighed down by the realization of his own mortality; he is to defy it.

The life a counterlife, the book not a compendium of reflections but a dramatic revelation, the sentiments scrupulous inversions of received romantic sentiment; what more logical than that Yeats should have modeled the successive phases of his testament on the traditional collections of miscellaneous poems, and (as he always did when he touched a tradition) subverted the usual implications? He dreamed as a young man of creating some new *Prometheus Unbound.* One applauds his wisdom in not attempting that sort of *magnum opus,* but it was not likely that he should forget the idea of a work operating on a large scale. Each volume of his verse, in fact, *is* a large-scale work, like a book of the Bible. And as the Bible was once treated by exegetists as the self-sufficient divine book mirroring the other divine book, Nature, but possessing vitality independent of natural experience, so Yeats considered his Sacred Book as similar to "life" but radically separated from it, "mirror on mirror mirroring all the show." In "The Phases of the Moon," Aherne and Robartes stand on the bridge below the poet's tower, where the candle burns late, and in mockery of his hopeless toil expound, out of his earshot, the doctrine of the lunar wheel. It is clear that they know what he can never discover; they toy with the idea of ringing his bell and speaking

> Just truth enough to show that his whole life
> Will scarcely find for him a broken crust
> Of all those truths that are your daily bread.

It is an entrancing idea:

> He'd crack his wits
> Day after day, yet never find the meaning.

But it is late; Aherne determines to pass up this satisfaction.

> *And then he laughed to think that what seemed hard*
> *Should be so simple—a bat rose from the hazels*
> *And circled round him with its squeaky cry,*
> *The light in the tower window was put out.*

Why is it put out? Because Yeats has finished writing the poem! Aherne, Robartes, the doctrine of the phases, the baffled student, all of them, we are meant suddenly to realize, are components in a book, and so is the man who is supposed to be writing the book. What we see in this mirror, the page, is reflected from that one, "life"; but the parallel mirrors face each other, and in an infinite series of interreflections life has been acquiring its images from the book only that the book may reflect them again. The book, then, is (by a Yeatsian irony) self-contained, like the Great Smaragdine Tablet that said, "Things below are copies," and was itself one of the things below; a sacred book like the Apocalypse of St. John, not like most poetry a marginal commentary on the world to be read with one eye on the pragmatical pig of a text.

"Day after day," Yeats wrote at the end of *A Vision*, "I have sat in my chair turning a symbol over in my mind, exploring all its details, defining and again defining its elements, testing my convictions and those of others by its unity. . . . It seems as if I should know all if I could but banish such memories and find everything in the symbol." On that occasion nothing came; the symbol was perhaps too limited. But the conviction remains with Yeats that a book, if not a symbol, can supplant the world; if not supplant it, perpetually interchange life with it. Nothing, finally, is more characteristic than his dryly wistful account of the perfected sage for whom the radiance attending the supernatural copulation of dead lovers serves but as a reading light:

Though somewhat broken by the leaves, that light
Lies in a circle on the grass; therein
I turn the pages of my holy book.

2. A Note on THE GREAT AMERICAN NOVEL[1]

THE PRETENSIONS INHERENT IN THE TITLE ARE PART of Dr. Williams' theme. The lad who was going to produce "The Great American Novel" as soon as he had gotten his mind around his adolescent experience is part of the folklore of the twenties, and the prevalence of this myth documents the awareness of the young American of thirty years ago that the consciousness of his race remained uncreated. The world of Henry James had always been special, and by now was long vanished; James apart, the job of articulating the American psyche remained about where Whitman had left it. Hence Williams' opening gesture:

> The Great
> American Novel
> CHAPTER I.
> THE FOG.

This is a parody of a beginner's beginning. It is also, though the beginner doesn't really know it, the place such a book should begin, because it is where the subject begins. (*"American poetry,"* the author of *Paterson* remarks, *"is a very easy subject to discuss for the simple reason that it does not exist."*) He continues, weaving in strands of Whitman, empty nature, monosyllabic primitivism, and the

---

[1] William Carlos Williams, *The Great American Novel*, Three Mountains Press (Paris), 1923. Limited to 300 copies.

30

sort of brainless pretentiousness that is really too authentic to be a pretense:

> If there is progress then there is a novel. Without progress there is nothing. Everything exists from the beginning. I existed in the beginning. I was a slobbering infant. Today I saw nameless grasses—I tapped the earth with my knuckle. It sounded hollow. It was dry as rubber. Eons of drought. No rain for fifteen days. No rain. It has never rained. It will never rain.
>
> . . .

A kind of innocence inheres in the attempts of the Thomas Wolfes and Ross Lockridges to swallow and regurgitate America whole. If they or their 1920 forerunners corrupted their material more there would be no point in parodying their gaggings and flounderings:

> Break the words. Words are indivisible crystals. One cannot break them—Awu tsst grang splith gra pragh og bm—Yes, one can break them. One can make words. Progress? If I make a word I make myself into a word. One big word. One big union. Such is progress. It is a novel. I begin small and make myself into a big splurging word: I take life and make it into one big blurb. I begin at my childhood. I begin at the beginning and make one big—Bah.

This maintains a remarkable poise, midway between spoof and earnestness. Yet the tone isn't genial, embracing these extremes, but irascible, polarizing them. The irascibility thrusts two ways, at the thankless job and at the entrail-searching of the Epigoni. The latter aren't disregarded or fended off as irrelevant, because their inchoate state of mind is part of the subject. So is the careful realism of a later para-graph:

> Leaving the room where the Mosquito Extermina-tion Commission had been holding an important fall conference they walked out onto the portico of the County Court House Annex where for a moment they remained in the shadow cast by the moon. . . . Com-ing to the car he said: Go around that side as I will have to get in here by the wheel. . . .

This is fashionable writing of the twenties, a note-book exercise. Its studied awkwardness, however, is in touch not only with journalism but with an au-thentic stratum of experience: a sleepwalking aware-ness of the inconsequential. The European tradition has no idiom for this state of consciousness, endemic among people who spend a great deal of time op-erating machinery.

In the opening pages of the book, in fact, various fashionable techniques and postures are being put to use as subject matter, blocks of verbal material. Here is another specimen:

> . . . Clean, clean he had taken each word and made it new for himself so that at last it was new, free from the world for himself—never to touch it—dreams of his babyhood—poetic sweetheart. No. He went in to his wife with exalted mind, his breath coming in pleasant surges. I come to tell you that the book is finished.
>
> I have added a new chapter to the art of writing. I feel sincerely that all they say of me is true, that I am truly a great man and a great poet.
>
> What did you say, dear, I have been asleep?

This doesn't parody *writing.* "He went in to his wife with exalted mind, his breath coming in pleasant surges": given the mood, a conceivable one, the words couldn't be better. It is the dream of a writer who hasn't written a word, and it parodies certain naïve motives for undertaking authorship which— once more—are part of Williams' subject. One can fancy the bloated abortion this "great man and great poet" might commit; in its place Williams offers a "Great American Novel" in exactly seventy pages of text, with no plot and no hero. And however often Williams prods lyrical themes, the words remain stunned. Though they go through all the motions of taking flight, they never bear the reader aloft. What the lyrical passages are about is ineffectual motions of flight. The afflatus of the young American romantic leads him to seek the elements of his subject in himself: hence the involuted values Williams is able to extract from the convention of a book about a man writing a book. On later pages, having exhausted the romantic's resources, Williams takes stock of a hundred modes of reality and vulgarity, also part of the subject, which no young poet will admit infest his soul.

One reason the words must be stunned is that the American language, or the part of it that interests Williams, is distinguished by a sort of amnesia. Though their colloquial vocabularies are restricted, their syntax simple, and their speech rhythms the reverse of Ciceronian, Americans don't utter a gelatinous Basic English. They have rhythmic and idiomatic means of concentrating meaning in these

counters, shifting the burden of the sentence with
a certain laconic grace from word to word, which
falsifies the unthinking novelist's assumption that
the way to extract the unuttered meanings of American experience is to assist these pidgin gropings with
the fuller cadences of European prose. European
prose, when it attempts to grapple with American
material, yields nothing but suave cliché. At the
beginning of Chapter II a European voice protests,

> *Eh bien mon vieux coco,* this stuff you have been
> writing today, do you mean that you are attempting to
> set down the American background? You will go mad.
> Why? Because you are trying to do nothing at all.
> The American background? It is Europe. It can be
> nothing else. . . .

This mind thinks in phrases, not in words: the up-
ward lilt between its punctuation marks is the signature of a habit of apprehension shaped by Latin
prose. A European would have imparted a more
elegant rhythm to the answering sentence, which
comes with Williams' own unmistakable flatness:

> As far as I have gone it is accurate.

These shadings of "far," "gone," and "accurate"
aren't in a European dictionary: they are imposed
by the tractorlike cadence. "Accurate," in this sentence, has forgotten its Latin past ("L. *accuratus,*
past part. & adj., fr. *accurare* to take care of, fr. *ad*
+ *curare* to take care, fr. *cura* care"). Its stress isn't
verbal, reflecting the care that has been taken, but
attributive, implying a scientific absolute achieved.

That the cadence in which words move controls

the degree of meaning they yield up, and that words
set in Jersey speech rhythms mean less but mean it
with greater finality, is Williams' chief technical perception. It underlies his intricate, inelegant verse
rhythms:

> —an old barn
> is peaked there also, fatefully,
> against the sky. And there it is
> and we can't shift it or change
> it or parse it or alter it
> in any way.

That "fatefully" has force but no plangence; and
"parse" doesn't receive the deliberative stress that
would make it a witty metaphor. It is the odd point-
lessness with which the line division (always Williams' principal instrument) bisects "change/it"
that flattens "parse" and all the adjacent words: a
more delicate feat than it looks.

In *The Great American Novel* Williams' skill at
exorcising from words the "pleasing wraiths of
former masteries" interlocks with a number of aphorisms about the irrelevance of traditional fiction:
"Permanence. A great army with its tail in antiquity.
Cliché of the soul: beauty." . . . "Europe's enemy
is the past. Our enemy is Europe, a thing unrelated
to us in any way." Hence the systematic eschewal
both of pseudo-Aristotelian plot with its stereotyped
climax, and of pseudo-Roman fine writing with its
spurious epithets and cadences. The subject yields
no plot, but it implies a wide range of textures:
Spanish explorers, Southern mountaineers, Aaron
Burr, the Presbyterian minister in Bonnie, Illinois.

No narrative, no analysis, nothing but a suitably balanced sensibility can hold them together. So the "Novel," bringing its lyric phases under progressively stricter control, acquires by cunning trial and error a reliable tone which in the final chapters can handle with a compositor's sureness a surprising variety of materials and effects: from "Particles of falling stars, coming to nothing. The air pits them, eating out the softer parts" to "The Perfection of Pisek-designed Personality Modes: A distinctly forward move in the realm of fashion is suggested by the new personality modes, designed by Pisek . . ."

At the end he returns to surer-footed parody. Coming after a survey of simple beginnings, the last two chapters ("Witness, O witness these lives my dainty cousins") borrow the journalist's congratulatory accents to suggest the apotheosis of commercial dreams:

> I had five cents in my pocket and a piece of apple pie in my hand, said Prof. M. I. Pupin, of Columbia University, describing the circumstances of his arrival in America in the steerage of the steamship Westphalie from Hamburg half a century ago.

One kind of Great American Novel, we remember, was written by Horatio Alger, the authentic folklorist of hustling America.

But the book doesn't close on this note of innocence; the climax, an interview with a successful rag merchant, rounds on Great American Novels and Great America alike:

Why one man made a million before the government stopped him by making cheap quilts.

He took any kind of rags just as they were collected, filth or grease right on them the way they were and teased them up into a fluffy stuff which he put through a rolling process and made into sheets of wadding. These sheets were fed mechanically between two layers of silkolene and a girl simply sat there with an electric sewing device which she guided with her hand and drew in the designs you see on those quilts, you know.

You've seen this fake oilcloth they are advertising now. Congoleum. Nothing but building paper with a coating of enamel.

¡O vida tan dulce!

Fluffy stuff, sheets of wadding, the mechanical patterns: a host of metaphors for shoddy art emerge from a passage which, like the artesian-well page in *Paterson*, achieves its sardonic suggestiveness by observing strictly the forms of simple documentation.

"Sardonic" isn't the right word: even this vulgarity is part of the subject. And since it is the fulfillment commercial America has agreed to prize, it is the fitting climax to an American affirmation:

> And there it is
> and we can't shift it or change
> it or parse it or alter it
> in any way.

3. With the Bare Hands

"**W**HAT SHOULD BE NEW IS INTENT UPON ONE THING, the metaphor—the metaphor is the poem. There is for them only one metaphor: Europe—the past. All metaphor for them, inevitably so, is the past: that is the poem. That is what they think a poem is: metaphor." In the five years during which parts One to Four of *Paterson* were appearing, the fact contained in these words of Dr. Williams rendered the appreciative unusually inarticulate. The poem was respectfully, enthusiastically received, and in unexpected quarters. But it isn't a metaphor, it isn't "about" *something else* (Europe—the past); so it seems undiscussable, except via "the inadequacy of Imagism" or some such trodden detour.

Neither does some familiar modus of meaning inform the novel materials of *Paterson*, nor is it the poet-physician's "view of life" that we are to listen for as we turn its pages. This is writing that by a Jacob's wrestle with words *gets down what happens*—

> they coalesce now
> glass-smooth with their swiftness,
> quiet or seem to quiet as at the close
> they leap to the conclusion and
> fall, fall in air! as if
> floating, relieved of their weight,
> split apart, ribbons; dazed, drunk
> with the catastrophe of the descent
> floating unsupported
> to hit the rocks: to a thunder,
> as if lightning had struck   [Book I:1]

38

—the language never reaching out of its proper dimension, level and solid as ice a foot thick, but
buoyed up by the whole depth and weight of the
profound reality with which it is in contact, and
whose contours it holds fast. This note of reality,
this sense of the poem being in touch with something dense, not something that the writer has densi-
fied by mixing quick-drying ideas with it, is everywhere in the book:

> a bud forever green
> tight-curled, upon the pavement, perfect
> in juice and substance but divorced, divorced
> from its fellows, fallen low—
>
>   Divorce is
> the sign of knowledge in our time,
> divorce! divorce!   [Book I:2]

❁   ❁   ❁

>   While in the tall
> buildings (sliding up and down) is where
> the money's made
>   up and down
>   directed missiles
> in the greased shafts of the tall buildings
> They stand in torpid cages, in violent motion
> unmoved
>   but alert!
>   predatory minds, un-
>   affected
>   UNINCONVENIENCED
>   unsexed, up
> and down (without wing motion) This is how
> the money's made   .   using such plugs
>   [Book IV:1]

Williams tells the story of a lady who wanted to
know "What is all that down in this left hand lower
corner" of a picture she admired and was thinking
of buying. The curator replied, "That, madam, is
paint." "This story marks the exact point in the transition that took place, in the world of that time, from
the appreciation of a work of art as a copying of
nature to the thought of it as the imitation of nature, spoken of by Aristotle in his *Poetics* . . . misinterpreted for over two thousand years and more.
The objective . . . is to imitate nature, which involved active invention, the active work of the
imagination."

> . . . without invention
> nothing lies under the witch-hazel
> bush, the alder does not grow from among
> the hummocks margining the all
> but spent channel of the old swale,
> the small foot-prints
> of the mice under the overhanging
> tufts of the bunch-grass will not
> appear: without invention the line
> will never again take on its ancient
> divisions when the word, a supple word,
> lived in it, crumbled now to chalk.   [Book II:1]

The invention that arranges the "paint" is fed by
preoccupation with dense fact. Williams has spent
some forty years listening to people talk, respecting
them, becoming them:

> Who are these people (how complex
> the mathematic) among whom I see myself

in the regularly ordered plateglass of
his thoughts, glimmering before shoes and bicycles?
They walk incommunicado, the
equation is beyond solution, yet
its sense is clear—that they may live
his thought is listed in the Telephone
Directory—

He has a sense of that unique thing, the American
community, a community built upon no past or fragments of a past, permeated by a dielectric that all
but baffles communication, united by symbols held
unexpectedly in common, parodying itself in its
every printed word; not the remnants of former
order the best modern poetry has learned to express
by using shards of older forms, the "unreal city" of
The Waste Land or the spezzato paradise of *The
Cantos*, not a great order smashed but a new one so
far voiceless

How to begin to find a shape—to begin to begin
again,
turning the inside out: to find one phrase that will
lie married beside another for delight   .   ?
—seems beyond attainment   .

*American poetry is a very easy subject to discuss for
the simple reason that it does not exist*

*   *   *

—of this, make it of *this*, this
this, this, this, this   .

*   *   *

—in a hundred years, perhaps—
the syllables
           (with genius)
                        or perhaps
two lifetimes

Sometimes it takes longer   .
                              [Book III:3]

Europe seems *there*, comprehended, more grasp-
able than America because it has a literature, a
provincial literature as well as the literature of the
Great Record that extends from Homer. American
literature has been with insignificant exceptions a
provincialized pastiche of the provincialisms of Europe: Europe's puritanism (New England), Europe's
mildewed grandeur (the South). Even Whitman,
the democracy snob, was an enlarged Byron, wel-
coming all men as fellow-aristocrats in the *Song of
Myself* and shaking the dust of the past from his
feet.

Hart Crane was another spiritual alien. Frost's
sense of community is rudimentary. Dr. Williams is
the first American writer to discover, not the phases
of America that reflect what was in Europe, but the
core of America that is itself, new, and so far un-
vocal. His sense of community is neither sociological
nor sentimental. Paterson, N.J., provides him neither
with cases for scrutiny nor with a background for
lyrical performance. One cannot, in a given passage,
zone out the compassion and the astringency. They
fuse to lead the reader, clue-like, into the unique
"feel" of the material. "A reply to Greek and Latin

with the bare hands," the author notes in an epigraph:

> To make a start,
> out of particulars
> and make them general, rolling
> up the sum, by defective means—
>
>   *   *   *
>
>   and the craft,
> subverted by thought, rolling up, let
> him beware lest he turn to no more than
> the writing of stale poems . . .
> Minds like beds always made up,
>   (more stony than a shore)
> unwilling or unable.

Because he is content to have devoted a lifetime to making a start, he gets the start made. *Paterson* expresses much more than its author's clinical individuality. From beneath the fractured words, the violences, the voiceless impasse of the mill-town citizen—

> Blocked.
>   (Make a song out of that: concretely)
> By whom?

—comes straining the ache of the mind, what the numb gestures would mean and the null words would express, straining to transcend the febrile "self-expression" that the citizen has become convinced he ought to want to intend:

>   in the pitchblende
>   the radiant gist

"Day in day out," writes Dr. Williams in his *Autobiography* (p. 359), "when the inarticulate patient struggles to lay himself bare for you . . . so caught off balance that he reveals some secret twist of a whole community's pathetic way of thought, a man is suddenly seized again with a desire to speak of the underground stream which for a moment has come up just under surface. . . . We begin to see that the underlying meaning of all that they want to tell us and have always failed to communicate is the poem, the poem which their lives are being lived to realize. No one will believe it. And it is the actual words, as we hear them spoken under all circumstances, which contain it. It is actually there, in the life before us, every minute that we are listening, a rarest element—not in our imaginations but there, there in fact." From the words that are going in at our ears "we must recover underlying meaning as realistically as we recover metal out of ore." The radiant gist: hence the long section of Book IV devoted to the heroism of the Curies

> A dissonance
> in the valence of Uranium
> led to the discovery
>
> Dissonance
> (if you are interested)
> leads to discovery   [Book IV:2]

The poem that is beneath the words doesn't localize, it inheres in the design of the whole. Its controlling image is the roar of the Paterson waterfall:

A false language. A true. A false language pouring—a
language (misunderstood) pouring (misinterpreted)
   without
dignity, without minister, crashing upon a stone ear.

                                     [Book I:1]

                ❋   ❋   ❋

These terrible things they reflect:
the snow falling into the water,
part upon the rock, part in the dry weeds
and part into the water where it
vanishes—its form no longer what it was: . . .

the whole din of fracturing thought
as it falls tinnily to nothing upon the streets   [Book I:2]

                ❋   ❋   ❋

     The language   .   words
without style! whose scholars (there are none)
  .   or dangling, about whom
the water weaves its strands encasing them
in a sort of thick lacquer, lodged
under its flow   .   [Book II:3]

The scholars dangle; but there are other lives. A
bewildered woman plummeted in; Sam Patch in the
1820s dove repeatedly into chasms, master of the
technique of communion, until the day of the exhibition jump when technique failed: "But instead of
descending with a plummet-like fall his body wav-
ered in the air—Speech had failed him. He was
confused. The word had been drained of its meaning. . . ."

Patch leaped but Mrs. Cumming shrieked
and fell—unseen (though
she had been standing there beside her husband half
an hour or more twenty feet from the edge).

:a body found next spring
frozen in an ice-cake; or a body
fished next day from the muddy swirl—

both silent, uncommunicative   [Book I:2]

This roar, this speech to which Dr. Williams
listens that he may make a replica—

I must
find my meaning and lay it, white
beside the sliding water: myself—
comb out the language—or succumb
[Book III:3]

—is modern cousin to the murmur that fills books:

A cool of books
will sometimes lead the mind to libraries
of a hot afternoon, if books can be found
cool to the sense to lead the mind away.

For there is a wind or ghost of a wind
in all books echoing the life
there, a high wind that fills the tubes
of the ear until we think we hear a wind,
actual   .
to lead the mind away
[Book III:1]

They murmur and draw us down the wind, while
the falls roar; or they may lead us back to the pres-

ent, not quite to the falls but to the roar of the stream in our own minds:

> a reverberation
> not of the falls but of its rumor
> unabated
> [Book III:1]

Eliot goes unforgiven by Dr. Williams for giving poetry back to "literature" ("Europe—the past")— the wind of books and the rumor of the falls in the mind—just when the breakthrough to direct perception of the present, the actual falls in the stream, had seemed possible. The burning of the library in Book III is a complex image; it is part impatience with books, part purgation of them, part an image of live reading, a lending of blood and heat to the past (no longer "cool to the sense") as Pound, in parable of his own translator's activities, portrayed Odysseus serving blood to the ghosts in Canto I.

> Awake, he dozes in a fever heat,
> cheeks burning   .   .   loaning blood
> to the past, amazed   .   risking life.

> ❋   ❋   ❋

> The pitiful dead
> cry back to us from the fire, cold in
> the fire, crying out—wanting to be chaffed
> and cherished
>   those who have written books

> We read: not the flames
> but the ruin left
> by the conflagration

Not the enormous burning
but the dead (the books
remaining). Let us read

and digest: the surface
glistens, only the surface.
Dig in—and you have

a nothing, surrounded by
a surface, an inverted
bell resounding, a

white-hot man become
a book, the emptiness of
a cavern resounding.   [Book III:2]

Here we have the metaphoric clue to Williams'
celebrated "opacity," his eschewal of sonorities and
reverberations, of words exploited for the sake of
their "tentacular roots." A poem is a solid surface,
hollow, ringing; "depth" is an illusion. The most
startlingly successful imaginative leap in *Paterson*
is the page-long tabular record of specimens found
in the boring of an artesian well, ending with the
attempt abandoned, "the water being altogether
unfit for ordinary use. . . . The fact that the rock
salt of England, and of some of the other salt mines
of Europe, is found in rocks of the same age as this,
raises the question whether it may not also be found
here." This is in the section about finding language;
perhaps we were wrong to look for water; perhaps
there is rock salt under the Passaic; the European
analogy raises a possibility, not a prescription. In
the next book, however, comes an interpolation in
the unmistakable idiom of an old friend of the

poet's: ".   just because they ain't no water fit to drink in that spot (or you ain't found none) don't mean there ain't no fresh water to be had NO-WHERE . ." The table of well-bore specimens carries all this thematic weight by not seeking to be more than itself, by not being cramped into a metaphor. "Reverberation" will arise of itself from a bell with a hard enough surface; the surface is the poet's level of concern. Synthetic plangency is an illusion, a tampering with the reader's responses. Such incantations "lead the mind away" from the dissonant actual roar. They would introduce into Williams' poem a past not his past, or impose a rhythm which he does not hear but which the tranquil (conventional) mind would prefer to find.

> As Carrie Nation
> > to Artemis
> > > so is our life today   .

> They took her out West on a photographing expedition
> > to study chiaroscuro
> > > to Denver, I think.
> Somewhere around there   .
> > > > the marriage
> was annulled. When she returned
> > > with the baby
> > > > > openly
> taking it to her girls' parties, they
> > > > were shocked

> —and the Abbess Hildegard, at her own
> funeral, Rupertsberg, 1179
> had enjoined them to sing the choral, all

women, she had written for the occasion
and it was done, the peasants kneeling
in the background   .   as you may see

This is from Book IV; by so late in the poem, Dr.
Williams has so thoroughly presented the actual
Paterson world that he can afford to insert one
measuring point from the European past without
sentimental nostalgia. Similarly the unrhymed qua-
trains near the end of Book III ("On this most voluptuous night of the year") are presented not as a
climax but as a powerful undertow, the easy way
out of a poetic dilemma:

> Be reconciled, poet, with your world, it is
> the only truth!
>
> Ha!
>
> —the language is worn out
>
> And She—
> You have abandoned me!
>
> —at the magic sound of the stream
> she threw herself upon the bed—
> a pitiful gesture! lost among the words:
> Invent (if you can) discover or
> nothing is clear—will surmount
> the drumming in your head. There will be
> nothing clear, nothing clear
>
> He fled pursued by the roar.

Hence we find him in his bewilderment

—saying over to himself a song written
previously   .   inclines to believe
he sees, in the structure, something
                    of interest:

On this most voluptuous night of the year
the term of the moon is yellow with no light
the air's soft, the night bird has
only one note, the cherry tree in bloom

makes a blur on the woods, its perfume
no more than half guessed moves in the mind. . . .

Replying, in the pioneer fashion, "to Greek and
Latin with the bare hands," he must invent rhythms,
a measure, images, the whole articulation of a comprehensive poem; it is the struggle to do this that
the poem dramatizes, and in dramatizing succeeds
in doing. Everyone struggles, the roar is in everyone's ears, everyone in Paterson must either strive
as the poet does, or merge himself with the stream
in some direct despairing way like Patch and Mrs.
Cumming, or remain "blocked."

"With the bare hands" is to some extent over-
stated. If there are "no ideas but in things," yet
"Stones invent nothing, only a man invents." Williams draws on other inventors: Pound who in cutting *The Waste Land* and building *The Cantos* revised our concept of poetic structure, Joyce who
fused a man and a city and spent his life in astringent, compassionate cataloguing of banalities so as
to set them down and force them to utter the poetry
they ordinarily short-circuit. The very title is a

Joycean pun: Paterson is a city, a man (sometimes
a doctor), and Pater-son, the molecule of generative
succession.

Generative succession carries the poem forward
from the elemental male and female forms of the
opening through the days when

> the breathing
> spot of the village was the triangle square
> bounded by Park Street (now lower Main Street)
> and Bank Street

to the day ("October 10, 1950") when the twentieth-century poet contemplates the running-out of
his particular experience to the sea:

> Yet you will come to it, come to it! The
> song is in your ears, to Oceanus
> where the day drowns   .
>
> No! it is not our home.
>
> You will come to it, the blood dark sea
> of praise. You must come to it. Seed
> of Venus, you will return   .   to
> a girl standing upon a tilted shell, rose
> pink   .
>   Listen!
>
> Thalassa! Thalassa!
>   Drink of it, be drunk!
>   Thalassa
> immaculata: our home, our nostalgic
> mother in the dead, enwombed again
> cry out to us to return   .
>   the blood dark sea!

nicked by the light alone, diamonded
by the light   .   from which the sun
alone lifts undamped his wings
                    of fire!
                                [Book IV:3]

The penultimate image is not a merging and death,
but a dryly circumstantial rebirth; a man who
emerges from bathing, slides "his shirt on overhand
(the/sleeves were still rolled up)" and heads inland,
followed by his dog. The finale to Book IV with fine
inclusive irony gathers up Sam Patch, Mrs. Cumming, the violent who have recurrently illustrated
"a poverty of resource," the fade-out of an American
movie, the end of *The Hollow Men* (Fawkes on the
scaffold, "not with a bang"), and for better or worse
(*"La Vertue/est toute dans l'effort"*) the enterprise
of the poem itself:

John Johnson, from Liverpool, England, was con-
victed after 20 minutes conference by the Jury. On
April 30th, 1850, he was hung in full view of thousands who had gathered on Garret Mountain and
adjacent house tops to witness the spectacle.

This is the blast
the eternal close
the spiral
the final somersault
the end.

An image which Dr. Williams doesn't use in the
poem but which his whole career as physician and
poet urges on the attention, recommends itself as

the most adequate basis for summary and praise:
the obstetrician devoting in a few critical moments
his every wile, his concentration, so far as his capacity allows, of the entire tradition of medical science since Hippocrates, to the deliverance, with his
bare hands, into independent life of something he
did not make, the identity of which he unshakeably
respects, and which but for his ministrations would
die voiceless.

4. Dr. Williams Shaping His Axe

D R. WILLIAMS, INFINITELY SYMPATHETIC WITH THE
purposefulness of earnest coteries, is our cham-
pion contributor to the least-known magazines, into
which he empties his mind of its current obsessions.
Since he hasn't been all these years painfully developing a system (which means trimming one's
later ideas to fit the earlier ones: "order that cuts
off the crab's feelers to make it fit into the box"):
hasn't feared to risk in his fifties and sixties the kinds
of false starts that don't matter in one's twenties;
and has kept his mind at the moment of writing
fixed on some object or other that looms as oppres-
sively as the cat's head in the primitive painting ("a
cat with a bird in his mouth—a cat with a terrifying
enormous head, enough to frighten birds")—for all
these reasons random samples of his fugitive writings, gleaned from such copies of equally fugitive
magazines as come one's way, are apt to prove un-
fortunate. Hence the impression (on what has been
to date necessarily imperfect acquaintance) of a
bush-league avant-gardist, one foot still in the 1920s,
apt to be sent gaga by the latest surrealist. His tone
isn't soothing; he is himself the archetypal six-foot
cat's head; even when he makes an appearance
among the statuary of more securely capitalized
publications, virtually put on his honor not to
frighten the birds, commissioned for instance to review Shapiro's *Essay on Rime,* he is apt to throw

his overcoat onto the grand piano ("I hadn't prepared a damn thing"[1]) and begin—

> Suppose all women were delightful, the ugly, the
> short, the fat, the intellectual, the stupid, the old—
> and making a virtue of their qualities . . . made
> themselves available to men, some man, any man,
> without greed! . . . Take for instance the fat: If she
> were not too self-conscious, did not regret that she
> were not lissome and quick afoot, but gave herself,
> full belly, to the sport! What a game it would
> make! . . .

The man who jammed a notion like that into the
Kenyon Review can be credited with having extended our notions of the possible, but hardly with
an Eliotic platform manner. It is no wonder that he
isn't known as a major critic, especially since he
doesn't specialize in putting into hierarchies an
array of poems closed off forty years ago (Wyndham Lewis' "Dead arrangements by the tasteful
hand without") but concentrates on the *nature* of
writing, especially the writing that somebody ought
to be doing right now. No critic senses more ur-
gently the immediate relevance of his subject to
this year's necessary activities.

Poetry, for him, keeps thought clean; not by what
is vaguely called "the humanizing influence of literary studies" but by virtue of *what it says,* on the
rare occasions when the writing is sufficiently good.
Just any poetry won't do; the sea contains many
billionfold more water than it does whale, but that
is no reason for confusing the two. Dr. Williams

[1] Cf. his 1950 lecture at U.C.L.A.: *Autobiography,* p. 386.

writes to defend critic and practitioner alike against "belief in a complicated mystery of approach fostered by those who wish nothing done."

> The trick is delay; to involve the mind in discussions likely to last a lifetime and so withdraw the active agent from performance. The answer is, an eye to judge.—When the deer is running between the birches one doesn't get out a sextant but a gun—a flash of insight with proof by performance—and let discussion follow. If the result is a work of art the effect is permanent.

Amid boulders his shots often ricochet; this wouldn't happen if he were pelting his quarry with grapes, but it has condemned a good deal of his prose to mere eccentricity. In retrospect, fortunately, Williams can be trusted to identify his solid critical achievements, though unlike Pound and Eliot he hasn't up to now troubled to keep them pruned and in circulation. His *Selected Essays*—a collection of pieces that should have been widely known years ago (the gist of the book lurks in passages written before 1939, and the contents date from 1920) ought to scatter a good many pigeons. Its advent is nicely timed to disturb the afternoon peace of a bureaucracy that has lately been supposing all the major criticism of the present time to be well known and sifted, the orthodoxies established, the hammocks slung, the returns in, and nothing to do but execute philosophical doodles—pointless as freshman themes—while the grad students work at tabulations. Williams has the timely virtue of being sufficiently aphoristic to focus attention—on his clumps of words, not on the phases of some wafty argument—and the conjoint virtue of having coined aphorisms as little suitable for ruminative mastication as so many bricks:

. . . the usual "poem," the commonplace opaque board covered with vain curlicues. . . .

. . . the coining of similes is a pastime of very low order, depending as it does upon a merely vegetable coincidence. . . .

. . . beauty . . . truth incompletely realized. . . . The beauty that clings to any really new work is beauty only in the minds of those who do not fully realize the significance. . . .

His best insights, like Mr. Eliot's, whom he admirably complements, coagulate into aphorisms; with this difference, that to qualify Williams' obiter dicta one needs a cold chisel, not a scalpel. He isn't adjusting his absolutes to existing frailty; by and large, he is talking about writing so good it hasn't been done yet. His knowledge of what it will be like if anyone succeeds in doing it sustains his intensity of statement. Aspects of this unwritten writing he discerns in the contemporary work that interests him, work which he subjects (amid tut-tuts from the glowworms) to a scrutiny implacable as an electric furnace. The writing of this half-century will not find a more tenacious reader. Where Mr. Pound reads his contemporaries to find out if they are alive, and Mr. Eliot to see if they merit introductions, Dr. Williams reads and rereads them to find out what they mean. He tells his young contemporaries the simple truth: that he has "a will to understand them that they will not find in many another."

"The goal of writing is to keep a beleaguered line of understanding which has movement from breaking down and becoming a hole into which we sink decoratively to rest." Hence the virtual nonexistence of quotations in Williams' critical essays. He abhors the notion that the essential poetic *movement* can be represented by one or two of the points it traverses: as though a railway system were judged by its station architecture. This abhorrence sets him squarely against the tendency—not the principle— of nine-tenths of modern criticism: against the idea, originally a classroom strategy, that the poem is *in* a few of its detachable parts; that it consists of gems, for the sake of which it exists, united by neutral bits; that one ponders this image (what does it mean?), this image, and this image, and stops with a sum of images. The whole incorruptible bulk of Williams' critical achievement is dropped squarely athwart the beaten track of the ants.

It is not to be supposed that for details he substitutes "ideas."

> It is in the minutiae—in the minute organization of the words and their relationships in a composition that the seriousness and value of a work of writing exist—*not* in the sentiments, ideas, schemes portrayed.
> It is here, furthermore, that creation takes place. It is not a plaster of thought applied.

His point is that instances of this "minute organization" can't be as readily detached from the whole composition's trajectory as we have been led to suppose. What takes place in a work of art is not an accumulation of beauties but "an alertness not to let go of a possibility of movement in our fearful bedazzlement with some concrete and fixed present."

Eschewing quotations, then, his method—which less skillful hands would be ill advised to imitate—is to exercise his inventive faculty and write a solid piece of prose which will serve as a sort of equivalent for "what this writer's work amounts to." This doesn't, in his practice, mean going back to Sainte-Beuve or Saintsbury. It means an intense concentration on the intentions implied by the subject, not on the urbanities of a public-relations job. Occasionally Williams thinks into the subject perfections probably not inherent in it; when he does this, as in the remarkable essay on Gertrude Stein, the result is not silliness but illumination not so much of Miss Stein as of the nature of writing. He notes, for instance, that

> Music could easily have a statement attached to each note in the manner of words, so that C natural might mean the sun, etc., and completely dull treatises be played—and even sciences finally expounded in tunes.

Solid writing, however, tends to use the word "as reality" rather than "as symbol":

> Bach might be an illustration of movement not suborned by a freight of purposed design, loaded upon it as in almost all later musical works; statement unmusical and unnecessary. Stein's "they lived very gay then" has much of the same quality of movement

to be found in Bach—the composition of the words determining not the logic, not the "story," not the theme even, but the movement itself. As it happens, "They were both gay there" is as good as some of Bach's shorter figures.

Stein is a laboratory example; turning his method to writing one willingly rereads, Dr. Williams has produced, for instance, the only enlightening pages in print on Marianne Moore, and the meatiest comments on *A Draft of XXX Cantos* ever written. His ability to drive a spike with one blow helps single him out from the critics one wonders whether to take seriously or not. He writes when he knows what there is to be said, and conveys his gists without periphrasis. Of the Greek quotations in *The Cantos* ("knowing no Greek, I presume they mean something") he divines correctly, "They are no particular matter save that they say, There were other times like ours—at the back of it all." When the Ur-critics of *XXX Cantos* were fussing about Pound's pedantry or his aestheticism, Williams was staring hard at Pound's theme. Twenty-four years before *Rock-Drill* he defined it: "A closed mind which clings to its power—about which the intelligence beats seeking entrance": bull's-eye with one shot.

Preoccupied not by the standards of traditional excellence with which Pound, to the confusion of most readers, retains contact, but by his own hard-won perception of the nature of a responsible modern American poet's job, Williams wasn't alarmed whenever Pound stopped imitating a Grecian nightingale. He was able to see the early Cantos as if the

Van Buren and Adams sequences had already existed, classicism not an inert norm but a key-signa-
ture, one of several, controlling the movement of the
poet's intelligence.

> It is beside the question in my opinion to speak of
> Pound's versification as carefully and accurately meas-
> ured. . . . His excellence is that of the maker, not the
> measurer. . . .
>
> That is why he can include pieces of prose and
> have them still part of a *poem*. . . .

That is also, he might have added, why Pound
could include pieces of "poetry." When *Eleven New
Cantos* at length appeared, Williams had nothing to
unsay:

> There is a good deal to say about money in this
> series, 9 per cent, thousands, millions of cash and the
> ways of men with it—to the exclusion of love. And
> love. . . .
>
> It is the poet who has digested the mass of impedi-
> menta which the scholar thinks to solve by sinking
> up to his eyes in it and shouting that he has found it.

In the earlier Pound essay (1931) he noted,

> Pound's "faults" as a poet all center around his ran-
> cor against the malignant stupidity of a generation
> which polluted our rivers and would then, brightly,
> give ten or twenty or any imaginable number of mil-
> lions of dollars as a fund toward the perpetuation of
> *Beauty*—in the form of a bequest to the New York
> Metropolitan Museum of Art.
>
> In America this crime has not been spread over a

period of centuries, it has been done in the last twenty
or twenty-five years, by the single generation, fifteen
or twenty-five years older than I am, who have held
power through that slobbery period.

This suggests the co-ordinates of Williams' rancor
against "Beauty," his abnegation of poetic attempts
to secure it, and his suspicion of every proposal to
endow it—expensive universities, for instance, "for
the propagation of something that passes for the
arts," which he consigns to the bottom of a list of
amenities beginning with dog hospitals, canine cem-
eteries, and Palm Beach. "Beauty at its best seems
truth incompletely realized"; and to use "beautiful"
language "is to confess an inability to have penetrated with poetry some crevice of understanding;
that special things and special places are reserved
for art, that it is unable, that it requires fostering.
This is unbearable."

What fascinates him about Marianne Moore is
that while she is undeniably choosing the things she
puts into her poems, the principle of choice has no
relation to a notion of beauty inherent in the materials. "The baby glove of a Pharaoh can be so presented as to bring tears to the eyes," but Miss Moore
doesn't deal in baby gloves (Williams is careful to
say that her poems wouldn't *therefore* be bad if she
did). What Miss Moore does deal in is actions, intellectual progressions, the mind moving freely "unen-
cumbered by the images or the difficulties of
thought. In such work there is no 'suggestiveness,'
no tiresome 'subtlety' of trend to be heavily fol-

lowed, no painstaking refinement of sentiment." Sentiments are blocks of emotional stuff; the poet envisaged by Dr. Williams doesn't pause to refine what he encounters in transit, he passes through it like an x-ray. "A poem such as 'Marriage' is an anthology of transit. It is a pleasure that can be held firm only by moving rapidly from one thing to the next. It gives the impression of a passage through. There is a distaste for lingering, as in Emily Dickinson."

This is not only an admirable statement of Miss Moore's quality, it implies, once we remove the coloration of the particular example, a poetic of great interest. Though poems, for Dr. Williams, have a mode of being which differs from that of raw experience, they don't thereby inhabit a zone on the lower borders of the supernatural. Though the mystical quality "still seems to many the essence of poetry itself," poetry is a secular art, deriving its illuminations directly from the quality of the mind that has done the work. "There is a 'special' place where poems, as all works of art, must occupy, but it is quite definitely the same place as that where bricks or colored threads are handled." Since the poem is itself a force, it won't, while it remains chaste, incorporate objects by force. Though the characters, as Aristotle said, are included only for the sake of the action, we demand assurance that they are acting and not being pushed, and in the same way should demand images that aren't being conscripted. Again Miss Moore supplies the illustration: in her poems

. . . an apple remains an apple whether it be in
Eden or the fruit bowl. . . .

"dazzled by the apple"

The apple is left there, suspended. One is not made
to feel that as an apple it has anything particularly
to do with poetry or that as such it needs special
treatment, one goes on. Because of this the direct
object does seem unaffected . . . free from the
smears of mystery. . . .

These remarks are as valuable as Mr. Eliot's on
the metaphysical poets: which prompts the reflection that nine-tenths of Eliot's vastly influential
criticism is concentrated in a dozen or so formulations, some of them dangerously succinct and memorable, that have started people thinking, and frequently been applied with clumsy enthusiasm to all
sorts of locks they were never intended to open. The
home-made quality of Dr. Williams' mental furnish-
ings, if it wants ease, fends off glibness; it should be
evident that his *Selected Essays* probably contains
as many radioactive deposits as Mr. Eliot's book of
the same title, and that they really are intended to
be useful generalizations, not *ad hoc* formulations
(like the famous sentence about the objective correlative) which some readers allow the pervasive
urbaneness to invest with inappropriate universality.
Critical books also contain outcroppings of less valuable minerals, and of these Williams probably offers
a higher concentration per ton of rock fill than does
his eminent rival. His remarkable essay on "The
American Background," though not untinged with

crankiness, should be required reading for anyone
interested in American writing; Mr. Eliot on com-
parably panoramic topics (Humanism, for instance,
or Modern Education and the Classics) is after
twenty-odd years chiefly interesting to students of
Mr. Eliot. The mind behind Williams' book is probably not less catholic, though certainly less urbane;
to say that Matthew Arnold wouldn't have understood him is to bring out strength and weakness together. Against his impatience with much of the literary past one can weigh Eliot's rank incuriosity
concerning the present. If Williams ignores Donne
and is suspicious of Dante, Eliot was unable to say
why he found the later Joyce impressive, and
wrote of *The Cantos* that Pound's belief that they
meant something was sufficient for him. There can
be no question of the one writer superseding the
other. But we are not likely to find two valuable
critics each so perfectly the other's complement.

5. Whitman's Multitudes

THE LEAVES OF GRASS CENTENNIAL PASSED AMID ODDLY dispirited jollifications; hardly anyone would admit to an active liking for the book. There were public lectures, displays in libraries, and much hand shaking; Dr. Williams appeared between the same covers as J. Middleton Murry; a man skilled at distinguishing inks and assigning a chronology to revisions, but unprepared by previous experience "for the close investigation of the work of a nineteenth-century American poet," was turned loose on the brouillons of the third edition;[1] commemorators across the country splashed their whisky on the honored corpse in hopes that he might start breathing the air of 1955.

It was a deed that was being commemorated; draw attention to the book, and the company, with an uneasy look, began talking rapidly about something more tractable, like Democracy. Even more than Yeats, Whitman has been removed from the critic's province to the biographer's, the poems turned into a man; even more than Swift, the man has been turned into a case, unfailingly bewildering: the Genius as Impostor, say, or The Good Gray Pansy. There is even a sort of subcommittee ambitious to vindicate his sexual orthodoxy, and thus (somehow) his poetic validity, by deducing what are called "experiences with women." This sort of trifling at least has gone far enough to incur some reproof from

[1] Fredson Bowers (ed.), *Whitman's Manuscripts: Leaves of Grass, 1860* (University of Chicago Press).

67

critics who having delivered the indictment sign off
without having started to function critically. The
most audacious strategy for brushing aside the
celebrants was Malcolm Cowley's in the July 25,
1955, *New Republic;* cutting away the whole bloat,
he offered for our veneration simply the first edition
itself with its mere twelve poems, the *Song of Myself*
nearly half the 95-page book, dismissing curiosity
about the life that came before as irrelevant to this
"miracle," and shrugging aside both the postures and
the 400-odd poems that came after as mere corrup-
tions of it. This has the merit of removing from visi-
bility that tedious Whitman who isn't a man but a
cyclorama, and leaving us some poems rather Blakean
not in their cosmic sprawl (the usual common
ground of comparisons between Whitman and Blake)
but in the piercing authenticity of their suburban
primitivism:

. . . Or I guess it is the handkerchief of the Lord. . . .

It *is* a sort of miracle, like the talent of the Douanier
Rousseau, the grassy spears of whose dream-heavy
jungles ("Only the lull I like, the hum of your valved
voice") are painted one by one with the entranced
energy of a Whitman inventory of dustmotes. Mr.
Cowley quotes Walt's notebook description of ". . .
a trance, yet with all the senses alert—only a state of
high exalted musing—the tangible and material with
all its shows, the objective world suspended or sur-
mounted for a while & the powers in exaltation, freedom, vision—yet the *senses* not lost or counteracted."
Not even a deed, then, but a sort of anonymous

event, a hundred years ago; but the man to whom this event happened then substituted a succession of public Walts for the anonymity, and has been repaid by a dragging around every Troy on the critical map. "Who touches this book touches a man," he wrote; but he didn't know who; and spent his life trying to turn himself into that man. He wasn't a technician but a sort of mouthpiece; nothing is more obvious than his failure to develop, to do anything but repeat himself, shutting batch after batch of trashy dough into the oven with a little pinch of the first *Leaves of Grass* for leaven. Nor is the familiar work an authentic transvaluation of language; its crafty misspellings ("loafe," "Kanada"), its eccentric violations of diction ("kelson," "imperturbe"), its transgressions against its own decorum ("Of life immense in passion, pulse, and power") aren't creations but efforts at compromise between accessible language and the authentic naïve vision. What wouldn't lie down in the words he jammed in anyhow. The "original" features of Whitman's language aren't the ones that have worn well.

What has worn is his gesture of contempt for the pentameter rhythm, any fixed rhythm. He knew, in this one sphere, what not to do. The chief event of the centenary celebration was Dr. Williams' essay in a collection of tributes edited by Milton Hindus.[2] Instead of trying to make Walt out a seminal poet (which would mean to identify distinguished prog-

---

[2] Milton Hindus (ed.), *Leaves of Grass One Hundred Years After,* essays by William Carlos Williams, Richard Chase, Leslie A. Fiedler, Kenneth Burke, David Daiches, and J. Middleton Murry (Stanford University Press).

eny somewhere but among the political orators)
Dr. Williams presents him as a direct rebellious challenge, still good after a century, "to all living poets
to show cause why they should not do likewise." This
is carefully phrased; Dr. Williams is perfectly aware
that to echo a challenge isn't to take it up, to Whit-
manize once the gesture has been made (as Walt
himself did) is to do nothing; but to abstain from
doing likewise having first shown cause why not,
profiting not from Walt's practice but from his perception of the need to "break the old apart to make
room for ourselves," would be to write poetry as yet
unwritten.

> From the beginning Whitman realized that the mat-
> ter was largely technical. It had to be free verse or
> nothing. . . . He had seen a great light but forgot
> almost at once . . . everything but his "message"
> . . . and took his eye off the words themselves which
> should have held him. . . .
>
> Poems are made out of words not ideas. He never
> showed any evidence of knowing this and the un-
> resolved forms consequent upon his beginnings re-
> mained in the end just as he left them.

This is, once again, Dr. Williams' familiar critical
theme, that America has a language which American
poets, busy using the old one well, aren't by and
large aware of. It was worth his repeating it, to give
us a role in which to see Whitman. Once so seen, not
simply, as Mr. Cowley sees him, the anonymous
recipient of a miracle, but the man with a definite
address in time who noticed what ought to be done

though he failed properly to do it, he is set free for us to read what we like of him, immune from the otherwise inescapable itch to turn his peripheral pretensions into the outline of a Poet and then scratch through biographies looking for that Poet's principle of vitality.

And the first thing we see is just why the qualities one feels him to possess are so elusive. A rhythmic liberation, unaccompanied by either a positive rhythmic invention or a reliable strain of poetry otherwise generated, is a diffuse achievement. Walt Whitman the poet would seem to be the nearly accidental juxtaposition of a negative impulse, concerning rhythm, which we obscurely recognize to have been right, and an intermittent Blakean talent for naïve perception. The rhythm was subsequently freighted with miscellaneous gestures whose banality it makes shift to disguise, the sharp talent (often confined to single lines) got obscured amid pyrites, and in poem after poem a nullity by its nature almost indiscernible from the real thing was further camouflaged by the regularity of a habitual rhetorical structure—the short first line, the systole and diastole of self, cosmos, and self, a mechanism, readily mistaken for animation, which Mr. David Daiches blueprints for us without suspicion. It is no wonder that Mr. Kenneth Burke gets nowhere surveying the range of the vocabulary, associating with *Leaves* the various uses of the verb "leave," or that Mr. Murry gives it all up and writes a paean to Democracy, or that the foreigners in Dr. Allen's anthology *Walt Whitman*

Abroad [3] tend to take him as a prophet like Marx or Isaiah, or that everybody else gets somehow involved with biography.

It is impossible, by the usual documentary methods, to write a "life" of him, as Dr. Allen's massive, definitive *Solitary Singer* [4] inadvertently demonstrates; impossible not because there isn't a life to write, but because one can't pin down a person living it. Either the events must be clamped into a thesis, or they diffuse into the chronicles of Proteus, signifying nothing. If it is the feel of the personality you want, you can get it most easily from the Detroit Exhibition Catalogue: [5] for instance—

WORDS: WHITMAN'S NOTEBOOK FOR AN INTENDED AMERICAN DICTIONARY: Bound by Whitman, by means of cutting out all pages of a book and retaining the stubs so that sheets of paper, fragments, and clippings could be tipped in. The sheets of paper used are various: left-over green wrappers from the first edition of *Leaves of Grass*, yellow end-papers left from the second issue of *Leaves of Grass*, unused stationery of the City of Williamsburgh, etc. . . . The cover was pierced, so that two pieces of cord are holding front and back covers together. . . .

[3] Gay Wilson Allen (ed.), *Walt Whitman Abroad,* critical essays from Germany, Scandinavia, France, Russia, Italy, Spain, Latin America, Israel, Japan, and India (Syracuse University Press).

[4] Gay Wilson Allen, *The Solitary Singer, a Critical Biography of Walt Whitman* (Macmillan).

[5] *Walt Whitman, a Selection of the Manuscripts, Books and Association Items gathered by Charles E. Feinberg,* Detroit Public Library Exhibition Catalogue, 1955.

Some of the notes and memos read as follows: "There could easily be a dictionary made of words fit to be used in an English (American) opera—or for vocal-lyric purposes, songs, ballads, recitations, etc.— pantaloons—pants—trousers—breeches. . . . Words: *Effective*—[Fr] [Com] p. 429 Wb. Dict. . . . Ei-do-lon (Gr) phantom—the *image* of an Helen, at Troy instead of real flesh and blood woman.—Names of persons—These are very curious to trace out.—How came they? . . . —Aboriginal names always tell finely . . . —In names a suggestion. The woman should preserve her own name just as much after marriage as before," etc.

His notes on oratory are worth transcribing:

The Elocution should be *full of pauses* and of that style vocalism which makes a little matter go a great way in the delivery—yes—*short* lectures. Proposed titles are 'America', 'Arena', etc.

—and his memorandum to the managing editor of the New York *Times*:

To make a personal item or paragraph for 'Minor Topics.' qu? to commence for instance: With the bright crispy autumn weather Walt Whitman again makes his appearance on the sidewalks of Broad-way . . .

Amid all these painted balloons—the crafty old string saver, the reformer of marital nomenclature, the vaudeville hack, the self-appointed orator, the composer of advertisements for himself—a mere biographer can only assume a glazed objective stare and fuss with chronology. It is not as though there were anything to be found out, in this jungle, about the poems one willingly reinspects; indeed, in view of the nonpoetic pressures acting on all his verse after his public debut, there would seem no reason for anybody but a psychiatrist wanting to grasp Whitman entire. But it is probably not merely the cult of psychiatry that causes the most knowing contributors to Whitman symposia to be fascinated instead of embarrassed by Whitman the poseur. Mr. Richard Chase, for instance, contributes a well-written neo-Freudian attempt to derive the poet from his early life (which at most could derive the compulsions that shaped his "message," the least viable part of his poetry because never technically entrapped), and Mr. Leslie Fiedler chronicles with a mixture of condescension and excitement the succession of Whitmans invented first by Walt and then by his disciples; and both critics appear to regard their activities as central to an understanding of the poetry. It is hard to escape the conclusion that a corrupt bard is *wanted,* for sticking up in the fore-time of a corrupt America.

This brings us to the very heart of the Whitman cult as it is at present administered. Its gambit is to restore the poet, without attending to the verse. That is why one can be sure that its interests lie not in the written words, but somewhere else, among preoccupations Whitman can merely be made to confirm. It is only from considerations of what is on the page that literary discussions can set out and re-

main compellingly meaningful, and Mr. Fiedler is a
good example of the man of habitual perception de-
feated by omitting to make the initial perception, to
notice the exact location, and limits, of Whitman's
technical innovation. He is excellent on Whitman's
wit, by-product, he acutely discerns, of the initial
anonymity, modified but not canceled by the subsequent personae. The latter simply exploit a doubleness of self of which Whitman was always aware,
allowing him to make faces at himself from around
the piano, the persona of the moment indulging in
great public exchanges of winks with the discarnate
Voice. Having on these grounds undertaken to res-
cue Whitman "from parody as well as apotheosis,"
Mr. Fiedler draws back. We cannot, it seems, con-
front the text, but only the presently relevant stage
of the reputation. "Twenty-five years of dissent cannot be undone." It is time to proclaim, therefore,
"our *own* Whitman," who turns out to be—"the
elegiac Whitman, the poet of death."

> We find with relief in *Leaves of Grass* that "blackness
> ten times black" which Melville once thrilled to dis-
> cover in Hawthorne. . . . Those of us who know that
> poetry (God forbid that we should attempt to judge
> the *man!*) is precisely a matter of cardboard butter-
> flies on real fingers . . . are grateful to [sundry at-
> tackers] for having rescued Whitman from "life" . . .
> and having restored him to art.

It is obviously important to discover who "we" are
supposed to be, who know these bitter things, that

art is a fake but when vital has death somewhere at
its roots. Mr. Fiedler would seem to be appealing to
the collective wisdom of the Lonely Crowd who
make a cult of European decadence and mistake,
say, Kafka for a physician rather than a symptom.

So far, so banal; it is in the next paragraph (his
penultimate) that Mr. Fiedler allows a revelation
of some significance to escape:

> His duplicity is, I feel, a peculiarly American du-
> plicity, that doubleness of our self-consciousness,
> which our enemies too easily call hypocrisy . . . Con-
> demned to play the Lusty Innocent, the Noble Savage,
> by a literary tradition that had invented his country
> before he inhabited it, Whitman had no defenses.
> The whole Western world demanded of him the lie
> in which we have been catching him out, the image
> of America in which we no longer believe. . . .
>
> But he was not "America"; he was only a man,
> ridden by impotence and anxiety, by desire and guilt,
> furtive and stubborn and half-educated. . . .

This not only has the authentic vatic ring, it throws
a flood of light on the Whitman legend. To represent
an American poet in the 1850s or '60s as defenseless
before the demands of a European dream is to ob-
literate eight decades of American history: to throw
up behind Whitman a vast blank out of which no
sustenance was available: to place him, in Lincoln's
generation, at the inception of the American consciousness instead of at one of its foci of corruption.
This means obliterating not only John Adams' "revolution took place in the minds of the people . . . in
the course of fifteen years before Lexington," but

the whole novel tradition of an aristocratic government deriving authority from a popular franchise.
That is why an actively mythopoeic Whitman, not a
man aware of his American past but a man at the
beginning of a story written in France, without any
past, his back to the void, not a technical innovator
but a corrupted prophet, is essential to the current
liberal tradition, which satisfies itself by fondling
"a peculiarly American duplicity, that doubleness
of our self-consciousness." The conspiracy to suppose
that American political history begins, effectively,
with Lincoln, is of the same order; it is no accident
that the twentieth century's prairie Whitman should
be Lincoln's most industrious biographer, or that the
accomplished trumpery of "When lilacs last in the
dooryard bloom'd" should be the inescapable Whitman anthology piece. That Whitman's notions of
political process were rudimentary—the Civil War
merely "the foulest crime in history known in any
land or age"—is irrelevant, in this view, to his status
as a political prophet; so is the evasiveness concerning particular conditions of men—documented with
naïve thoroughness by Leadie M. Clark[6]—that lurks
inside his windy championship of the common man.
It would be worth asking why a man so shrewd understood so little of the past of his own country; but
that is not asked. That he disintegrates under biographical scrutiny like the scholiasts' Homer is thoroughly congenial to current fashion, for which he *is*
the Homer, behind whom nothing, of the American

[6] Leadie M. Clark, *Walt Whitman's Concept of the American
Common Man* (Philosophical Library).

dawn, of a swarming of pocket Hectors and ant-hill Agamemnons ("the word En-Masse"). It all fits, even Mr. Chase's neat presentation of Whitman as a ple- beian James on grounds of shared misfortunes and neuroses; one notes as an overlooked feature of the James revival that it is only to a neurotic James that it has been thought safe to entrust an aristocratic tradition.

It seems just now for some reason important to present an America dominated by an image of itself as egalitarian paradise, equally important to make this image not only batten on corruption but to be corrupt from its inception. (One might here invoke Mr. Warren's *Brother to Dragons.*) Hence the cult of de Tocqueville, who as Senator Thomas Hart Benton observed "may pass, in Europe, for American history." Hence the obliteration of Adams, whose letters are American literature, and the transforma- tion of Jefferson into a figure as mute as Washington, only given to tinkering and obiter dicta. Hence, then, the cult of a bard whose expansiveness lends energy to the notion of an American consciousness diffused across the sidewalks of Manhattan. It is after the most distinguished men in the United States cease to be discoverable in Washington that American history, not as a chronicle but as a significant process reaching to us, is allowed to begin; and the trumpery Whitman of legend gets promoted as its flawed epon- ymous bard, the anonymous Homer of a fortuitous concourse of pygmies.

That is what the centennial celebration would appear to mean, the part of it that is not mere scholarly thumb twiddling and dedication of statues. Though Mr. Cowley and Dr. Williams have shown where to begin, there is still room for the separation, in his verse, of ore from pyrites and of both from mud.

6. Faces to the Wall

SEVENTY-FIVE YEARS AFTER MATTHEW ARNOLD'S EX-
pansive prophecy—"More and more mankind
will discover that we have to turn to poetry to interpret life for us, to console us, to sustain us. Without
poetry our science will appear incomplete; and most
of what now passes with us for religion and philosophy will be replaced by poetry"—we observe, among
other symptoms, a student population so illiterate
it cannot read poetry at all, being herded through
a succession of huge anthologies scientifically designed to teach it how.

Arnold in 1880 apparently assumed (by extrapolation) that the Poetry lecture rooms of 1955 would
be crowded by undergraduates stuffed, like so many
young John Stuart Mills, with serried facts (as if by
expert packers in a pencil factory) and requiring
only to have their emotional natures awakened and
ordered. Instead we have, as every teacher knows,
not merely occasional sad sacks who wonder whether
Apollo is in the Bible or Shakespeare, but whole
roomfuls of sophomores who can't follow Marvell's
"Definition of Love" because no one present knows
what the North Pole is[1] (except that it's a very cold
place, which doesn't seem to fit). Their plight is met
by survey courses which grow so bloated with de-
partmental hobbies that they must occasionally be
trimmed down in committee ("If we put in *Hamlet*
we'll have to take out *She Stoops to Conquer*." "Do

[1] *Testor scriptor.* When asked what in heaven's name they
studied in school they reply, "Oh, history . . . economics . . ."

80

we want *She Stoops to Conquer?*" "Well"—the eighteenth-century specialist's jaw setting—"they ought
to know about it" [2]).

It is idle to pretend that a defensible idea of literary tradition or function presides over such delib-
erations. Mr. Eliot's classic description of the historical sense—"a feeling that the whole of the literature
of Europe from Homer and within it the whole of the
literature of his own country has a simultaneous
existence and composes a simultaneous order"—no
longer defines something widely if obscurely felt: it
is part of a controversial document useful for eluci-
dating the work of poet Eliot, who already belongs
to a vanished age. No comparable formulation today
would mention Homer. Literature in English is supposed to exist on its own, and so is any particular
work within it: suppositions buttressed by the Ricardian heresy that, given the appropriate techniques
for deciphering, one can extract the nourishment
from any poem while considering it as an isolated
event, or as though it were the only poem in the
world. This doctrine goes down well with undergraduates who want to read as little as possible, or
who like to think of poems as tidy little patterns of
imagery (like Scrabble layouts), and hence recommends itself to their teachers. Father Walter J. Ong
has noted (*English Institute Essays, 1952*, p. 150)
that the bulk of "mediaeval philosophy" was shallow
and diagrammatic because its discussion was confined to universities where students became M.A.s
at twenty, and at present, for the second time in

[2] Reported from western Canada.

Western history, "thought" and pedagogy are becoming one thing.

These parochial confusions have stemmed implacably from the attempt, now a half-century current, to treat English vernacular poetry as a cultural norm. The extreme interest at this juncture of the Chinese Book of Odes (*The Classic Anthology Defined by Confucius,* translation by Ezra Pound, Harvard, 1954) consists in the fact that these 305 lyrics do constitute a cultural norm and have been nutriment for the civilization of China for about 2,500 years. Whether Arnold would have found this fact intelligible is difficult to say; he found his "healing power" in the Grand Style—

. . . and what is else not to be overcome . . .

whereas the Odes extend from "Yaller bird, let my corn alone" to ". . . ancestral manes pass . . ." It should also be noted that though Confucius said that a man who hadn't worked on the first twenty-five Odes was like one who stands with his face to a wall, he never claimed that the Odes alone would guarantee civilization. He didn't invite his followers to turn to poetry to "interpret life for us, to console us, to sustain us"; he said,

> Aroused by the Odes;
> Established by the Rites;
> Brought into perfect focus by Music.

Achilles Fang writes in his Introduction to the volume, "The word *li,* essentially a code of behaviour, is generally rendered as 'rites' when that behaviour is directed toward the supernatural or the manes, and as 'etiquette' when it concerns man's relation with his fellow men. . . . Perhaps the late Ku Hung-Ming had insight when he rendered *li* as 'tact'. It could, as well, be translated 'character'." Kung leaves no place for the dilettante, nor does he try to make reading poetry a substitute for religious observance. Analogies for all these components—Odes, Rites, and Music—functioned in the West during the ascendancy of Catholic Christianity. They still exist but they don't function. Music is the property of the impresario. Poetry is what is taught in sophomore surveys. Exiguous rites are transacted inside churches; in a more comprehensive sense, the term requires a long footnote.

While the Odes were in Kung's view only part of the civilizing process, yet they aren't a miscellany of poems propped and forced into coherence by the rest of the civilized usages. The great Anthology, beginning with fifteen books of Folk Songs or "lessons of the states," gathering weight and direction in the two political divisions (eight books of Elegantiae Minores and three decads of quasi-epical Greater Odes), and reaching a climax with forty Ceremonial Odes (the last five of which constitute the oldest part of the anthology), provides, coherent and free of irrelevancies,[3] a sacramental corpus on which Chinese civilization perpetually feeds. "Less a work of the mind than of affects/brought forth from the

[3] An editor of genius—Confucius himself, it used to be thought —seems to have selected the 305 pieces from an accumulation of some 3,000.

inner nature," wrote a Manchu prince seeking to describe their massive anonymity: "all order comes into such norm." "Have no twisty thoughts," was Confucius' summary of the entire anthology. It is not, like Palgrave's *Golden Treasury*, a collection of miscellaneously interesting poetic documents. It was apparently the translator's concern for emphasizing the shape of the whole, and the way each poem's significance consists in its being part of the whole, that kept him from publishing bits separately in advance of the entire volume. A poem like No. 86—

> So he won't talk to me when we meet?
> Terrible!
> 　　　　I still can eat.
> So clever he won't even come to dinner;
> Well, beds are soft,
> 　　　　　　and I'm no thinner.

—doesn't, like a poem by Laforgue, imply a cycle of similar poems; it doesn't express an attitude to life, it is a posture possible to a supple sensibility, an unstudied response to the behavior of a particular man. The next poem is saucier—

> Be kind, good sir, and I'll lift my sark
> and cross the Chen to you,
> But don't think you are the only sprig
> 　　　　in all the younger crew. . . .

—but the next transforms indurated flippancy into pathos:

> A handsome lad stood in the lane,
> Alas, I asked him to explain.

A rich boy came for me to the hall
and I wasn't ready. How should it befall?
     Who wants a lady? . . .

A few pages away we find a different kind of experience and a different poetic language:

Dry grass, in vale:
          "alas!

"I met a man, I
        met
        a man.

"Scorched, alas, ere it could grow."
A lonely girl pours out her woe.

"Even in water-meadow, dry."
Flow her tears abundantly.
        Solitude's no remedy.   [Ode 69]

—and a few pages from that, a different poignancy
(since no one theme monopolizes the emotions):
the plight of the Emperor's divorced mother whom
decorum forbade to return to court:

Wide, Ho?
A reed will cross its flow;
Sung far?
One sees it, tip-toe.

Ho strong?
The blade of a row-boat cuts it so soon.
Sung far? I could be there
(save reverence) by noon
           (did I not venerate
           Sung's line and state).
               [Ode 61]

This isn't inflated to the dimensions of tragedy, yet the expression is perfectly adequate to the emotion. It is perhaps the absence of inflation in these poems that makes them welcome one another's company; none tries to engulf the world. It is only in the eighteenth century that we find European poets so sure of what, in the poem at hand, the moral theme is; the English Renaissance and Romantic writers are, in different ways, opportunists who can't be counted on not to stick in anything moving that comes to mind.[4] Yet the eighteenth-century poet, inheritor of the scholastic discussion of moral themes, specialized his themes to the point of etiolation and then "amplified" his *language*. Racine could have turned the divorced dowager Empress's situation into a play on the conflict of Inclination and Duty, but because he would have thought it discussable in those terms it would have been, for all its brilliance, a less moving performance than the anonymous Chinese Ode.

The gnomic sentences in the Odes are equally unassuming:

> My heart no turning-stone, mat to be rolled
> right being right, not whim nor matter of count,
> true as a tree on mount. . . .   [Ode 26]

This is both explicit and comprehensive; it has the bite of great poetry; but it doesn't offer itself, like comparable bits of *The Essay on Man*,

> —Know then this truth (enough for Man to know)
> 'Virtue alone is Happiness below'—

[4] Cf. "He is not long soft and pathetick without some idle conceit"—Johnson on Shakespeare.

as a picture postcard of the Universe. Neither,
though it echoes Housman's tone, does this:

> . . . Nor fine nor coarse cloth keep the wind
> from the melancholy mind;
> Only antient wisdom is
> solace to man's miseries.   [Ode 27]

By contrast with this tranquil decorum, Housman,
when he is being sententious, implies too much:
commits himself to statements about the way things
are, that beg more questions than they allay, and
exclude more experience than they evoke:

> . . . Therefore, since the world has still
> Much good, but much less good than ill,
> And while the sun and moon endure
> Luck's a chance, but trouble's sure,
> I'd face it as a wise man would,
> And train for ill and not for good. . . .
> > [*A Shropshire Lad,* LXII]

This is a more *provincial* utterance than the Chinese;
it does not "imply a recognition of other kinds of
experience that are possible"; its Stoicism belongs to
a time, not a tradition. Pound's use of Housman's
idiom in the translation implies a criticism of Housman, the most interesting because the least categorical kind of criticism.

To say that the poems as rendered by Pound don't
"sound Chinese"—which means in practice that
their rhythm isn't limpid or their prevailing color
blue—is to register both their advance on *Cathay,*
and the extent to which *Cathay* has trained us—and
trained a dozen other translators of less sharpness—

to expect of Chinese verse in English a tranquillity, rather aesthetic than lively, that accords with the era of Whistler's Japanese prints. *Cathay* (1915) begins,

Here we are, picking the first fern shoots
And saying, when shall we get back to our country?
Here we are because we have the Ken-nin for our foe-
men,
We have no comfort because of these Mongols. . . .

The 1954 version of the same poem (Ode 167) runs:

Pick a fern, pick a fern, ferns are high,
"Home," I'll say: home, the year's gone by,
no house, no roof, these huns on the hoof.
Work, work, work, that's how it runs,
We are here because of these huns.

This is a much more convincing soldier's song; the Odes, all of them, really were sung, and some of them were danced to.

But the new work, with its array of implied tunes and sinewy rhythms, doesn't undo the finest parts of *Cathay*—"The River Song," for instance, or "Poem by the Bridge at Ten-Shin," the originals of which in any case postdate the Odes by nearly a thousand years; rather, it provides them with a context. Pound wrote the *Cathay* poems when his ambitions were still engaged with visions of a cultural renaissance, envisaged by him (see *Patria Mia*) as a liberation of artistic impulses by intelligent patronage. It was an Edwardian dream, already anachronistic by 1915; but his symbiosis with the T'ang poet Li Po (miscalled via Fenollosa's Japanese scholarship Rihaku) was perhaps in part catalyzed by the attractiveness of Li Po as a persona: an artist who ornamented a resplendent dynasty, wasn't condemned to journalism or the task of harassing impercipient editors, didn't need to campaign or form "movements" or take account of any but the least worrisome themes, had no responsibility thrust upon him but that of perfecting his craft, and could write

South of the pond the willow-tips are half-blue and
     bluer,
Their cords tangle in mist, against the brocade-like
     palace,

and feel with the lamented H. S. Mauberley that

> The month was more temperate
> Because this beauty had been.

Hence the immediacy with which Pound, whose best translations are always profoundly vitalized by his concurrent interests, was able, as Eliot once put it, to "invent Chinese poetry for our time." It was an invention; the poems of "Rihaku" didn't come out of familiarity with Chinese, but out of a sensibility caressed by Henry James, Whistler, and a vision of peaceable perfection. In the subsequent forty years Pound greatly extended his grasp both of the Chinese language and of English versification; the Odes aren't less Chinese, merely less Edwardian. Here is another vision of perfection, quickened in a manner wholly alien to *Cathay* by the grotesque and the legendary:

> . . . The King stood in his "Park Divine,"
> deer and doe lay there so fine,

so fine so sleek; birds of the air
flashed a white wing while fishes splashed
on wing-like fin in the haunted pool.

Great drums and gongs
hung on spiked frames
sounding to perfect rule and rote
about the king's calm crescent moat.

Tone unto tone, of drum and gong.

About the king's calm crescent moat
the blind musicians beat lizard skin
as the tune weaves out and in.   [Ode 242]

Having now learned, in his own phrase, to "control
the procedures" of a remarkable number of poets,
Pound is able, by drawing on dozens of chronological
and formal conventions, to convince us that we are
handling, in English, an authentic Sacred Book with
a long history. This is the *use* of his awesome technical mastery, of his ability to manage the most intricate effects with the air of one improvising, or add
an extra dimension to a small lyric by echoing as he
renders its plain sense the mood of some vernacular
genre or the turn of phrase of some familiar English
anthology piece. The use of the Miracle Play idiom
in portions of Part III is the most striking instance of
this technique; the élan of a chronicler whose mind
is on the most important facets of his subject comes
through the rhythmic primitiveness of the "Creation"
Odes as it would not through a more enameled
surface:

As gourd-leaves spread, man began
leaf after leaf, and no plan

overgrowing the Tsü and Ts'i,
living in caves and in stone hives
ere ever they knew a house with eaves.

[Ode 237]

The "freshness" of, say, the Towneley Shepherd's
Play, its sense of contact with living beliefs, arises
from a comparable directness:

God is made youre freynd: now at this morne
    He behestys,
At Bedlam go se,
Ther lygys that fre
In a crib fulle poorely,
    Betwyx two bestys.

More sophisticated idioms abound. The intricate
Provençal and Tuscan rhymes, first put by Pound to
creative use in his 1931 version of the *Donna mi
priegha* and greatly elaborated in the Choruses of
the 1953 *Women of Trachis*, now chime, to suggest
the visual and aural interrelation of the ideograms,
through Ode after Ode:

Pine boat a-shift
on drift of tide,
for flame in the ear, sleep riven,
driven; rift of the heart in dark
no wine will clear,
nor have I will to playe. . . .   [Ode 26]

Eleven words in these six lines are coupled by rhyme
or assonance, to articulate the kind of subject for
which the Tuscan aesthetic of rhyme was developed.
In another Ode, with a more public and general
subject, the eighteenth-century couplet

(Another Age shall see the golden Ear
Imbrown the Slope, and nod on the Parterre)

contributes its assurance of inclusive social order:

Full be the year, abundant be the grain,
high be the heaps composed in granaries,
robust the wine for ceremonial feast
and lack to no man be he highest or least,
neither be fault in any rite here shown
so plenteous nature shall inward virtue crown.

[Ode 279]

Elsewhere an anxious young Emperor echoes a
Shakespearean sonnet:

Whenas my heart is filled with kings and deeds
seeking to avoid the cause of new regret. . . .

[Ode 289]

The praise of an ambiguous woman begins in the
cadence of later Yeats:

Go with him for a life-long
with high jewelled hair-do. . . .

—but ends in an expressive blend of Elizabethan
definiteness and Swinburnean facility:

Splendour of court high guests to entertain,
erudite silk or plain flax in the grain,
above it all the clear spread of her brows:
"Surely of dames this is the cynosure,
the pride of ladies and the land's allure!"

and yet?

[Ode 47]

In a very entertaining banquet Ode the meter of
L'Allegro, flavored with Uncle Remus, commits itself to quite un-Miltonic indecorum—

Guests start eatin', mild and even
The sober sit an' keep behavin',
but say they've boozed then they do not.
When they've boozed they start a-wavin' an' a-ravin',
Yas' sir they rise up from the ground
and start dancin' an' staggerin' round

—but suddenly returns to its Miltonic keynote with
a perfect seventeenth-century line:

each to his own wild fairy fancy. . . .

[Ode 220]

The more we explore the *Classic Anthology* the
more such echoes we find; but it is always the "procedures," never the personal features, of an older poet's
style that Pound imitates. This is strength, not weakness; the trick of personality (a poetic impurity) is
much easier to catch. The version of the Fifty-eighth
Ode owes a great deal to the Browning of *Men and
Women* without incorporating a single one of his
mannerisms. Moreover, numerous Odes display no
discernible technical debt, only a decorum and quiet
virtuosity exempt from singularity, as expressive
amid the harmonies and echoings as a bar of silence:

There was no fuss about the fall
of the sash ends, there was just that much to spare
and it fell, and ladies' hair
curved, just curved and that was all

the like of which, today, is never met;
And I therefore
express regret.   [Ode 225]

There is reason in these echoings; Pound's book is
in part meant as a compendium of English poetic
procedures, set in order, all put to work expressing
not a chaos of preoccupations but something coherent. The various themes, devices, and tones of
English verse are the accents of successive phases
of a civilization, but the elements of a *paideuma*
don't reside in them. Nothing comparable to the Shi
King, no such compendium of sustenance as Arnold
half-implies, can be assembled out of existing English poetry, for all its range, for all its magnificence,
for all the genius that has gone into its composition.
Its history since Chaucer's time—Chaucer is the last
thoroughly civilized English writer—is a history of
mobilized doctrines and counterobsessions, of foreign injections, chiefly French and Italian, of dubious
systems and astonishing random talents, all consti-
tuting a cultural chronicle but not a cultural *norm*.
Arnold's claims for poetry may have been badly expressed, but it wasn't, at least, on behalf of vernacular poetry that he made them. He saw English
vernacular poetry as part of an order founded on
Homer, Vergil, Sophocles, Dante: on the classics
that do constitute a norm for the Western spirit.
Pound's list in *How to Read* may be regarded, in this
light, as his attempt to do for Western culture what
Confucius or whoever selected the 305 Odes did for
Chinese: nominate the contents of what W. B. Yeats
used to call "a new sacred book of the arts": the

things one must know to be fully human in a Western context (taking "know" to mean "incorporate into oneself").

It is arguable, then, that however hard he works on twenty-five English poems or 250, the "English" specialist must stand, in Confucius' phrase, with his face to a wall. His circumvallation, an eighty-years' labor of pedagogic expediency, is now nearly complete. Arnold wasn't a professor of English, he was a professor of Poetry; he lectured on translating Homer. It was after his time that "English Departments" began to appear, charged with disseminating works so miscellaneous as Parkman's *Oregon Trail,* Shakespeare's *Othello,* and Cardinal Newman's *Apologia,* plus Dante, the Bible, and Greek Mythology, not to mention Critical Method and How to Use the Library. For such responsibilities the English Professor of Raleigh's or Quiller-Couch's generation was, not surprisingly, unprepared. He was accustomed to getting his disciplines from what he remembered of the classics, and treating the English writers (i.e., the poets; prose seemed more serious) as diversions. ("If I am accused on Judgment Day of teaching literature," wrote Raleigh, "I shall plead that I never believed in it and that I maintained a wife and children.") Hence the habit described by Dr. Leavis, of treating English literature "in terms of Hamlet's and Lamb's personalities, Milton's universe, Johnson's conversation, Wordsworth's philosophy, and Othello's or Shelley's private life": neither a subject nor a discipline nor a *paideuma,* but a collection of hobbies. Hence also the adoption of historical and

philological method from the German universities;
the professor who introduced into the poetry seminar
the stooped shoulder and the 3 x 5 card didn't modify his conviction that English poetry is essentially
frivolous; all he wanted was a procedure for dealing
with it that would give his students something rigorous to do and be graded on. The New Criticism—in
practice a new pedagogy—was yet a third strategy
for milking carrots. Its valuable initial polemics
against "Q's" eclecticism and the graduate school's
Wissenschaft having consumed the available fuel, its
American exponents have been spending the past
ten years arranging the terms of a truce with the
MLA, while in England Dr. Leavis, his attempt to
erect a scheme of values from the close study of
English literature alone having led insensibly to the
piecing together of a tradition uniting chiefly those
writers who had no foreign interests to speak of,
trickled off into a series of desultory articles on
D. H. Lawrence and finally shut down his review.

The New Critics discerned that literature was being taught, at the time they arrived on the scene,
as a species of history. This is a simple corollary of
the fact that an anthology of English poetry is, when
comprehensive, a history of taste, not a thesaurus of
values that would interest an Italian or a China-
man. When stringent, it is—like Pound's *ABC of
Reading*—largely a succession of fine performances
in a succession of modes or implying a succession of
norms not native to the English temperament but
imported from France, from Italy, or direct from
the constantly rediscovered classics. No other kinds

of anthology are possible, using strictly English materials. The kind used to teach poetry courses result from an attempt not to compile the historical kind while ignoring the fact that the other kind implies background work that is pedagogically embarrassing; one can't keep telling innocent freshmen that they should have read Catullus in high school, and one's college, as likely as not, has no classics department. Hence the recourse to methodology; hence also the tendency, as time passes, to allow the undoubted benefit that the least knowing students can get from studying a few poems carefully to pass itself off as the whole of what literature has to offer.

So *The Classic Anthology Defined by Confucius* is unique in English, not only as a piece of resourceful translating, but also with respect to the kind of book Pound has translated (and insisted on publishing *in toto*), a kind otherwise impossible in English: a block of lyric material all ventilated, coherent, implying a full set of civilized values. The constant echoing of existing modes implies not only the variousness of the original but a criticism, an attempted ordering of the resources of English poetry, deliberately undertaken by a specialist of genius whose mind has been occupied with the uses and implications of available idioms for forty-five years. Most of the time it is the interest of the Chinese original that predominates, its wisdom and its strangeness; but over and over we are made aware of Pound's judgment on some nuance or other of the native tradition: here is where this would fit in, here is how a full scale of values would use it.

Poem 58, for instance, opens as a folk song:

> Hill-billy, hill-billy, come to buy
> silk in our market, apparently?
> toting an armful of calico.

A few lines later, however, we are apprised that the convention of the Browning monologue is governing the whole poem; with an effect reminiscent of Browning's slang minus Browning's personality, the lilt modulates into colloquial modernity—

> . . . and then I asked for a notary.
> I said: It's O.K. with me,
> we could be spliced autumnally,
>   be not offended.

"Be not offended" complicates the sensibility behind the poem; this woman was never cheap and is not now hard: she remains in adversity the shiftless pedlar's sworn wife. The pathos of the next lines is too economical to be Browning's:

> Autumn came, was waiting ended?
> I climbed the ruin'd wall, looked toward Kuan pass.
> On the Kuan frontier no man was.
> I wept until you came,
> trusted your smiling talk. One would.
> You said the shells were good and the stalks all clear.
> You got a cart
> and carted off me and my gear.

At this point an Elizabethan pastiche intervenes as lyric interlude—

> *Let doves eat no more mulberries*
> *While yet the leaves be green. . . .*

—its clear melody not tied to the song books but
weighted, like a song of Ophelia's, by the specific
situation from which its arises and to which it leads
us back:

> The mulberry tree is bare,
> yellow leaves float down thru the air,
> Three years we were poor,
> now Ki's like a soup of mud,
> the carriage curtains wet, I ever straight
> and you ambiguous
> with never a grip between your word and act.

Midway through the final sixteen lines we come
across a cunning acknowledgment to Browning—

> "Grow old with you," whom old you spite. . . .

—which is at once a note of homage, an intensifica-
tion by contrast ("Grow old along with me! The best
is yet to be!" [5]), and a perfectly natural phrase
whether one thinks of Browning or not. By the close
of the poem we are aware that this tour de force,
making use of at least three identifiable English traditions to articulate a subject handled by none of
them, has been fitted into a moral context determined
by adjacent poems in the anthology: much of what
is valuable in Browning, for instance, salvaged from
his nineteenth-century optimistic Protestantism.

A few poems from Pound's version of the *Classic
Anthology* will no doubt in time find their way into
the English Anthologies, or turn up on the American
Lit. survey curricula; one hopes this won't have taken

[5] *Rabbi ben Ezra.*

place before the import of the book as a whole has been absorbed, showing what an autonomous vernacular literary tradition (if any Western language could have one) would look like, and how unfocused, for the lack of one, are interests confined to vernacular poetry. In an ideal world the effect of the *Classic Anthology* would be to send readers—and educators—back to the occidental classics.

7. Subways to Parnassus

Walter Blair & W. K. Chandler, *Approaches to Poetry*, revised edn., Appleton-Century-Crofts, 1953. (Original edn. 1935.)

Cleanth Brooks & Robert Penn Warren, *Understanding Poetry*, revised edn., Holt, 1950. (Original edn. 1938.)

Wright Thomas & S. G. Brown, *Reading Poems*, Oxford, 1941 (tenth printing, 1950).

Charles W. Cooper, *Preface to Poetry*, Harcourt Brace, 1943 (revised edition not to hand).

Fred B. Millett, *Reading Poetry, a Method of Analysis with Selections for Study*, Harper, 1950.

Mark Van Doren, *Introduction to Poetry*, Sloane, 1951.

N. C. Stageberg & W. L. Anderson, *Poetry as Experience*, American Book Company, 1952.

Leonard Unger & William Van O'Connor, *Poems for Study*, Rinehart, 1953.

Clyde S. Kilby, *Poetry for Study*, Odyssey Press, 1953.

Etc., etc.

ONE CAN FIND MUCH OLDER BOOKS WITH TITLES LIKE these, but most of them are either graduate-school handbooks on prosody, essays in the classification of classifications, or more or less chatty historical treatises. The present books deal with the technique of reading poetry, which became a textbook "subject" in the late thirties, as the implications of Richards' *Practical Criticism* (1929) spread through the pedagogical mind like a deep stain. A dateline can be pretty exactly drawn; the Blair &

Chandler book (1935) remains a souvenir of the old order even in its 1953 revision; the revolution was touched off, if not exactly masterminded, by Messrs. Brooks and Warren in 1938. Today the market for how-to-read-poetry books seems inexhaustible; the revised Brooks & Warren (1950) was promptly adopted, according to its publishers, by over 250 institutions; at least five new publishers clambered aboard the bandwagon in the succeeding three years; disseminating poetic taste among college freshmen has become a big business.

Blair & Chandler's "Approaches to Poetry" are three: via types (Narrative and Lyric), via schools (Metaphysical and Neoclassical), and via personalities (in the first edition, Keats, Whitman, and Vachel Lindsay; in 1953 the latter two were replaced by T. S. Eliot, with appropriate fanfare from the publisher). Within these categories are subcategories introduced by decorous essays ("Ballads and Imagery in Poetry"; "Epics and Sublimity in Poetry"; "The Ode and Thought in Poetry"). In the last-mentioned we learn that "the song or sonnet is sufficient for the expression of a simple emotion or thought, but, for the presentation of a complex emotion or thought, longer and perhaps more complex forms are necessary. For such themes poets have long favoured the ode. . . ." Turning back after this to "The Sonnet and Diction in Poetry," we are hardly surprised to find Mr. Guest and Miss Millay among the sonneteers, or to be told that while poets may mention "kine" or "herds," the word "cows" is not poetic: "cows cannot make very inspiring poetic flights."

This principle is hardly compatible with the bottoms of Mr. Prufrock's trousers, and when Eliot's poems came into the revised edition, the bit about cows went out. Watts-Dunton's description of the Shakespearean sonnet-form as "the sweetest of all possible arrangements in English versification" was, however, retained, so the editorial principles can't be said to have undergone serious questioning. The book in fact is still permeated by exactly the notion Brooks and Warren sought to combat: that some magic inheres in forms, so that if you understand what the sonnet-form, the lyric-form, the ballad-form, etc., are good for, and possess in addition a smattering about Schools and Personalities, particular poems will give you no trouble.   .

It was I. A. Richards who effectively undermined this theory, by showing that intelligent but fatuously civilized Cambridge undergraduates, bamboozled by Critical and Technical Presuppositions, Doctrinal Adhesions, and Stock Responses, could imagine that they were interested in poetry while being totally incapable of telling live poetic tissue from dead or synthetic: a state of affairs no biology department would have tolerated. Over most of the recent textbooks broods Dr. Richards' implication that if the values conventionally ascribed to good poems really exist, there ought to be some way of teaching a freshman to see them for himself.

The manifesto of the pedagogical new order, Brooks and Warren's "Letter to the Teacher," is neither comprehensive nor sanguinary, though it appears to have been vastly influential. It amounts to a tactful plea that poetry be taught "as poetry." "As poetry" is an easier phrase to understand than to gloss: one gathers that poems should be read as adequately as possible instead of being put to documentary or didactic uses, and that such critical generalizations as are indulged in should emerge from the ordered and inspected experience of as many poems as possible. The resulting textbook, *Understanding Poetry*, is pretty substantial under light loads, and if not especially exhilarating, is free from specious exhilaration of the hark-to-that-caroling-dickeybird order.

The mind that is docile when told *about* poetry is apt to turn hostile when asked to *look at* it; hence the editors' interminable bedside manner. Their great insight was that the salient hostility is likely to be that of the teacher. It is really the teacher who is being soothed and cozened in the questions and discussions that occupy almost exactly half of this 700-page anthology, though his face is saved by the apparent aiming of all the commentary at the student (who can probably be trusted not to read it). With muted affability and infinite tact, the editors apply a steady gentle pressure in the direction of good sense. The audience, as they gauge it, is however by turns touchy and sluggish; so the proportion of emollient to verse is startlingly high and sometimes strangely distributed. Three sketchy questions on one of Shakespeare's most difficult sonnets are followed by a four-page demolition of Kilmer's "Trees." Eight-line and six-line poems by Yeats are followed by six-page and four-page commentaries on their metrics. There are four pages of "Prufrock" and eleven pages about it; two pages of "Ode to a Nightingale" and eight pages of discussion. These discussions aren't especially incandescent: the one on "Prufrock" begins, "This poem is a dramatic monologue. As in Tennyson's 'Ulysses' or Amy Lowell's 'Patterns,' a person utters a speech that implies his story and reveals his characters." Of the reader who this late in the book (p. 433) still needs assurance that the dentist isn't going to hurt, one might fairly conclude that he will never turn into a reader of poetry. Unfortunately, as Messrs. Brooks and Warren well know, he is probably teaching an "Introduction to Poetry" course. Such courses remain in many institutions curricular poor relations like Remedial Grammar, likely to be assigned either to young instructors with the grad-school grave-smell still on them and still, like Frankenstein's monster at an early stage, a bit helpless and mechanical; or else to gray-suited unpromotables who are capable of telling a class that the "Ode to a Nightingale" is very beautiful, but aren't markedly resourceful in the face of "Prufrock" or "The Garden." Of the available books, *Understanding Poetry* comes closest to coping with the conditions under which poetry is actually taught; it remains open to doubt whether this is the best way of teaching it.

A textbook, one would assume, should provide a selection of salient facts set down as cogently as possible by someone sufficiently interested in the subject to know them. This would presuppose a teacher equally interested.[1] As things are, the postulate that neither students nor teachers care much about poetry requires that each grain of information be dissolved in nine ounces of pedagogy, blandly flavored.

The patience required to control this sort of reader —like coercing a neurotic elephant into a boxcar— affects not only the strategy of presentation but the choice of poems. The choice, in *Understanding Poetry*, tends to get subordinated to a sort of working understanding about the nature of poetry in general, in which the stress is rather on communication than on content. As in the old argument for studying algebra or Latin in order to improve one's reasoning powers, poetry tends to be offered as a subject on which one can sharpen one's reading skills. It is not the body of knowledge uniquely available in poetry —Mr. Pound's "news that stays news"—that the commentaries stress, but the efficiency with which the poet can organize an appeal to quite commonplace intellectual appetites. "Even though the account of a painful accident or a sordid murder seems almost as far removed as possible from poetry, it arouses the kind of interest which poetry attempts to satisfy, and, as we have already said, comprises the 'stuff of poetry'." This approach seems connected with the editors' apparent preference for moderate voltages. There is surprisingly little from Shakespeare among the 200-odd poems: four sonnets and two

---

[1] To guard against misunderstanding, I had better put on record my admiration—based on a two-hour classroom visit in 1950—for the skill and enthusiasm with which Mr. Brooks can guide beginning readers.

songs, plus a few snatches from plays used to illustrate critical points. The total is less than 125 lines. Pope is represented only by *The Rape of the Lock* (entire) and a few lines about Sound and Sense; Donne by six poems open to discussions of wit and paradox but no "Ecstasie"; four contemporary American Southerners usurp a third more space than Shakespeare and Donne together. Linguistic difficulties no doubt account for the absence of Chaucer. The most exploited poet is Robert Frost (eleven poems, one of them five pages long). The criterion seems not to be intensity but discussability; and the discussion seems meant to be almost tepidly well bred.

The most useful available selection of verse is probably that of Thomas & Brown (*Reading Poems*). They assume a pretty good teacher and tend to keep out of his way; which is perhaps just as well, since their accents when they do intrude are utterly naïve. ("This and the following poem by Landor are noteworthy because so much meaning is distilled from so few words": this isn't a gambit but the entire comment. "What is Keats's experience recorded in lines 12–14? Do these lines re-create the experience?" One wonders how either of these questions can possibly be answered.) Messrs. Thomas and Brown's comments are all buried out of the way, in small print in the back of the book. So, unfortunately, is the authorship of the poems. This device seems to have been derived from Dr. Richards, who was using it rather as a laboratory control than as a pedagogical tool. One can't imagine what purpose it serves with students so innocent as to be grateful for the level of commentary that is offered; this book would do even less than Brooks and Warren's to develop the historical sense.

Developing the historical sense and learning to read poetry should, it seems obvious, go on together. A poem isn't a cat in an oxygen tank, nor can one, granted the appropriate techniques, simply contemplate the interaction of its 183 words as though no others existed. That way lies the conception of language as a set of signs classified in a dictionary, which, when people called poets manipulate them, can produce the fascinating psychological phenomena we call poems. A desire to frustrate the kind of teacher who turns a course in poetry into a course in history has, however, led several text authors to court this Scylla by eschewing chronological arrangement as thoroughly as possible.

Mr. Mark Van Doren's chronological orthodoxy, on the other hand, marks not a recoil from Scylla but a fondness for the conventional. "The aim of this volume is to introduce its readers to some poems with which they may fall in love." They include Miss Millay on Euclid, Kipling's "Recessional," and Yeats' worst poem, "The Ballad of Father Gilligan," concerning the ending of which Mr. Van Doren writes, "There is only this hymn, this lyric conclusion, with its rapturous repetition of 'He Who' and its innocent enumeration of God's grandeurs, to prove that Father Gilligan did understand. Of such for him was the kingdom of heaven. Of such for us is the kingdom of poetry."

As for Messrs. Unger & O'Connor, they provoke

not blame but something less than admiration. Their
book is not deadly dull, merely dull. It won't harm
any student who has a good teacher. It seems hardly
fair to the editors to record that their most memorable page is the one on which the phrase "Dead
cats" is scanned as an iamb.

After these Laodiceans there remain the Muscular
Christians. Mr. Cooper and the Messrs. Stageberg
and Anderson believe in Experience. Mr. Cooper
bounds in from the nearest YMCA to disabuse us of
our habit of confusing poets with flat-chested pan-
sies. We are to "get into the swing of the lines," to
be "conscious of responding physically to the strains
and tensions suggested in the poems." Having read
a poem about a foot race and one about a hammer
thrower, we are asked whether we have indeed re-
sponded in this way. Then we are asked:

> Would it seem to you that the writers of these
> poems are effeminate? Or that reading them is just a
> waste of time?
> Or that they are somehow addressed to the high-
> brows?
> I believe not.

Like Donne, Mr. Cooper can be as physical as he
pleases. He devotes a page to the structure of the
eye, and the saccadic movements that enable us to
read a poem "with the book held at the proper angle." He discusses the role of chest, diaphragm, and
abdomen in enabling us to read Shakespeare "aloud,
with vigor and gusto." A good poem, he tells us, "is
one that bursts upon the reader as he experiences it

—delights, titillates, surprises, dazzles, stimulates, engages, puzzles, provokes, rewards, challenges, satisfies! Not so the *bad poem*. . . ."

Stageberg & Anderson are less sweaty; their use of "experience" is Ricardian (see *Principles of Literary Criticism*, ch. xxx) and their terminology reeks of the laboratory. "A spoken vowel is a complex voice-tone consisting of two basic parts," commences the section on Assonance, which includes a table of characteristic frequencies of common vowels and refers us to an Appendix where the International Phonetic Alphabet (abridged) offers further assistance. *Poetry as Experience*, the blurb tells us, "makes use of the scholarly work of such men as John Dewey in philosophy, Wertheimer, Köhler, and Koffka in psychology, and Bloomfield, Jespersen, and Sapir in linguistics." Its axes for poetry are less clear. The selections are capricious, the annotations eclectic ("When Yeats wrote this poem in 1916 he was a bachelor of 51"), and the deference to commonplaces preposterous ("Of this line John Livingston Lowes has remarked, 'The music of the line . . . is due to the nice conjunction of recurring consonants with subtly varying vowels' ").

Mr. Millett doesn't prate of Experience, but he is just as depressingly methodical. He provides a six-page scheme of "Directions for the Analysis of a Poem," for instance:

II. Psychological Values.
    A. Emotional.
        Make a diagram representing the succession of

feelings and emotions that you experience as
you read the poem again and again. . . .

He discusses the five kinds of poetic values, Factual,
Psychological, Technical, Symbolical, and Ideational,
and observes, for the benefit of *very* bright freshmen, that "the distinction between the philosophical-
ethical approach to poetry and the discrimination of
the ideational values in a poem may be difficult to
keep in mind, but it nevertheless exists." Embedded
in this discourse on method are exactly fifty poems.
That doesn't seem many, but application of the
Method to each poem takes quite a bit of time, so
the semester will presumably be filled up. "Almost
every student that I have had has carried out all the
Directions for Analysis with an assiduity and com-
prehensiveness far beyond the call of duty. . . .
They will never again read a literary work quite
superficially."

It is appropriate that the latest-come[2] of these
awful books should be an attempt by a professor at
Wheaton College (Illinois) to reconcile all of them.
Mr. Kilby's *Poetry and Life* opens with the proposi-
tion that "a rich, full life is itself a poem, and a great
poem is the image of fruitful human experience."
Poets, he notes, have "often been men of affairs.
David was a king, Aeschylus was a soldier . . . de la
Mare was for eighteen years an employee of the
Anglo-American Oil Company. . . ." The table of
contents teems with subject headings like "Poetry
is Sane," "Poetry is Greater than its Rules," "Poetry

[2] As of late 1953.

is Subject to Critical Abuse," "Poetry and Science
Are One in Their Highest Reaches." This camp-
meeting atmosphere isn't dissipated by the use of
poems like the one which begins

> What is a word?
> A word is a pulley
> To raise up a city in the wilderness . . .

or by the citation of Mr. J. Donald Adams against
"the literary fashion created by these poets and
critics with their 'secret by-paths' and 'cerebral
gymnastics'." Against Mr. Kilby, for whom Milton
"had the finest ear of all English poets," for whom
the "Ode to a Nightingale" is difficult "because the
specific occasion of the poem is not known," for
whom Guiterman and Don Marquis exist in un-
abashed democratic ragtime a bare three pages from
John Donne—against Mr. Kilby no one is going to
prove narrowness, addiction to "secret by-paths," or
want of somewhat guarded solidarity with sixty
thousand professors.

Whoever protests that it is unfair to snipe at these
books because they were called forth by a situation
much more confused than they are, should explain
why, in a state of affairs so desperate, he considers
poetry worth teaching at all. It is perhaps the word
"poetry" that is causing much of the confusion. "Poetry," once we consider it as a "subject," breeds
every variety of pedagogic fungus. To study Poetry
requires an unusually tenacious mind, fortified by
a wide acquaintance with poems. It is doubtful
whether very many people should be encouraged to

undertake such a study. But the proposition that, whatever his notions about Poetry, there are *certain poems* every civilized American should be familiar with, seems not to be commonly advanced. It is tenable that a curriculum should consist of these plus certain other poems which buttress them, though only a persistent and experienced reader is likely to realize the solidity of the unspectacular buttresses. Whoever set out to nominate a list of poems, *with reasons,* would be in for a lively time; but he would perhaps prove to have done more for pedagogical enlightenment than the editors of a dozen textbooks who at bottom don't care which poems the student has read, so long as he has learned how.

8. Tales of the Vienna Woods

IT CAN VERY NEARLY BE CLAIMED FOR THE SUBJECT
of Dr. Jones' biography[1] that he has been the
presiding genius of the early twentieth century. That
he is already as dated as William Archer or *Trilby*,
and may come to seem as quaint as Boehme or
Swedenborg, are considerations that don't alter this
historical fact. An age in flight from diversity is de-
lighted by one-page explanations of all human phenomena, and Freud has seemed for many years the
most plausible of those investigators in whose name
such pronouncements can be issued. Since the early
nineteenth century the dominant philosophy of the
West has been some guise or other of German pessimism: of this Freud's utterances-at-large are a clinical variant. In the climate of all these philosophies
what a person takes to be his undertakings and
achievements are really just details of some process
he doesn't comprehend: the class war, or the struggle for survival, or the Decline of the West, or the
apotheosis of Emergent Will. What people think
they are doing, and so their conscious life in general, gets consequently devalued; the illusion of
being conscious, and of intending and willing, is represented as no more than an indispensable self-
deceit. So it is not surprising that the sequence of
doctrines represented by Schopenhauer, Darwin,
Marx, and subsequently Spengler should have
reached equilibrium with Freud's promotion of the

[1] Ernest Jones, M.D., *The Life and Work of Sigmund Freud*,
Vol. I: The Formative Years and the Great Discoveries, 1856–
1900 (Basic Books).

unconscious mind. "He would," his biographer writes, "have endorsed the view of the great anthropologist Tylor that 'the history of mankind is part and parcel of the history of Nature, that our thoughts, wills and actions accord with laws as definite as those which govern the motion of the waves'" (p. 366). The difficulty with all previous attempts to convince Mr. Everyman that he is the pawn of some Zeitgeist or other has been to demonstrate a linkage between its actions and what he persists in regarding as his own. In the wake of psychoanalysis this difficulty vanishes. Mr. Everyman carries his portion of the demiurge around with him in a sack labeled "the unconscious"; and it is useless for him to protest that he has never known this, for it is by definition unknowable, is it not?

That the spirit of these remarks seems irreverently remote from science must be ascribed to Freud himself, who was more often out of his depth than not, and continually the victim of bright ideas. Even the very short book (*An Outline of Psychoanalysis*, written in 1938) intended as a last résumé of his considered doctrines contains (p. 96) a pot-shot quasi-identification of Shakespeare with the Earl of Oxford, whose family history provided the materials for a really splendid Oedipus Complex.[2] His lucid and cogent analyses of the machinery of certain mental happenings—dreaming, forgetting, recollecting, abridging, and substituting—were soon sub-

[2] Though as late as 1931 he gave his imprimatur to an edition of *The Interpretation of Dreams* which adduces, apropos of *Hamlet*, biographical data about the Stratford Shakespeare (*Basic Writings*, Modern Library, p. 310).

merged in his theatrical conviction that human affairs are transacted in a sort of omnipresent Venusberg. "He was apt," writes Dr. Jones, "to be careless and imprecise in his use of terms, using, for instance, 'perception' as interchangeable with 'idea,' and the like" (p. 371). He was even "ill-informed in the field of contemporary psychology and seems to have derived only from hearsay any knowledge he had of it" (p. 371). His work, it may be maintained, presents a small viable corpus of the observed and comprehended, entrained and nearly smothered in an interminable afterbirth.

Dr. Jones unintentionally makes it especially easy for us to see Freud in this way, as one of the vastly influential philosophic amateurs of the nineteenth century, peddling his own brand of gloomy monism. His properly scientific work—the anatomizing of unconscious mental processes in pursuit of a technique for curing hysteria and other psychoses—didn't, the biographer makes clear, come easily to him; in order to concentrate on observing something, he had to suppress a massive desire to speculate. We hear of

> . . . a reply Freud once made to my question of how much philosophy he had read. The answer was: "Very little. As a young man I felt a strong attraction towards speculation and ruthlessly checked it." [p. 29]

The adverb is characteristic; Freud shared the belief of his time that the man of science had to be a pretty heroic fellow, "ruthless," "fearless," "uncompromising," and so on. "Nature," he wrote of himself in 1883, "endowed me with a dauntless love of truth, the keen eye of an investigator, a rightful sense of the values of life, and the gift of working hard and finding pleasure in doing so" (p. 118). On that occasion he was on his dignity, writing beneath the eye of his betrothed. Here is a more romantic version, excerpted from an effusion to a male intimate: "I am not really a man of science, not an observer, not an experimenter, and not a thinker. I am nothing but by temperament a *conquistador* . . . with the curiosity, the boldness, and the tenacity that belongs to that type of being" (p. 348).

This volume, the first of three, takes the career of the hero only to the year 1900, and the Freud it shows us isn't, despite these self-characterizations, the familiar figure of the later photographs, the graying Mephisto with the cigar, gazing in bleak comprehension on the dismal panorama of Civilization and its Discontents. The Freud of "The Formative Years and the Great Discoveries" was a victim of "neurotic suffering and dependence" the kinks in whose soul included a melodramatic phobia of traveling by train (which he later connected with fear of losing "his home and ultimately his mother's breast": p. 13), a lust for violent attachments (he "panted"—p. 301—for rare but compulsively necessary meetings with a rhinologist and numerologist named Fliess, to whom for some years, until a violent quarrel, he wrote weekly letters, and whose quasi-astrological jugglings with the numbers 23 and 28 he tried for years to build into the foundations of psychoanalysis); and an equally remarkable compulsion to alienate violently anyone he distrusted (about Josef Breuer, co-author of the *Studies on Hysteria,* he later used language so strong the biographer refrains from quoting it, and of his fiancée he demanded that she withdraw all affection from her mother and her brother—"this on the grounds that they were his enemies, so that she should share his hatred of them"—p. 123). The difference between this Freud and the more familiar one Dr. Jones, like a good Freudian, ascribes to the self-analysis begun in 1897. From this "there emerged the serene and benign Freud, henceforth free to pursue his work in imperturbable composure" (p. 320).

Incipit Vita Nuova; it makes a fine climax for Volume One, and presumably by the time he gets into Volume Two it will have blurred in the faithful reader's mind sufficiently to evade embarrassment. The orthodox Freudian who conceived the plot of this trilogy, however, is somewhat undercut by the chronicler who incautiously included in Volume One a few glimpses of the "serene and benign" Freud of later years. The following incident, which took place in 1912, is recorded within three pages of the sentence just quoted. At a luncheon with five disciples in a Munich hotel—

> . . . he began reproaching the two Swiss, Jung and Riklin, for writing articles expounding psychoanalysis in Swiss periodicals without mentioning his name. Jung replied that they had thought it unnecessary to do so, it being so well known, but Freud had sensed already the first signs of the dissension that was to follow a year later. He persisted, and I remember

thinking he was taking the matter rather personally.
Suddenly, to our consternation, he fell on the floor in
a dead faint. The sturdy Jung swiftly carried him to
a couch in the lounge, where he soon revived. His
first words as he was coming to were strange: "How
sweet it must be to die"—another indication that the
idea of dying had some esoteric meaning for him.
[p. 317]

This was fifteen years after the self-analysis started.
As for his having, as we were told on p. 13, been
able to "dispel" the traveling phobia by analysis, we
learn on p. 305 that "he retained in later life relics
of it in being so anxious not to miss a train that he
would arrive at the station a long while—even an
hour—beforehand."

In attending to trivia of this sort we are following
Dr. Jones, whose *bosse professionnelle* is an almost
comic preoccupation with anything that would ordinarily pass as too petty for extensive remark.[3] We
are told that the hero still wet his bed at the age of
two (p. 7), and once urinated in his parents' bedroom at the age of seven (p. 16); that matches in
Paris in 1885 cost him a whole penny a box (p. 184),
and that he applied chemical tests to the green cur-
tains in his hotel bedroom there "to make sure they
did not contain arsenic" (p. 183); that twenty years
after his first piece of laboratory work, an inconclu-
sive investigation of the gonadic structure of eels,
he bore a faint grudge against the teacher who had

[3] Though Mr. Paul Goodman in the *Kenyon Review* (Winter
1954) complains that the early part of the book is skimpy: "Jones
mentions not a word about toilet-habits and there is no history of
masturbation or its absence."

set him a task in which he could not make "some
brilliant and original discovery" [4] (p. 38); that an
overseer he disliked was exactly the age of his half-
brother, "the imagined rival with his mother in early
childhood," while one he admired was a contemporary of "his omniscient and beloved father" (p.
39). This half-brother is the theme of one of the
funniest paragraphs in the book, the one that deals
with the two-year-old Freud's growing suspicion
"that some man was even more intimate with his
mother than he was" (p. 14). A baby, the infant
Hercules noted, was on the way; "jealousy of the
intruder, and anger for whoever had seduced his
mother into this unfaithful proceeding, were inevi- .
table. Discarding his knowledge of the sleeping conditions in the house, he rejected the thought that
the nefarious person could be his beloved and perfect father." So he elected to hate the half-brother;
and "his intelligence was given a task from which
he never flinched until, forty years later, he found
the solution in a fashion that made his name immortal."

Dr. Jones is of course quite insensitive to the inherent comedy of these solemn remarks. The Freudians, most readers must have noticed, are funnier
than Freud, though the Master, with his usual penchant for overplaying his hand, did psychoanalyze
Moses, and did commit himself to the view that
small boys want to be engine drivers because of the

[4] Dr. Jones' footnote is worth reproducing: "One is tempted to
make the perhaps irrelevant remark that the future discoverer of
the castration complex was disappointed at not being able to find
the testes of the eel."

sexual stimulation afforded by "shaking sensations experienced in wagons and railroad trains" (*Basic Writings,* p. 600). His American translator, Dr. Brill, unsmilingly relates the case of a scopophiliac who "was able to *sublimate* the tendency for perverse looking" by becoming a dealer in optical instruments (*Basic Writings,* p. 18), and gives us an equally Flaubertian image of conversation at the staff dinner table of the Burghölzi Clinic in Zurich:

> No one could make a slip of any kind without immediately being called on to evoke free associations to explain it. It did not matter that women were present —wives and female voluntary internes—who might have curbed the frankness usually produced by free associations. The women were just as keen to discover the concealed mechanisms as their husbands. [*Basic Writings,* p. 27]

This, plainly, is a sort of comedy not covered by Freud's celebrated analysis, since no unconscious energy is being liberated. Its principle is the unwitting disclosure of a monomania. The only thing of which Dr. Jones, for instance, appears to be unconscious is the extravagance of his admiration for his subject. He is more objective than Freud's other intimates, he tells us; "my own hero-worshipping propensities had been worked through before I encountered him" (p. xiii). Yet with the warmth of Bouvard commending Pécuchet he shakes his head in dignified admiration whenever the Master opens his mouth or sets pen to paper. The letters Freud wrote to his betrothed "would be a not unworthy contribution to the great love-literature of the world.

The style is at times reminiscent of Goethe"[5] (p. 99). Of Freud's touristic descriptions of the various cities he visited ("Brussels was wonderfully beautiful, an enormous town with splendid buildings. . . .") he remarks on the "unusually keen powers of observation" and announces their separate publication (p. 182). His portentousness has a flavor all its own. Freud's fantasy of reproaching the Almighty for not giving him a better brain was "the remark of a man not easily satisfied" (p. 35). His ritual of devoting the last half-hour of every day to further self-analysis was "one more example of his flawless integrity" (p. 327). When he forsook physiology for psychology "the struggle must have been titanic" (p. 286). Of "his most heroic feat—a psychoanalysis of his own unconscious"—Dr. Jones remarks with fatuous awe, "no one again can be the first to explore those depths" (p. 319).

Behind these gaucheries lies the reason for the extraordinary fascination of this book. Through a lucky combination of professional solemnity and professional regard for minutiae, Dr. Jones has given us all the material we need to see Freud embedded in his time and place, pursuing a representative nineteenth-century career. The nonconformists of that age—Flaubert, Ibsen, and, in his special way, James Joyce, are familiar examples—seem to have

---

[5] "Woe to you, my Princess, when I come. I will kiss you quite red and feed you till you are plump. And if you are froward you shall see who is the stronger, a gentle little girl who doesn't eat enough or a big wild man *who has cocaine in his body.*" We are cautioned that much is lost in translation, though *"Meine geliebte Braut. Soweit das Schreiben. Was nun folgt ist Umschreibung"* is offered in illustration of the evanescent humor of the letters.

been locked into a biographical pattern possessing a number of standard elements. These are (1) a youth distinguished by both emotional turmoil and devotion to an ideal of thoroughness (Cf. Dodgson and Carroll; Freud performed a number of apparently unimpeachable pieces of physiological research); (2) a period of stormy relationships with other people, characterized by a loud insistence on utter and complete understanding which is always getting snagged on the unwillingness of the other people to be taken possession of in that fashion; (3) a phase, setting in at about the fortieth year, in which the life work ruthlessly pursued erupts suddenly into publicity and bourgeois scandal; and (4), immediately thereafter, a prolonged middle age during which, from behind a mask of majestic indifference, the hero, all passion supposedly spent, watches himself being turned into an institution. This last phase—Joyce in Paris, Flaubert coaching Maupassant, Ibsen returned from exile—is too common a feature of the *Heldenleben* to require the adduction of a Freudian self-analysis in explanation. Dr. Jones just isn't aware how commonplace is the shape of the life he is writing.

Nothing is more "period," for instance, than Freud's passion, so impressive to Dr. Jones, for threshing matters out. The theme of the long chapter about the four-year betrothal is "His hatred for half-measures and his determination to probe the truth to the bitter end, however bitter" (p. 123). The end, in those days, was always supposed to be bitter. "Their relationship must be quite perfect;

the slightest blur was not to be tolerated" (p. 110).
Having sent Martha's mother a tart letter, he wrote
Martha, "I have put a good deal more of my wrath
in cold storage which will be dished up some day.
I am young, tenacious and active; I shall pay all my
debts, including this one" (p. 123). Dr. Jones should
not ask us to suppose that in reading passages like
these we have a finger on the pulse of Freud's
genius; what throbs through the pages in question
is the shiny brass engine of nineteenth-century implacable rectitude. The identical beat is discernible
in many speeches from *Exiles,* which is about this
state of mind, or in Ibsen's letters to his sister Hed-
vig. Freud's conception of human relations was
rather provincial than otherwise, and this thirst—
masquerading as a love of sincerity—for subduing
other people's wills to his own, was exaggerated by
the social climate of bourgeois Austria, where no
mean seems to have been conceivable between utter
repudiation of another's right to existence and standing on his feet while breathing protestations of
friendship into his face. Here is part of the saga of
Fritz, who trifled with Martha's affections:

> Then Fritz called for pen and paper, and wrote a
> letter to her on the spot. Freud insisted on reading it,
> and it made the blood rush to his head. . . . Freud
> tore the letter in pieces, at which Fritz left in mortifi-
> cation. They followed him and tried to bring him to
> his senses, but he only broke down in tears. This sof-
> tened Freud, whose own eyes became moist; he seized
> his friend's arm and escorted him home. But the next
> morning a harder mood supervened, and he felt

ashamed of his weakness. "The man who brings tears
to my eyes must do a great deal before I forgive him.
I am made of harder stuff than he is, and when we
match each other he will find he is not my equal." . . .
[p. 112]

Every fact supplied by the biographer confirms
Wyndham Lewis' judgment of thirty years ago, that
Freud's is "the psychology appropriate to a highly
communized patriarchal society in which *the family*
and its close relationship is an intense obsession,
and the obscene familiarities of a closely-packed
communal sex-life a family-joke, as it were" (*The
Enemy*, No. II, p. 68). He seems never to have
questioned the universality of the family customs
and practices of bourgeois *Mitteleuropa*. For instance, the severest trauma of a small boy's life, "the
central experience of the years of childhood, the
greatest problem of early life and the most important source of later inadequacy" depends on his
mother threatening him with castration as a disci-
plinary measure; and Freud as late as 1938 seems to
have thought that the practice of issuing this threat
was as universal as the practice of breathing. By the
nature of psychoanalytic theory, once a practitioner
gets an idea like this into his head, nothing can get
it out; patients who protest that it never happened
to them merely illustrate the way the event is "so
completely forgotten that its reconstruction during
the work of analysis is met by the adult's most determined scepticism" (*Outline of Psychoanalysis*, p.
95).

"I always find it uncanny when I can't understand

someone in terms of myself," Freud wrote in 1882
(p. 320). To this romantic subjectivism, reinforced
by the *Mitteleuropäisch* norm of hysterical oscillation
between coldness and intimacy and by the German-
idealist emphasis on the will as the only thing real
or meaningful, we have only to add the Helm-
holtzian tradition of scientific determinism, in which
Freud was trained and which he never forsook, to
arrive at a working model of both the man and his
doctrines.

"Like most adolescents Freud had the need to
'believe in something,' and in his case the something
was Science with a capital" (p. 40). This religion,
which he shared with so many eminent Victorians,
came to him in a form "deeply imbued with the
principles of causality and determinism, so pronounced in the Helmholtz school that had dominated his early scientific discipline" (p. 245). The
moment we can imagine this faith placed at the
service of his preoccupation with how people felt
about other people—especially about him—we have
the key to his severe pursuit of trivia, his stern determination that the verbal slip you uttered in his
presence, or the name he was himself unable to remember (for he was as hard on himself as on anyone) *meant something.* And of course his "passion
for threshing things out" intervened on the spot. We
shall *have this out,* here and now! And since "he
never abandoned determinism for teleology" (p.
45), the meaning of the slip which you persisted in
treating so lightly—to the scorn of this Sinaitic will-
specialist—lay in the past. Backwards, then, the

threads of "free association" were to be traced, if necessary back to the cradle. The instant unbroken trains of rigid causality are posited, one is committed to saying that the events that control one's behavior now, occurred in remote infancy. It was Freud's distinction that he pursued these consequences with fanaticism to the end. He even thought of pursuing them beyond the womb; in a footnote to a chapter on the Oedipus Complex we read, "The possibility cannot be excluded that a phylogenetic memory-trace may contribute to the extraordinarily terrifying effect of the threat [of castration]—memory-trace from the prehistory of the human family, when the jealous father would actually rob his son of his genitals if the latter interfered with him in rivalry for a woman." Though we have no record of this jealous caveman, we have Freud's assurance that "dreams offer a source of human prehistory which is not to be despised." The Darwinian view that ontogeny repeats phylogeny was another premise he never forsook (*Outline of Psychoanalysis,* pp. 50, 92).

Freud's philosophical achievement—like that of a chess master who contrives an impregnable opening —was to combine the ambient premises of nineteenth-century continental pessimism into the most impenetrable of orthodoxies. By transforming Schopenhauer's "will" into "the unconscious" he placed the whole complex of interdependent doctrines beyond discussion. The axioms of psychoanalysis are not statements about things in general, nor about a sort of Lockean working model to be considered with dispassion, but statements about *you;* and when you question one of them the Freudian cocks a caustic eyebrow and inquires into your motives for evading self-knowledge. Discussion, for that matter, always nettled Freud, whether because he took it as a personal affront or because he recognized the futility of its attempts to penetrate the machine he had constructed. At any rate, in deference to his wishes, it has always been forbidden at Psychoanalytic Congresses. His last book begins with the tart warning that the teachings of psychoanalysis "are based upon an incalculable number of observations and experiences, and no one who has not repeated those observations upon himself or upon others is in a position to arrive at an independent judgment of it" (*Outline,* p. 9). In another late work he says that "the recognition we afford to sexuality is— whether they confess it or not—the strongest motive for our opponents' hostility to psychoanalysis. But are we to let ourselves be shaken on that account? It only shows us how neurotic our whole culture is, when apparently normal people behave no differently than neurotics" (*The Question of Lay Analysis,* p. 54). So the mere inquirer hasn't a chance. Neither had associates. Breuer, when his feet cooled on the threshold of Venusberg, was hurled amid maledictions into limbo. Jung was excommunicated (or severed himself; accounts differ —Volume Two throws less light than one might wish on that mysterious affair).

From the final volume, we may perhaps expect to learn more about the extraordinary spread of Freud's doctrines. It was of course to be expected that a body of statements so involuted as to be capable of absorbing, like a Venus Flytrap, the inquirer who perches on the rim of its most peripheral conclusions, would achieve a sort of underground popularity, especially among individuals anxious to appear interesting to themselves. And the constant incitement to introspection (since you cannot safely examine your neighbor's unconscious) has led many readers into a process of self-examination so inexact it would convince them that all their dreams were symbolically related to elephants, if that was what they had been told they would find. Again, the British literary and artistic avant-garde of the twenties and thirties constituted a powerful engine of publicity. Nothing gives the "feel" of that period more vividly today than the plexus of notions its languid literati were absorbing. It seemed pleasant, apparently, to be told that your inability to rival Michelangelo was the result of a neurosis, or that the trivialities that flicker at the threshold of a consciousness that isn't attending to anything were the forked tips of subterranean flames. No one, in that milieu, seems to have found the unconscious *dull*, though a glance at the files of, say, *Transition* will convince us that nothing is deader than "automatic writing" and no one drearier than a synthetic primitive. There is no Poe-esque energy in those morbid dungeons beneath the stratum of conscious life: nothing but the same dreary Oedipus Complex, universally distributed. Freud's Id, one would think, could inspire a *frisson* in nobody. Perhaps it was modish to despise *frisson;* the Freudian years in Anglo-Saxonry were the enervated decades of ("yes, oh dear yes") Forster and Mrs. Woolf.

For Freud the conscious part of the mind does nothing but mediate between the monotonous demands of the Id and an external reality which can be called "real" only by courtesy: an external world whose phenomena manifest only two sorts of character—either they comply readily with the Id, or they don't. There is no question of the mind *knowing* them, or of its life drawing nourishment from their intelligible species. Rather, there may be such questions, but Freud isn't interested; and so interlocked are his expositions that he soon gives the impression of ignoring their existence. His is a world in which, ultimately, nothing possesses any interest at all, except for the sort of tumid interest people can always derive from themselves.

It nettled him a little that "the pleasure principle requires a reduction, or perhaps ultimately the extinction, of the tension of the instinctual needs (that is, a state of *Nirvana*)": in other words that what the machine tries to do is discharge its batteries and drift. But this parallel with the concept of *entropy* advanced by his contemporaries in physical science didn't arrest him; he merely remarked that the difficulty "leads to problems that are still unexamined" (*Outline*, p. 109). A year before he died of cancer he was writing that we all die of the death-wish (*Outline*, p. 23).

Freud made a number of irrefragable discoveries which haven't enjoyed nearly the acclaim of his theatrical generalizations. His account of how dreams work, and where their material comes from, and their function as protectors of sleep, seems sound, whether or not it covers all dreams; and so does his investigation of the symbologizing activities of the relaxed mind. Symbols thus created aren't interesting symbols, just as the jokes dissected in *Wit and the Unconscious* aren't good jokes. Nevertheless some symbols and puns do get made in the manner he described, and, properly scrubbed and sterilized, his descriptions make valuable instruments for investigating the highly peculiar art and literature of his own century, when writers were accustomed to let the creative faculty be hypnotized by prosodic superficies while a florid dream-work went on beneath. Of his therapeutic achievements I am unqualified to speak. But he was unwilling not to explain the world; and the stuff of his explanation, as Dr. Jones unintentionally convinces us, was the philosophic flotsam of his time. It dates more cruelly with every decade, and the decades that swallowed it most avidly—the twenties and thirties, pursuing their predilected nexus with the hothouse nineties—date today most of all.

9. Provision of Measures

BOOKS HAVE THEIR DURATIONS. THE *Guide to Kulchur* belongs to a small category that before they pass into nothingness or into history enjoy a greater or lesser period of active usefulness. This category should be distinguished from two others: the very large one comprising books that never get off the ground, and the very small one of books that achieve a sufficient "escape velocity" to stay up permanently. One can read the *Odyssey* as though it had been written yesterday, but not, after two centuries, Pope's *Odyssey*. Pope's *Odyssey* wasn't a failure, however, nor is it simply a mark in Pope's career. It was a useful and seminal work for some sixty years. A hundred other English *Odysseys* have been stillborn.

It is a mistake to suppose that writing *ad hoc*, including most "critical" writing, aims or ought to aim at immortality, or should be judged as if it did. The critic who thinks he is writing literature is very unlikely to write anything useful. He is the more likely to hit the target in proportion as he understands what he is aiming at, and insofar as his work achieves its function it ought to render itself unnecessary. Pound's aim in 1938 was to help "fit the student for life between 1940 and 1960"; the duration he forecast for the *Guide* at the time of writing was probably about twenty years. Time-lags being what they are, it seems likely to be useful for another thirty, before it turns into a highly delectable curiosity. If such a document had been left over from

132

the nineteenth century, it would be regarded today
as that century's most fascinating book. A certain
amount of it—surprisingly little after two decades
—already seems limited by Pound's view of what
was going on in 1938.

More of Pound's work is worth reading than that
of most prolific writers, because he doesn't play soli-
taire with general ideas. He has been so prolific
because he has had things to say. He has seldom
claimed to be saying the last word, but his least
squib has the validity of some perceived fact with
rudiments of context. His mind has always been taking in material, and it has always been at work. It
has three main ways of working. The first way,
which accounts for the bulk of his writing, is to seize
a new fact and set it in relation with known facts:
in a letter of 1928 he perceived a relationship between Rémy de Gourmont and Confucius. The second is to discern amid these facts the necessity for
some action or other, and urge this action upon the
general reader or upon whatever individual is
handy: in the thirties he was demanding a bilingual
edition of the *Ta Hio*. The third is to ruminate and
digest, a process which goes on continually behind
the constant intake of new facts, and is perhaps
slower for Pound than for people who call a halt to
all other mental operations while they "think over"
two new ideas: by 1945, nearly thirty years after
first discovering Confucius, he had found out sufficiently what Kung's text meant to make a version
that renders the long enthusiasm intelligible.

Though he often finds out what alignments of fact

mean years after first perceiving them, Pound has seldom been embarrassed by his earliest formulations. He is fond of quoting Brancusi's *"Toutes mes choses datent de quinze ans"* and has remarked that "one of the pleasures of middle age is to find out that one WAS right, and that one was much righter than one knew at say 17 or 23." If it was sixteen years after writing Canto XLV that Pound made a definition of Usura ("A charge for the use of purchasing power, levied without regard to production; often without regard even to the possibilities of production"), the moral is not that he was bluffing in 1937, but that he could identify Usura and see where it fitted in long before he could enclose it in his mind and say exactly what it was.

That is why the meaning of the *Cantos* is cumulative, and why Pound was able to embark on his long poem without having thought out a rigorous scheme. If there is more depth of felt meaning in the Homeric allusions of *The Pisan Cantos* than in the Odyssey extract of Canto I, that is because Pound was penetrating and gaining possession of that particular subject during the intervening thirty years. Yet he saw at the start how Odysseus' voyage would lock in with his other materials in certain important ways. In the same way, he recognized that T. S. Eliot was an important poet at once, without necessarily realizing *what* Eliot's poetry was. And when he helped revise *The Waste Land,* he knew that Phlebas the Phoenician was necessary to its structure at a time when Eliot wanted to throw the section out; and he was able to give this practical advice without necessarily realizing what the significance of "Death by Water" was.

The passage from knowing *that* a thing is to knowing *what* it is always takes a long time. It may be wrong to assume that many people can negotiate it faster than Pound, but it is safe to say that he is unique in our time for the speed with which he seizes on the first essential, that there is something or other here to repay attention. In due time the *what* seems to take care of itself, if you have the gift of seeing the *that,* and then don't fake. *The Spirit of Romance,* his earliest prose book, is still readable after nearly fifty years, because of the energy with which it recognizes the existence and relevance of a number of facts. The value of the book inheres in its schema; the facts aren't very deeply penetrated, but our attention is called to them, and many of their implications arise from their very collocation. The value of the ideogrammic method is that it enables you to make statements that don't exceed your knowledge. Of course you can always improve the wording. The translations as given in the latest reprint have been much revised since 1910; some of this revision was done between 1929 and 1932 for an abortive French reprint, some is more recent. Though stripped of "hath" and "doth," they still sound very pre-Raphaelite. The prose has been less retouched; Pound was apparently aware that rethinking the material "in depth" would require a wholly new book. The Pound of 1910 encloses the nature of a topic by disjunct statements and comparisons: "Petrarch refines but deenergizes." The

Pound of 1929, having better grasped many of these
topics, can spring the appropriate image in a word
or two: "No, he doesn't even refine, he oils and
smooths over the idiom . . ."

As for the Pound of 1938, he presents in the *Guide
to Kulchur*, as one might expect, all three sorts of
mental activity: things he is just discovering, things
he has long explored, and innumerable programs for
action. The facts he has lived with longest have
been assimilated into a kind of wisdom ("Culture
begins when one HAS 'forgotten-what-book'") in
which the incitements to action and the tessellations
of his most recent facts have their setting.

The overall intention is clearly stated on p. 23:
"Certain ground we have gained and lost since
Rabelais' time or since Montaigne browsed over 'all
human knowledge.' Certain kinds of awareness mark
the live books of our time, in the decade 1930–40.
Lack of these awarenesses shows in the mass of dead
matter printed." And eleven pages later, a distinction between "ideas which exist and/or are discussed in a species of vacuum, which are as it were
toys for the intellect, and ideas which are intended
to 'go into action,' or to guide action and serve us
as rules (and/or) measures of conduct. Note that
the bloke who said: all flows, was using one kind,
and the chap who said: nothing in excess, offered a
different sort."

In a later chapter the author reverts to Rabelais
and Montaigne, from whom "you would, I believe,
acquire curiosity by contagion, and in a more mel-
low form than from the 18th century collectors of

heteroclite items laid out all of 'em from the same point of view, all dealt with by an identical process, whereas Montaigne and Rabelais are handling them with a more general curiosity." Pater's *Renaissance,* he reminds us, "made a limited circle of readers want to know more of a period"; a few pages later there is a reference to "general incuriosity, while faddists and university infants carded out again the overcombed wool of a limited set of 'classics.'"

The Spirit of Romance is an orderly book; the contents of the *Guide* on the other hand aren't grouped under familiar headings. One reason for this is that the *Guide* images Pound's own extremely interesting mind, which at any given moment holds a multiplicity of related topics, some newly gripped, some wholly digested, the rest at various intermediate phases. Another reason is strategic: Pound wishes at all costs in this book to incite curiosity, the *sine qua non* of the world he would open up for the reader. His own limitless curiosity has made him the poet he is, and it underlies the fact that virtually every sentence in the *Guide* registers a mental effort, an inquiry, a setting of things in relation, a reach for the appropriate analogy. "Bad writing," he has said, "comes from insufficient curiosity." The incurious mind won't *look at* the subject long enough to discover its shape, an act which is the prerequisite for finding the right words; nor will it reach far enough for those words. And whether its activity is intended to issue in written words or not, the incurious mind will float within the tepid confines of received curriculum divisions, studying now history, now currency, now poetry, now mathematics, without ever seeing the world of interacting processes in which these are not "subjects" but ways of discussing a single complex subject.

There are, in short, several different kinds of material in *Kulchur,* and their interrelation in the nature of things isn't simple. It is foolish, Pound thinks, to suppose that a single abstract statement like "everything flows" would have made Heraclitus' reputation among a people that prized "the quite H. Jamesian precisions of the *Odyssey."* More likely he was respected for trying to "carry a principle through concrete and apparently disjunct phenomena and observe the leaves and/or fruits of causation." The principle carried through disjunct phenomena was what Fenollosa noted in the Chinese sentence, "Man sees horse," wherein all three of the ideograms have legs: not only the man and the horse but the moving eye that unites them. Fenollosa, and Pound after him, prized the "continuous moving picture" by which the Chinese syntax depicts what is in fact a process, not a mere relation between two entities. "A true noun," wrote Fenollosa, "an isolated thing, does not exist in nature. Things are only the terminal points, or rather the meeting points, of actions, cross-sections cut through actions, snapshots. Neither can a pure verb, an abstract motion, be possible in nature. The eye sees noun and verb as one: things in motion, motion in things."

Apply this to history, and you have what Pound calls the "totalitarian" grasp, a good term that has unluckily gotten spoiled. He notes the blankness of those who have tried to study history from historians, and don't read verse. "Can we," he asks on another page, "sort out 'greek thought' from the iron money of Sparta, and the acute observer who remarked that the great mass of gold in Athens served merely to assist the Athenians with their arithmetic? . . . Does any really good mind ever 'get a kick' out of studying stuff that has been put into water-tight compartments and hermetically sealed? Doesn't every sane ruler feel that Plato was a faddist? . . ."

If you can't divide the study of Greece into art, thought, monetary custom, language, etc., neither can you so divide "Culture." "The one thing you shd. not do is to suppose that when something is wrong with the arts, it is wrong with the arts ONLY." This observation is connected with Pound's often-repeated dictum that there is no necessary place from which a general education ought to start, so long as you eventually get the whole of it. There aren't, for the kind of knowledge he seeks to impart, first principles from which the others can be deduced. He has written, for instance, a great deal about poetry without implying that the subject necessarily starts from imagery, or from narrative, or any of the other textbook starting places. In fact the *ABC of Reading* is prefaced with the remark that it doesn't matter which leg of the table you make first, so long as it eventually stands up. When you get it made, no one will doubt the interrelation of the parts.

This amounts to saying, not that study—that thought—has no method, but that the existing categories are misleading and even deadening. They imply divisions where the facts have none, separating Plato-as-philosopher (philosophy) from Plato-as-faddist (Realpolitik), and cauterize sets of facts just when they are reaching out into the domain of other facts, or into action. In an illuminating page devoted to Leo Frobenius, Pound quotes, "Where we found these rock-drawings, there was always water within six feet of the surface," and comments, "That kind of research goes not only into past and forgotten life, but points to tomorrow's water-supply." Frobenius couldn't have made an observation of that kind had he been content to be an art critic.

The allusiveness of modern poetry needn't be a sign of cultural breakdown, but a manifestation of one of poetry's oldest functions. Confucius listed among the uses of poetry that it helps you remember the names of many birds, animals, plants, and trees. In the schools of Rome and of the Middle Ages, whole tracts of knowledge now dealt with separately as "subjects" were discussed in the grammar and rhetoric classes as ancillary to the exegesis of Homer and Vergil: botany, strategy, history, geography. "Real knowledge," Pound notes, "goes into natural man in titbits, a scrap here, a scrap there: always pertinent, linked to safety, nutrition, or pleasure." The teacher of modern poetry finds himself discussing the Grail legend, Heraclitus, Cuchulain, the *Odyssey*, Dante's trimmers, Chinese ideogram, the culture of Provence, usury, spirit writings, the *Noh*.

What justifies the use of such materials by the poet is that they are worth learning about anyway.

The *Guide to Kulchur* aims to teach us to deal with knowledge as the poet does. There is always, as in a poem, a relation between two adjoining sentences or paragraphs, but it isn't the traditional textbook relation of common categories. Hence one may expect to find on a single page (56) Cambridge economics, Dante's interest in living, the effect of Schönbrunn on a visitor of sensibility. The thread that runs through these particular three coins is a discussion of live vs. dead learning. At the end of one chapter (p. 75) Pound warns the reader that "these disjunct paragraphs belong together. Gaudier, Great Bass, Leibniz, Erigena, are parts of one ideogram, they are not merely separate subjects."

This isn't to imply that Pound regards the intellectual world as an endless circle of bright sayings. In addition to inciting to curiosity and indicating tissues of relationship, the book has a third aim, the provision of measures. A measure, a criterion, of directness in working through the medium of one's art is implied in a reference to a picture in the Prado in which a fire in the background "is there with two strokes or perhaps ONE of the brush." One may connect this observation with the author's exemplification, in an essay now forty years old, of the kind of poetic effect that is highly charged without any "device" beyond common words in a prose order. Another measure is supplied in the advice on how to see works of art: "Think what the creator must perforce have felt and known before he got round to creating them." This may be connected with Frobenius' distinction between "knowledge that has to be acquired by particular effort, and knowing that is in people, 'in the air.'" The artist's knowledge is of both kinds. There is yet a third measure in the remark that "The moment a man realizes that the guinea stamp, not the metal, is the essential component of the coin, he has broken with all materialist philosophies."

The conception of the critic as one who gathers specimens and aphorisms for his reader to use in measuring whatever else he encounters is Pound's major critical discovery. The *ABC of Reading* contains a long series of examples, each illustrating some specific quality of verse at its highest potential. Matthew Arnold's "touchstones" by contrast all illustrated the same thing, not a variety of qualities, though Arnold deserves credit for realizing that criticism must proceed by comparison rather than deduction. In the *Guide*, a book to help one read many kinds of other books, Pound undertakes to provide useful measures for a very wide body of experience. Such an undertaking is by its nature a challenge; the contents aren't meant to be swallowed as dogma. One would like, and presumably Pound would like, to hear an intelligent Aristotelian's detailed comments on Chapter 54, for instance, or an intelligent musician's evaluation of Chapters 7 and 42. The critic's intelligence would have to be pretty high to make the commentary of any interest; neither sneers nor corrections of detail will damage the book. In longing, as he did when the book was first published, for someone both learned enough and intelligent enough to take issue over some of the points he raised, Pound was setting forth yet another measure for *"Kulchur,"* one that has always dominated his mind: the possibility an age affords for conversation between intelligent men.

10. Remember That I Have Remembered

I

"TO KNOW WHAT PRECEDES AND WHAT FOLLOWS," the translator of Confucius reminds us, "is nearly as good as having a head and feet." That "the Present can only be revealed to people when it has become Yesterday" is unfortunately a concomitant maxim, as Wyndham Lewis, who formulated it, long knew to his cost. The map of English literary events for the first third of this century is only now at long last emerging; the importance of the republication of Ford Madox Ford's *Parade's End* a quarter-century after it was written is that an entire continent has been added, and it is now possible to explain to people why they can't sail directly from Naturalism to Joyceland across the Freudian sea.

The working hypothesis of putative good will confronted by "modern literature" used to be that "modern psychology" explained its differences from Tennyson and Thackeray. The Unconscious and Free Association wrote and underwrote the vagaries of Woolf, Lawrence, Eliot, Joyce, Auden, Pound, and even Miss Stein. It is now becoming possible to publicize the fact that Lawrence, the only one of these writers who couldn't be suspected of using "Freudian" techniques, was the only one exhibiting a relatively uncritical interest in Freud; that the key to twentieth-century English poetry is nineteenth-cen-

144

tury French prose; and that the writers of the half-century just closed "weigh" in exact proportion to their grip on this key.

As Mr. Pound has been telling us for forty years, Stendhal's repudiation of "poetry with its fustian à la Louis XIV" was a crucial event in the history of letters. "At that moment the serious art of writing 'went over to prose,' and for some time the important developments of language as means of expression were the developments of prose. And a man cannot clearly understand or justly judge the value of verse, modern verse, any verse, unless he have grasped this." Again, "No man can now write really good verse unless he knows Stendhal and Flaubert."

It was Ford, and Ford almost alone, who in the first decade of this century absorbed and retransmitted the discoveries of Stendhal and Flaubert on an English wavelength. It was a long time (1915— *The Good Soldier*—aetat. 42) before his practice really caught up with his conversation; but from the time of his collaboration with Conrad at about the turn of the century until the emergence of the Pound-Eliot-Lewis "Vortex" in 1914 he was virtually alone in his tireless insistence on (1) the adequation of language to the thing perceived or the sensation undergone rather than to an overriding concept of "style"; (2) the importance of making every episode, sentence, and phrase *function*—carry forward the total effect (*"progression d'effet"*); and (3) the principle of juxtaposition without copula of chapter with chapter, incident with incident, character with character, word with word, as the mainspring of poetic effect.

The quality of Bouvard and Pécuchet's rapture at their inheritance is both rendered and placed in twelve words by just one collocation of enthusiasms: *"Nous ferons tout ce qui nous plaira! nous laisserons pousser notre barbe!"* In the technique of that sentence lies all modern letters in embryo: the exact words, the thematically relevant detail, the *hokku*-like juxtaposition of imperial felicity and an unchecked beard. It has nothing to do with the unconscious or private associations; neither has anything in *The Waste Land*. And it was Ford who discerned and propagated that technique.[1]

Mr. Yeats had frequented the Symbolists but not the prose writers of France; Ford the prose writers but not the Symbolists. The young Ezra Pound in the London of 1912 or so, seeing Ford in the afternoons and Yeats on Monday evenings, effected some

---

[1] In *The March of Literature* (1939) Ford traces the principle of juxtaposition to, for contemporary purposes, Stendhal or perhaps Jane Austen. "The point," he adds, "cannot be sufficiently laboured, since the whole fabric of modern art depends on it." A page or two later he adds, "Nothing in the way of incident or character sticks far out of the story, but the effect of ordinariness set against ordinariness in a slightly different plane gives precisely the effect of not ill-natured gossip, which to the average intelligent mind is the most engrossing thing in the world, and of slight surprise which is the prime quality of art." A comparable and much more elaborate account is given in the invaluable third part of the Conrad memoir. The term "gossip" should be noted. Ford's unobtrusive good manners made it necessary for him to efface these principles by washes of casual verisimilitude. He got no further than a sophisticated impressionism, but as the English novel stood (and largely stands) it was a major innovation to get so far.

transfusion of ironic discipline into Yeats as well as a notable synthesis in himself. Joyce acquired independently a corresponding synthesis of the same French components. So did Wyndham Lewis. Assimilating Gautier at Pound's instigation, Mr. Eliot acquired a "hardness"—ultimately Flaubertian— that underlay his great work of the twenties.

Hence the "Vortex" of 1914–16; Pound, Lewis, Eliot, Gaudier-Brzeska, with Joyce a saluted ally; perhaps the only time—certainly the only time since 1600—when a group of masters was doing things in English that had not been done better on the continent. And as if in certification of his magisterial status, Ford's first masterwork, *The Good Soldier*, commenced serial appearance in the Vorticist organ, BLAST.

That World War I dissipated the Vortex may yet prove to have been its most far-reaching effect: as though the Armada had broken off English intellectual life in 1588. The mind of England was abandoned to Bloomsbury, to its perdition. Some half-baked milieu or other becomes the intelligible context of the career of each of the surviving vorticists: Eliot's ironic truce with Bloomsbury and Lewis' ferocious anatomizing of its fauna, Joyce's involvement with the *Transition* gang, Pound's quest of new vortices in Paris and Rapallo (maelstroms in bathtubs) and Ford's in Paris and New York. Hemingway, Mrs. Woolf, the Sitwells, all writers subsequent to the Vortex, however disparate in quality, are dominated if not bounded by such milieux.

II

The false dawn and nightfall we have been out-
lining is in effect Ford's lifelong theme, though it
is not at that level of realization that it engages his
attention. It does not detract from his honor, but
does a great deal to illuminate his orientations, that
he never really knew what the Vorticists were doing.
They knew what he was doing;[2] they printed him in
BLAST; yet BLAST seems the oddest possible context for his prose. His subsequent avuncular ironies
about the impatient young "parading those respec-
table streets in trousers of green billiard cloth and
Japanese foulards" connote equal amusement with
the paraders and with the respectability. Ford was
to that extent allied with the morning-coat ethos.
That alliance was perhaps a condition of the skill
with which in *Parade's End*—his second master-
piece—he achieved its indestructible record. For
that is very largely what *Parade's End* is.

The artist who can actually get down on paper
something not himself—some scheme of values of
which he partakes—so that the record will not
waver with time or assume grotesque perspectives
as viewpoints alter and framing interests vanish, has
achieved the only possible basis for artistic truth and
the only possible basis for literary endurance. Homer
so registered values and was the educator of Greece.
It is the hardest and rarest of jobs. This or that novel

[2] One at least was only half-persuaded. "I am afraid an invention of Ezra's," said Lewis of Ford, November 1956. As to what
of Ford's most needed preserving, Pound answered, "The tradition of his intelligence" (September 1953).

which we in haste mistake for a mirror of the age—
The Forsyte Saga, for instance—usually turns out to
be a reflection in moving water. Language alters,
connotations slither, the writer leans on what his
audience understands, and that understanding does
not endure. What Pope meant by "Nature" and
"Reason" in the *Essay on Criticism* must be labori-
ously filled in by the archaeologist of traditions; that
is the technical failure of a firmly intended effort at
definition, clear in Pope's mind, that it is now impossible to praise as Dr. Johnson, living closer to its
terminology, could praise it. Thirty years' subsequent work made possible the almost lexicographi-
cal exactness of the fourth book of the *Dunciad*. The
point at which a writer *defines* something, whether
one moral term—"wise passiveness"—or an entire
civilization—Cummings' *Eimi*—is the point at which
he drives his peg into the cliff. That was the work
Ford undertook for the values of gentlemanly England. It was in its way a harder job than Dante's,
since it is the essence of those values that they com-
port with extreme conventionality of articulation. *La
sua voluntate è nostra pace* relies not only on the
image structure of the *Paradiso* (*ella è quel mare*)
but on a tradition in which terms were defined.
Despite Ford's thirty years' cultivation of every technical wile, only his vastly allusive diffuseness could
have done the job for " 'Bad form!' she exclaimed.
'You accuse me of bad form.' " I am not prepared
to say that he needs every word on his 836 pages;
but he needs nine-tenths of them.

The two young men—they were of the English public official class—sat in the perfectly appointed railway carriage. The leather straps to the windows were
of virgin newness; the mirrors beneath the new
luggage-racks immaculate as if they had reflected very
little; the bulging upholstery in its luxuriant, regulated
curves was scarlet and yellow in an intricate, minute
dragon pattern, the design of a geometrician in Co-
logne. The compartment smelt faintly, hygienically of
admirable varnish; the train ran as smoothly—Tietjens
remembered thinking—as British gilt-edged securities.
It travelled fast; yet had it swayed or jolted over the
rail-joints, except at the curve before Tonbridge or
over the points at Ashford where these eccentricities
are expected and allowed for, Macmaster, Tietjens felt
certain, would have written to the company. Perhaps
he would even have written to the *Times*.

That is the train that was, figuratively, wrecked
at Sarajevo. Its "mirrors, immaculate as if they had
reflected very little," convey with sufficiently potent
wit the limitations of the Tietjens world, limitations
which generate the agonies and catastrophe of parts
II and III of the tetralogy. Yet the great achievement of the first quarter of the work is the weight
with which Ford manages to invest the code of
"Some do not," hitherto accessible to Americans only
via the stridently understated snobbery imparted in
the public schools to the sons of drainage inspectors.
This felt and realized sense of a flexible, scrupulous
order cannot be illustrated by quotation; indeed the
paragraph just quoted is almost the only one in this
gargantuan novel that has something of its full effect
alone, because it is the first. *Progression d'effet*—the

reliance of every word on all the words that have
come before—has hardly been carried so far in English. A sort of scrupulous lexicography working by
the exact reproduction of the tones of numerous
speaking voices invests the numb counters of "right,"
"wrong," "honour," and "gentleman" with the context of sensitive values informing the best minds of
Edwardian England. "Admirable," in that first paragraph—"admirable varnish"—is such a counter. It is
a recurrent word; and in what novelist but Ford is it
anything but a clumsy blur of approval? To have
registered a code in which "admirable" denotes a
definite, complex congeries of values is a technical
achievement sufficiently astonishing.

One test of Ford's method is that the pseudo-values
of the lacquered, ingratiating upstart Macmaster are
demarcated without caricature from those of Tietjens. "Macmaster was obviously Scotch by birth, and
you accepted him as what was called a son of the
manse. No doubt he was really the son of a grocer in
Cupar or a railway porter in Edinburgh. It does not
matter with the Scotch, and as he was very reticent
as to his ancestry, having accepted him, you didn't,
even mentally, make any enquiries." This in its context is not snobbery; it registers exact and—again,
in context—perfectly acceptable mental processes.
Here is Macmaster enacting what he conceives to be
pre-Raphaelite grand passion:

. . . He heard himself quote:
"Since when we stand side by side!" His voice
trembled.
"Ah yes!" came in her deep tones: "The beautiful

lines. . . . They're true. We must part. In this
world. . . ." They seemed to her lovely and mournful
words to say; heavenly to have them to say, vibrat-
ingly, arousing all sorts of images. Macmaster, mourn-
fully too, said:

"We must wait." He added fiercely: "But tonight, at
dusk!" He imagined the dusk, under the yew hedge.
A shining motor drew up in the sunlight under the
window.

"Yes! yes!" she said. "There's a little white gate from
the lane." She imagined their interview of passion and
mournfulness amongst dim objects half seen. So much
of glamour she could allow herself.

Afterwards he must come to the house to ask after
her health and they would walk side by side on the
lawn, publicly, in the warm light, talking of indifferent but beautiful poetries, a little wearily, but with
what currents electrifying and passing between their
flesh. . . . And then: long, circumspect years. . . .

This is magnificently "placed." It is handled more
sympathetically than the analogously derivative
amours of Gerty Macdowell; but no less critically.
Parody is the clue to everything in Joyce, because his
subject is itself a parody: aristocratic values preserved in Ireland, but preserved in alcohol; pickled
fetuses; paralyzed. Ford's subject, on the other hand,
is not a parody but a wraith; values obeyed but never
enunciated, or merely felt against Philistine disobe-
dience, or enunciated with ineffable monosyllabic
clumsiness.

"God's England!" Tietjens exclaimed to himself in
high good humour. " 'Land of Hope and Glory!'—F
natural descending to tonic, C major: chord of 6-4, sus-

pension over dominant seventh to common chord of C
major. . . . All absolutely correct! Double basses, 'cel-
los, all violins, all woodwind, all brass. Full grand organ,
all stops, special *vox humana* and key-bugle effect. . . .
Across the counties came the sound of bugles that his
father knew. . . . Pipe exactly right. It must be: pipe
of Englishman of good birth: ditto tobacco. Attractive
young woman's back. English midday midsummer.
Best climate in the world! No day on which a man may
not go abroad!"

This, with its ironically technical choric imagery,
must not be confused with mere prose Rupert
Brooke. It is as near articulation as Tietjens ever
gets. And Ford builds it up from thousands of careful
observations of cadence, idiom, tone, and gesture.
The recorder and re-creator is at work: at work, not
asprawl.

This point needs to be made. There is every reason
to suppose that the Ford boom, like the recent
Mozart, Austen, and Pope booms, is bottomed by
nostalgia for an innocent bucolic order.[3] All these
artists were "civilized" in a leisurely and ample manner: so we are told, despite Miss Austen's sardonic
"regulated hatred" and Pope's explicit feeling of living at the verge of the darkness of the Uncreating
Word: as he was. One might have supposed, to read
some reviews, that

> There's some corner of a foreign field
> That is forever England. . . .

[3] Written in 1950. Eight years later it only remains to be added
that the boom was indeed a puff of smoke, and *Parade's End* was
remaindered.

was, for some 800 pages, Ford's substance. A Brooke
revival, really, would have made in these terms considerably more sense. Ford's constant concern is to
record and anatomize, not to wallow. The reasons
for the impending smash (the matter of parts II and
III of the tetralogy) are thoroughly implicit in *Some
Do Not*. And the postwar world in which *"There will
be no more parades. . . .* No more Hope, no more
Glory, no more parades for you and me any more.
Nor for the country . . . nor for the world, I dare
say" emerges in *The Last Post* with as much tough-
ness and as little nostalgia as, given the données of
the novel, could be desired. The English Horatian
ideal, now half-wordless and hence fated ("But what
chance had quiet fields, Anglican sainthood, accuracy
of thought, heavy-leaved, timbered hedge-rows, slowly
creeping plough-lands moving up the slopes? . . .
Still, the land remained"), bore in its increasing re-
gressiveness the seeds of doom. George Herbert,
Tietjens remembers, wrote *Sweet day, so cool, so
calm, so bright, the bridal of the earth and sky;* but
as for Tietjens, "the basis of Christopher Tietjens'
emotional existence was a complete taciturnity—at
any rate as to his emotions. As Tietjens saw the
world, you didn't 'talk'. Perhaps you didn't even think
about how you felt." Ford takes ample account of
the "other England" (the ruling classes as distinguished from the governing class) who inhabit Mr.
Pound's scabrous Hell (Cantos XIV and XV). The
inarticulate Tietjens order with its massive tolerance
permitted these to rise. Tietjens' thorough approval
of the right of every man to use his own weapons is

what, in a sense, undoes him and his world; Groby
Great Tree that a Yankee tenant cuts down in the
final pages, wrecking half the house and ending an
era, represents not only the Tradition but its suicidal
component. "It had always been whispered in Groby,
amongst the children and servants, that Groby Great
Tree did not like the house. Its roots tore chunks out
of the foundations and two or three times the trunk
had to be bricked into the front wall of the house."
Yet its presence was not only tolerated but revered:
"Christopher set great store by the tree. He was a
romantic ass. Probably he set more store by the tree
than by anything else at Groby. He would pull the
house down if he thought it incommoded the tree."
Ford, it should be noted, sought without irony his
final audience and milieu among the compatriots of
the Yankee tenant.

III

This order incompatible with the very exertion by
which it might save itself corresponds with whatever
prevents Ford from ranking as a very great writer.
He is great enough. Such writing, page by page,
phrase by phrase, mass by mass, employing every
wile with utterly self-effacing virtuosity, can scarcely
be equaled in English. But there is a component of
softness—not etiolation as in the late Henry James,
a reflex of the remorseless urge to *explain*, but something here and there a little closer to whimsy than is
comfortable in an extrapolation from Flaubert. When
he was not yet thirty Ford had written in the final
paragraph of his second collaboration with Conrad,

"And, looking back, we see Romance—that subtle
thing that is mirage—that is life. It is the goodness
of the years we have lived through, of the old time
when we did this or that, when we dwelt here or
there. . . ." It is remarkable how early in life he
began writing memoirs. *Memories and Impressions*
is dated 1910 (aetat. 37), and it is at least the fourth
volume drawing on Ford's pre-Raphaelite childhood.
His first books, fairy tales and historical romances,
regress in an analogous way. From 1910 till his death
his eyes are turned backward; the original title of
The Good Soldier was, we remember, *The Saddest
Story*. Pathos, until the Tietjens tetralogy, was his
métier: pathos superbly controlled and objectified,
but a little soft, a little naïvely susceptible to Edwardian ladies cool and finely gowned.

That his marvelous childhood had ended, then that
his Edwardian years had ended, were successive
themes of Ford's early books. *The Good Soldier* is
probably the best of these books because it holds
these themes of loss in a rarely articulated and deper-
sonalized balance. And *The Good Soldier* plus all
that the War implied gives us *Parade's End*: im-
mensely complex personal misery plus the shattering
of all the externals of the order that had sustained
the poise of gentlemen. An important strand of
Parade's End, then, leads us back to Ford's youth
and out to his public persona of incorrigible remi-
niscer. On this strand may be blamed such lapses as
occur.

Nice to be in poor old Puffles' army. Nice but weari-
some. . . . Nice girls with typewriters in well-

ventilated offices. Did they still put paper cuffs on to keep their sleeves from ink? He would ask Valen . . . Valen. . . . It was warm and still. . . . On such a night . . .

That "poor old Puffles" passes because it is Tietjens' word, but Tietjens at his least exigent. Tietjens here as often is a little too close to being Ford himself, vastly wearied and regretful, and whimsical. One doubts whether *in propria persona* Ford would have troubled to invent a better name than "Puffles," or cast a better phrase, because he too felt like that: as we can tell from reading *Great Trade Route* or *It Was the Nightingale*. Tietjens, that is, is much more literally Ford—as to his emotional quality—than, say, Prufrock is Mr. Eliot.

The success of *Parade's End* depends upon the way it exploits all Ford's skill while using just the material that will conceal his defects. They are the defects, however, which deprive him of co-status with Pound, Eliot, and Joyce, a little anachronistic, writing from a basis a little closer to the time in which the novels are set than to that in which they were conceived. The fact that he seems never to have noticed Eliot gives us one way of bringing this out. (The writer recalls two references to Eliot, both ironic, in the whole of Ford's oeuvre with which he is acquainted; and *The Waste Land* does not appear in *The March of Literature* reading lists, whose standards are not so exigent as to exclude Auden, Masefield, Cummings, and Rupert Brooke.) Impressionism, Pound justly observes, meant something to Ford that it did not mean to Arthur Symons or

George Moore; it meant a technical rigor that es-
chewed "fine writing" in the interests of the subject.
But symbolism meant something to Mr. Eliot that
it didn't to Ford, who seems not to have undergone
the Symbolist impact at all.

Intensity, for Ford, was a matter of mass: *progression d'effet.* He saw this dimension alone in Eliot's
work, apparently; and at the level of *progression
d'effet, Prufrock,* however sound, was nothing more
remarkable than the verse Ford himself could turn
out in a morning. (His *On Heaven* was at this level
skillful and moving enough to be—deservedly—an
Imagist wonder in 1916 or so.) Ford presumably saw
something absurd in the massive reputation erected
by Eliot on a very slender output. Slender, that is,
by Impressionist standards. Sound enough, but short-
winded.[4] Confronted by

> *I should have been a pair of ragged claws*
> *Scuttling across the floors of silent seas*

Ford would have recalled Bouvard's *"J'ai envie de
me faire saltimbanque sur les places publiques!"* and
reflected that the technique was easy after all. The
"tentacular roots" of those precise images, "reaching
down to the deepest terrors and desires," would not
have seemed relevant to him. He describes the effort
of the good stylist to make sure "that the word
chosen was not too *juste.* A too startling epithet, however vivid, or a simile, however just, is a capital

---

[4] Mr. Pound has supplemented this account by remarking that
Ford was the only man in London who foresaw the likelihood,
and the consequences, of Eliot's becoming a literary dictator.

defect because the first province of a style is to be unnoticeable." "Impressionism" implied author-suppression at that level. The Eliotic "impersonality"—an anonymity quite compatible with great local intensity, so that line after line lodges in the memory—apparently did not strike him as a meaningful extension of that principle. He could not have started a poem with the word "Polyphiloprogenitive." The Impressionist aim—"above all, to make you see"—immolates language to subject in a futile as well as a salutary sense. The poet's *language* is something vastly more than himself; it contains the past of the race and, in its potentialities for juxtaposition, the intelligible species of all the mysteries. His *subject* is, as it reflects his pattern of interests, something much more like himself, invested with his limitations of emotion and vision. *Parade's End* is a fine and moving novel because its author was a great and massively honest craftsman, and a fine and serious and sensitive person. But apart from Joyce's oeuvre there is still no fiction—unless some of Lewis'—great, as is much poetry, because the language, which does not merely extend the author but transcends him, has gone into independent action and taken on independent life.

IV

To talk about other possible novels is not to wish that Ford had written a novel other than the one in hand. It would be worth most novelists' while to spend some years of study and emulation on the

procedures and felicities of *Parade's End*. It opens
slowly, amid a multitude of leisurely and supple
flashbacks, because Ford must begin by getting down
that age now gone in all its complexity and implication. Christopher Tietjens, whether or not he "comes
off" as a detachable human being (which is irrelevant), succeeds as the multifaceted incarnation of
the virtues of an age; nor even confined to an age,
but backed by the traditional mass of centuries. The
counterpointing of Tietjens' marital troubles and the
debacle of Tietjens' England achieves with enviable
tact what would in clumsier hands be *Cavalcade*
superimposed on *Goodbye, Mr. Chips*. And the rich-
ness of the dozen marvelous closing pages is backed
by the elaborately differentiated planes of reference
of the preceding hundreds. It is into the overgrown
but still unblocked tunnels to dialect and faery England that the dying Mark Tietjens glimpses: it is
from them that he extracts his legacy for the living:

> "How are we to live? How are we ever to live?"
> "Now I must speak," Mark said to himself.
> He said:
> "Did ye ever hear o't' Yorkshireman. . . . On Mount
> Ara . . . Ara . . ."
> He had not spoken for so long. His tongue appeared
> to fill his mouth; his mouth to be twisted to one side.
> It was growing dark. He said:
> "Put your ear close to my mouth. . . ." She cried out!
> He whispered:
> " 'Twas the mid o' the night and the barnies grat
> And the mither beneath the mauld heard that."
> . . . "An old song. My nurse sang it. . . . Never

thou let thy barnie weep for thy sharp tongue to thy goodman. . . . A good man! . . . Groby Great Tree is down. . . ."

He said: "Hold my hand!"

* * *

She said:

"Perhaps it would be best not to tell Lady Tietjens that he spoke.

. . . She would have liked to have his last words. . . . But she did not need them as much as I."

11. Conrad and Ford

THE OLDEST OF THESE BOOKS HAS BEEN ACCESSIBLE for fifty years, the youngest for thirty.[1] All three are books the reader of novels cannot afford not to know. All three are faintly old-fashioned now; their solidity is Edwardian; the novel has moved on. Joyce solved problems Conrad never faced; Wyndham Lewis in *The Revenge for Love*—the finest "unknown" book in fifty years—brought politics into fiction in a way that has been neither surpassed nor examined; Ford himself, in *A Call* and elsewhere, developed Jamesian latencies that escaped the later interests of James and so made possible the finest parts of *Parade's End*. Joyce, however, goes unexamined except by card indexers; *The Revenge for Love* was ignored in England and suppressed in New York; and the recent Ford boomlet confined its interests to what seemed "safe." The critical avant garde is busy discovering *Under Western Eyes* (1911), "appallingly corroborated by events that have become ominous reality in modern history" (introduction by M. D. Zabel), *Nostromo* (1904), an image of "man . . . precariously balanced in his humanity between the black inward abyss of himself and the black outward abyss of nature" (introduction by Robert Penn Warren), and *The Good Soldier* (1915), the sort of novel of which one can ask, "But are not these 'realities,' in effect, 'appearances'?" while in the course of reading it "we slowly learn to

[1] Joseph Conrad, *Under Western Eyes* (New Directions).
Joseph Conrad, *Nostromo* (Modern Library).
Ford Madox Ford, *The Good Soldier* (Knopf).

read ourselves" (introduction by Mark Schorer). It should be possible to see them better than that in mid-century, though it is something that they are seen at all.

The three books are thoroughly "written." Conrad and Ford—it is becoming commonplace to observe —accepted from Flaubert the view that the novelist's job is to find words, sentence by sentence, for the unique instance, the particular case, the light of torches making the letters of an inscription leap out black from end to end of a long wall, the plash of fountains from the mouths of stone dolphins, a terrified student looking down a staircase: "Gazing down into the black shaft with a tiny glimmering flame at the bottom, he traced by ear the rapid spiral descent of somebody running down the stairs on tiptoe. It was a light, swift, pattering sound, which sank away from him into the depths: a fleeting shadow passed over the glimmer—a wink of the tiny flame. Then stillness." This—from *Under Western Eyes*— not only neatly illustrates Conrad's formula, ". . . above all, to make you see," it illustrates the mode of his most memorable effects. One is made to see not a man going down stairs, but a certain man, Haldin, with his characteristic manner of running, descending the stair of Razumov's lodging house with the lamp at the bottom, running out of Razumov's life (the sound "sank away from him into the depths") to a police trap and doom ("a wink of the tiny flame. Then stillness"). The whole first part of *Under Western Eyes* is a tour de force of pregnant writing, the presented fact become the economic metaphor. Haldin, a political assassin, had come to Razumov for asylum, because he supposed Razumov was a kindred spirit. Razumov declined to compromise his own future and arranged the trap. The next sentence reads: "Razumov hung over, breathing the cold raw air tainted by the evil smells of the unclean staircase. All quiet." The air of freedom, the smell of his own treachery. Then composure: "He went back into his room slowly, shutting the door after him. The peaceful steady light of his reading-lamp shone on the watch. Razumov stood looking down at the little white dial. It wanted yet three minutes to midnight. He took the watch into his hand fumblingly." The imbalance of his composure is reserved for the last word in the fourth of these sentences; "fumblingly" strikes the reader with much the same surprise as the fact that his hand was unsteady must have struck Razumov. Such minutely dramatic writing, never overtly "symbolic" but always in touch with larger meanings through the presented facts which hold the reader's attention from sentence to sentence, carries Flaubert's techniques into areas where Flaubert, the Stoic comedian, never ventured. *Under Western Eyes* affords ninety-nine such pages, unbroken.

Then Conrad's devotion to "the way of doing a thing that shall make it undergo most doing" takes over. The Western Eyes of the elderly language teacher are interposed between the reader and the Razumov saga, and the narrative never really regains momentum. This frustration for the unsophisticated reader, in quest of a story, corresponds, it is important to note, to a disappointment for the critical reader. It is not that the change of the perspective breaks the action; there are artistic reasons for breaking it. It is rather that the presented fact is withdrawn to a considerable remove from our attention; commentary, the arranging and presenting consciousness of the detached man who is supposed to be editing Razumov's diary and narrating what came under his own observation, becomes a medium through which, so to speak, the subsequent events—often crashingly melodramatic events—are reviewed. The phony revolutionaries who begin to swarm—Peter Ivanovitch, Madame de S.—don't weigh as they should against the genuine moral dilemma of the Razumov whom they take for an ally, because they don't exist. They coincide too closely with the skepticism of the elderly narrator to have a life of their own; that they are bundles of quite predictable mannerisms isn't an ironic element in their character but a defect in their presentation, for we come to see this fact as a mere manifestation, a cruder manifestation than is the narrator, of the temperamental skepticism which Conrad is determined to inject into the book. Conrad's ironies of character are almost always facile; *The Secret Agent,* for instance, is a less interesting book than current accounts suggest. "Technique," in the "detached" parts of his books, becomes a cover-up for the fact that his mind has ceased to be obsessed by the reality of his subject, that he has withdrawn from his material and begun to manipulate it, as he considers, philosophically.

Nostromo, as much his most anxiously meditated fiction, is the fullest case of this curious phenomenon.

Much of the time—when he is "creating" the town
and characters—one can see very little. It is exactly
when the narrative breaks loose—in the marvelous
night voyage of Decoud and Nostromo with the
treasure—that the prose unclogs and one reads on
unfatigued. *Nostromo* is a brilliantly excogitated
book, wrought detail by detail with barely a chink;
but Dr. Leavis' grudging verdict that its reverberation "has something hollow about it" corresponds
to a pervading forced "significance" that localizes
itself in analytic images like "The sense of betrayal
and ruin floated upon his sombre indifference as
upon a sluggish sea of pitch" and statements like "In
our activity alone do we find the sustaining illusion
of an independent existence as against the whole
scheme of things of which we form a helpless part,"
which are neither sufficiently grounded in the presented facts of the book nor sufficiently backed by a
communicated sense of the author's experience. This
last sentence is part of the analysis of Decoud's
breakdown, but it doesn't stay within its données;
it comes as a portentous aside from Conrad. The
minutely wrought solidity of *Nostromo* derives, as
much as anything, from its being willed into existence, the characters created to illustrate a theme, the
theme worked out in an elaborately balanced plot
with appropriate symbols in incident and setting,
every detail arranged, and the whole painstakingly
focused so that Conrad's essential want of belief in
the reality of what he is presenting is disguised as a
"detachment" intrinsic to the book's philosophy. It
is perhaps the very intimacy of the creative impulse,

in this instance, with the philosophical that has won *Nostromo* its reputation as Conrad's supreme achievement; it is certainly an achievement of sheer scrupulousness that the result appears so solid, but there is very little in *Nostromo* as immediate as whole sections of *Under Western Eyes*. Conrad, at bottom, doesn't know what his attitude to his events and characters is, and that is what "detachment" conceals; nor will Mr. Warren's Kafkaesque speculations about "the true lie," "fidelity," "moral infection and redemption" bring the book really to any but a willed life.

Ford had no "philosophy"; that is perhaps the reason for his long neglect. Far more impressively than Conrad has he the ability to invent exactly the right words from moment to moment; the prose texture of *The Good Soldier* is unfailingly vivid: "I had forgotten about his eyes. They were as blue as the sides of a certain type of box matches. When you looked at them carefully you saw that they were perfectly honest, perfectly straightforward, perfectly, perfectly stupid. But the brick pink of his complexion, running perfectly level to the brick pink of his inner eyelids, gave them a curious, sinister expression—like a mosaic of blue porcelain set in pink china. And that chap, coming into a room, snapped up the gaze of every woman in it, as dexterously as a conjuror pockets billiard balls." *The Good Soldier* is in more than one way a tour de force. Ford arranges words so as to produce constant surprise, constant small shocks to the attention. He arranges incidents in the same way. Theme words drop into place, key scenes recur in new contexts, an intricate tangle of cross-reference conveys the illusion of living complexity assuming no more and no less order than life assumes. With a technique of far greater virtuosity than Conrad's goes a far greater sense of flexible life. Ford's heroes, like Conrad's, undergo mute ordeals, but without suggesting to the reader a "symbolic" remoteness. If Conrad wrote out of his capacity for skepticism, Ford wrote out of his capacity for compassion and worry. Worry is the stuff of his situations; on Edward Ashburnham is heaped a worry so intolerably complex that he breaks. As in *Parade's End*, the impasse is adulterous; it is essential to the structure of *The Good Soldier* that it shall be an impasse. The narrator suffers on his own account as much as on Edward's; he is himself in fact a party to the impasse. Within this simple matrix Ford deploys with consummate virtuosity his trivial, melodramatic incidents. A book was never, from one point of view, better written.

There is no pretense of detachment; the whole is ordered by a shocked narrator. And the narrator's bewilderment is Ford's most serviceable device; for it prevents him from having to resolve the book. The convention of the book is that the narrator resolves it by writing it: the last turn of Ford the technician's screw. If one seeks for a center, one is driven through ironic mirror-lined corridors of viewpoint reflecting viewpoint, and this is of the book's essence; an optical illusion of infinite recession. Ford, one uneasily supposes, doesn't himself know what his attitude is to the situation he presents. The gap between presentation and "values" is never bridged. Ford's presented values are those of the craftsman; the man Ford, most compassionate of novelists, is himself in an impasse, an impasse of sympathy for all sides.

It is impertinent to turn to biography: Ford's Catholicism, his adulteries, and the unresolved conflicts of his life. At ease, he threw off in his memoirs (in some respects, his best fiction) masks of himself so engaging as to make these factors of negligible weight. But that he presents himself more convincingly than he does any other character throws light on what the virtuosity of *The Good Soldier* is masking; a suspension of judgment that looks like technique and is in fact bewilderment. If Conrad forced into "philosophy" a naïve nineteenth-century skepticism: man alone in a meaningless universe, making fictions to live by, Ford forced into "technique" a more permanent plight: that of a man incapable of squaring his values with his actions, incapable of repudiating anything that has once laid claim on his sympathy.

Though his achieved fictions haven't Conrad's weight, Ford should have come nearer to being a great novelist; he had more to work with; Conrad's central theme may well in another fifty years seem as dated as *In Memoriam*. Both of them might have been weightier if technique hadn't seduced them, hadn't persuaded them that they had solved at the level of judgment problems which they were accustomed to coping with at the level of literary presentation. But technique seduced them because it was important; no one but Henry James, in those years,

understood its claims so clearly; almost alone they
had to redeem the English novel for the intelligent
world. They did that, and they wrote memorable
pages. They might have done more in another language, or at another time; but perhaps they did more
than we might reasonably expect. It was no small
achievement to maintain an artistic conscience in
Balfour's England, to wrestle in those times of facile
writing with the exact enduring word, Razumov
leaning over the banister listening to the light swift
pattering sound which sank away from him into the
depths, or Edward Ashburnham, sentimentalist to
the last, speaking with the penknife in his hands the
precise last words that will epitomize a sentimentalist's life: "So long, old man, I must have a bit of rest,
you know."

12. In the Wake of the Anarch

POPE WAS AWARE, WITH MORE THAN YEATSIAN LUCID-
ity, that in his lifetime millennial traditions were
suddenly fading. The Universal Darkness into which
he gazed with such prophetic horror was no mere
sensational reflex of a provincial inability to grasp
the mutability of cultures. Misled by a look of grad-
ualness, however, we suppose that he was misled.
When Mr. Eliot reminded us that the eighteenth
century was, "like any other age," an age of transition, he was speaking of its poetic sensibility, which
"alters from generation to generation, whether we
will or no," impelled by the accumulation of events,
retarded by the tenacity of human habit, not a seis-
mograph to register intellectual cataclysms but a
turbid fluid medium of awareness holding in suspension their settling dust. The gradual downward
sloping of the arts into the Romantic century mis-
leads us into supposing that Pope's age modulated
into Shenstone's just as Dryden's modulated into
Pope's; but to approach history through poetry anthologies, with an ear for the morphology of sensibility, is to apprehend not events but their protracted
reverberations. Scholarly ears, attuned to this mull of
sound, readily suppose that when Pope spoke of Art
after Art going out he was "exaggerating magnificently" (as his Twickenham editor puts it) the death
of an age which he refused to believe was like all
ages mortal: a first trombonist standing up in the pit
to announce the extinction of music because the

171

phrases allotted for the passage of which he bore the burden were drawing to a close.

Yet it is easy to show that he was not exaggerating: the proof is that Pope himself became in fifty years all but unintelligible. His editors could not read him; his commentators cannot read him. Though our dictionaries contain all his words and our handbooks all his allusions, his poems have grown as inaccessible as (to exaggerate magnificently) those of the Etruscans. We are situated, since the Romantic explosion, on another planet; in the finale to the *Dunciad* we intuit a desperate vatic urgency and applaud a pomp of sound, but suppose that the same thing is being said over and over. On the contrary: a most precise analysis goes forward, according to premises desperately in need of recovery.

> She comes! She comes! the sable throne behold
> Of Night primeval and of Chaos old!
> Before her Fancy's gilded clouds decay
> And all its varying rainbows die away.
> Wit shoots in vain its momentary fires . . .

The light that is being negated is no mere blurry metaphor for intelligence, but an illumination whose modes of operation are conceived with speculative exactness. Fancy stands in relation to it as sunset colors and rainbows to the sun: the clouds and raindrops not objects made visible but pretexts for a tenuous virtuosity of the luminescent principle itself, to be anticipated (Coleridge, Shelley) just after the full light has vanished. Wit in its absence is condemned to be self-luminous and transient, a fugitive display (Byron, Peacock)—

The meteor drops, and in a flash expires.

The sun of learning has set before, but in a previous Dark Age the stars held their places: an Erigena put Greek tags in his verses, a stray monk took bearings from Vergil. But this time the primal light itself is being withdrawn from all things luminous:

> As one by one, at dread Medea's strain,
> The sickening stars fade off th' ethereal plain,
> As Argus' eyes, by Hermes' wand opprest,
> Closed one by one to everlasting rest,
> Thus at her felt approach, and secret might,
> Art after Art goes out, and all is Night. . . .

The arts are stars as civilization's steering marks, flowers as its products and ornaments, eyes as its guardians; now the flowers fade, the eyes close, the very stars are occulted. Hermes, the undoing of the many-eyed Argus, was the god of luck and wealth, the patron of merchants and of thieves: in Pope's usage, emblem of the opacities of commerce. The booksellers and the money spinners of the City are among the efficient causes of the *Dunciad*'s action.

The "Universal Darkness" that buries all is therefore a negation of a universal light concerning whose functioning Pope was willing to be more specific than elocutionists suppose. We hear about it, in fact, as early as the *Essay on Criticism*, published when he was too young (twenty-three) to have done any more than intuit a set of regnant intellectual conventions.

> Unerring NATURE, still divinely bright,
> One clear, unchanged, and universal Light,
> Life, force, and beauty must to all impart,
> At once the source, and end, and test of Art. . . .

This Light comes, by a long tradition, out of St. John's gospel: it shone in the darkness and the darkness did not comprehend it, it was in the beginning with God, and it was the Word, the Logos which the Romans, lacking a single term, denominated as *ratio et oratio.*

> In some fair body thus th' informing soul
> With spirits feeds, with vigor fills the whole,
> Each motion guides, and every nerve sustains;
> Itself unseen, but in th' effects remains.

These passages, to be sure, are flaccid gestures toward the conventional: but a lost convention. The identity of the Universal Light and the Universal Reason was a commonplace of a thousand sermons; St. Augustine's doctrine of human knowledge, never abandoned from the fourth century to the Cambridge Platonists, turns on this identity. The Holy Spirit, furthermore, stood to the world in the same relation as the human soul to the body; hence a tissue of analogies whereby the polysemous "Nature," divine, human, and created, could be "at once the source, and end, and test" of a human activity which paralleled that of the Divine Artificer. All this, by Pope's time, had come to be believed "in memory only, reconsidered passion"; and Pope for his part reports

no visions of the light, though he talks about it
with a born paraphraser's suavity. He has nothing
comparable to Dante's

> *Chè la mia vista, venendo sincera,*
> *e più e più intrava per lo raggio*
> *dell' altra luce che da se e vera,*

or even Mr. Pound's

> that the body of light come forth
> from the body of fire . . .

He handled the ideas that were in circulation, and
rubbed them smoother; he was content enough in
Locke's ambience, and allowed Bolingbroke credit
as a philosopher, and wrote about

> strong connexions, nice dependencies,
> Gradations just. . . .

What rouses him to visionary intensity isn't metaphysical radiance but the processional triumph of
obfuscation:

> She comes! she comes! . . .

The *Dunciad*, as Mr. Aubrey Williams shows in his
well-mannered, vastly informative study,[1] plays its
energies on a process of thickening and fattening,
perceived with hallucinatory particularity: literature
inertly copied from other literature, drama no longer
aspiring to conceive with austere passion an action
like a moving arrow, plunging instead into stupefy-
ing sensation, the stage manager rather than the

[1] Aubrey Williams, *Pope's Dunciad, A Study of Its Meaning*
(1955).

dramatist "immortal";[2] the prestige of learning become an inducement for pedagogy to ally itself with
advertisement and scholarship to agitate itself like
a tireless worm:

> Let standard-Authors, thus, like trophies born
> Appear more glorious as more hack'd and torn,
> And you, my Critics! in the chequer'd shade
> Admire new light thro' holes yourselves have made.
>   Leave not a foot of verse, a foot of stone,
> A Page, a Grave, that they can call their own.

It is a terrible, compelling apocalypse, and when its
detractors complain of spleen its champions have
found nothing better to do than concede exaggera-
tion, albeit magnificent.

One would never guess from Mr. Williams' genteel
manner that he had walked into the professional
Popeans' Natchez-Augustan manor with the components of a time bomb under his raincoat. Possibly
he doesn't guess it either. In his first two chapters
he appears to be setting up the equipment for a
lantern lecture, complete with map. The impatient
reader may well start on the last four chapters, which
are informative enough to discount the lecturer's
tone; and then reflect that the large perspectives of
learning there afforded may well be more systematically accessible to Mr. Williams' generation than

---

[2] "Immortal Rich! how calm he sits at ease
 'Mid snows of paper, and fierce hails of pease;
 And proud his Mistress' orders to perform
 Rides in the whirlwind, and directs the storm."
As for the spectator, he goggles like a tourist in Radio City:
 "Joy fills his soul, joy innocent of thought;
 'What pow'r,' he cries, 'what pow'r these wonders wrought?' "

they were to Pope's. As one may sail along coasts
without a map, or any idea of what a map would
look like, so a reader living in Pope's age would
have encountered the capes and headlands of the
poem with a readiness of habitual response which
the historian, mistaking tradition for doctrine, can
extrapolate into a statement of principle the Augustan might not have recognized. The way to profit by
Mr. Williams' exposition is to transpose it into the
specific assumptions behind Pope's local devices.

The chief technical device in the *Dunciad* is to
mime perversity by systematically perverting what
we are meant to recognize as the normative images
of orderly encomium. Bentley's great paean to the
scholars affords a condensed instance:

Like buoys, that never sink into the flood—

his learning a mark to steer by, he and his fellows
fixed points amid tempests and opinions; it seems a
neatly predictable image, until the denouement—

On learning's surface we but lie and nod.

In the passage about standard-Authors, the first
couplet perverts into Yahooesque jubilation the
regimental pride and orderly decorum of armies, the
second into simian self-congratulation a tranquil
pietism about the fullness of age. We are meant to
recall how Waller had written,

The Soul's dark cottage, batter'd and decay'd
Lets in new light thro' chinks that time has made;

but the plenitude of senescent wisdom gives way to
its parody, the annotator's idiotic delight that new

beams penetrate a text (which before his arrival on the scene had been merely an impediment to the light) every time his forefinger punches a hole in it.

Pope's way of moving mock earths requires his taking a stand on such minimal and cliché-ridden orderliness as can still be evoked; he postulates the intelligibility of created things, the normality of their symbolic functions, the rationality of poetic images. We hear much about the aptness of his literary parody; but the literary order upon the prestige of which Pope depends for so many effects isn't to his mind venerable because it happens to exist, but radiant because sanctioned by those very analogies between divine and human intelligence which permit and render fructive the ready resemblances between wise men and seamarks, light and intelligence, the Playwright and God; which enable the writer to see in ordonnance an image of order, to co-operate with his material rather than fight it, and make with ease intelligible statements about the intelligible: which in short reveal a world interesting enough to write about.

When no one believed such things any longer, no one could read in depth what had been so written. The mind coming close slips over Pope's mirrorlike surface, and drawing back sees reflected there its own banalities. "Not a classic of our poetry," said Arnold, "a classic of our prose." Pope opened his fourth book with a prophetic apostrophe to the powers of oblivion:

> Ye Powers! whose mysteries restored I sing,
> To whom Time bears me on his rapid wing,

> Suspend a while your force inertly strong,
> Then take at once the Poet and the Song.

It was so: a criticism which assumed that the writer situated before an opaque world expressed only himself, transformed Pope into a spiteful little hunchback.

Which is the point d'appui of Mr. Donald Davie's book on syntax.[3] If Mr. Davie, the most gifted British critic now functioning, has opened up a subject for which his book isn't ambitious enough, he has gone beyond any previous theorizer in opening it up. Syntax postulates an intelligible world; whoever frames a sentence claims to have performed an analysis, corresponding in complexity to the articulation of the sentence. "Jack threw the ball and Will caught it": we have observed these activities, and concluded that they were disjunct. "Jack threw the ball to Will": either a different throw, or a closer analysis.

> The thriving plants ignoble broomsticks made,
> Now sweep those Alleys they were born to shade.

—syntactic neatness miming a perception that Fortune's wheel can turn with headlong precision. But an arrangement like the following, though officially a sentence, corresponds to no observed architectonic of events:

> There was rapture of spring in the morning
> When we told our love in the wood.
> For you were the spring in my heart, dear lad,
> And I vowed that my life was good.

[3] Donald Davie, *Articulate Energy, an Enquiry into the Syntax of English Poetry* (1955).

The only identifiable event ("told"; for one can't believe "vowed") buries its face in a subordinate clause
shielded by a falling rhythm; while the first and third
lines expend their clockwork confidence in saying
nothing. The tawdry appeal the poem puts forth (it
is Poem IV in I. A. Richards' *Practical Criticism,*
where it is shown to have pleased 53 per cent of the
college readers on whom it was tried) depends on a
mere Gestalt of reliable words: rapture, spring,
morning, love, dear lad. Any gimmickry that will set
these partners jigging in a suitably brief stanza will
suffice, or any gelatine that will hold them in conjoint suspension. The syntactic machinery is plainly
a sham.

  * Now Mr. Davie's argument is that it is not merely
bad poems that trifle with counterfeit syntax in that
way. It has become customary for the best poets
to either (1) dispense with syntax altogether, employing "a language broken down into units of isolated words, a language which abandons any attempt
at articulation," or else (2) utilize a pseudo-syntax,
"syntax as music," which he analyzes subtly and
persuasively in his brilliant third chapter, and which
makes use of syntactic units—sentence lengths,
phrases—as elements in "a silent music, a matter of
tensions and resolutions, of movements (but again
not rhythmical movements) sustained or broken, of
ease or effort, rapidity or languor," playing for a sort
of empathic response to a Swedish drill of movement, communicating before it is understood or even
when there is nothing to understand, in which "noth-

ing is being lifted, transported, or set down, though
the muscles tense, knot, and relax as it were."

Music flourishes in the dark; and at the end of
Chapter 5 Mr. Davie makes it clear that he is attempting a fundamental account of the poetic strate-
gies that have prevailed since Pope's Great Anarch
dropped the curtain and engulfed us in the romantic
night-world: "The point I want to make is this: in
the 17th and 18th centuries poets acted on the assumption that syntax in poetry should often, if not
always, carry a weight of poetic meaning; in the 19th
and 20th centuries poets have acted on the opposite
assumption, that when syntactic forms are retained
in poetry those forms can carry no weight. I have
sought only to make those assumptions explicit, so
that we may know just what we are doing, and what
we are turning our backs upon, when we agree with
the symbolists that in poetry syntax turns into music.
Is Pope's handling of poetic syntax really so irrelevant to the writing of poetry today? And are we
really so sure of ourselves that we can afford to
break so completely with the tradition he represents?"

Since twentieth-century poetry has all along conducted its affairs on the principle that we can afford
to sacrifice much of the nineteenth, Mr. Davie's
lumping of these poets and those in one regretful
but firm dissent seems open to suspicion. So does his
principal strategy, a joining together of Susanne
Langer, T. E. Hulme, and Ernest Fenollosa, whose
interests don't overlap, to make a sort of tripartite

advocatus diaboli whose principles, with a little adroit give and take, will blanket twentieth-century literature, and, with a little dampening, smother it. Mrs. Langer can be used to define the key concept, "syntax as music," the morphology of feeling without specific content, which we may facetiously graph,

? . . . . ! . . . .

Hulme champions imagery without structure, for instance

. . . on rose and icicle the ringing handprint . . .

(The example is from Dylan Thomas, on whom Mr. Davie has some exact and disabling comments.) As for Fenollosa, he applauded specific images and transitive verbs, as in Shakespeare, but has, it appears, been co-opted to sanction doing without sentences, as, we are told, in Pound. Generally speaking, Hulme will cover the barbarous cases, Mrs. Langer the subtle; and the polemic use of Fenollosa consists in showing that his views, being illuminating but incomplete, must insofar as they have been translated into twentieth-century poetic practice, condemn that poetry to attempts at running on one leg.

Mr. Davie's unpromising procedure nevertheless opens enough incidental doors to convince us that he has something of fundamental usefulness to say. He is absolutely right in focusing our attention on the eighteenth century if we want to see the beginnings of a landslide; that was also, we recall, where Pope cautioned us to look. It may also be deduced that the standard accounts of post-symbolist poetry are in a state of confusion, since a poetry answering in essence to those accounts would deserve all Mr. Davie's suspicions. It seems worth while to attempt some restatement.

One might begin by applauding what Mr. Davie says about Hulme, whose status is symptomatic of an important muddle. Pope, we saw, stood for a world interesting enough to write about; Hulme, to put his position briefly, doesn't; which may explain why he never finished any of his projects. "One could make an impressive list from the present volume alone of the works which Hulme announced he would write but didn't," notes his latest editor. He left no books, numerous notebooks and uncompleted mss. quarried by Herbert Read for the 1924 *Speculations,* a diary and a few dozen hand-to-mouth articles quarried by Sam Hynes for the 1955 *Further Speculations,* letters, a legend, and the memory of much conversation. He participated in the Cartesian nightmare, and described its sensations so picturesquely that they sounded like a new and authentically twentieth-century *Weltanschauung.* The world is random, chunky, and irreducible: he compared it to a heap of cinders. In satisfaction of an appetite, we impose words on it and pretend that their elisions and fluidities betoken a coherence in the world. This gives us the Cartesian satisfaction ("Why is it that London looks pretty by night? Because for the general cindery chaos there is substituted a simple ordered arrangement of a finite number of lights"[4]).

[4] *Speculations,* 221.

Thus "The ideal of knowledge: all cinders reduced
to counters (words); these counters moved about on
a chessboard, and so all phenomena made obvious." [5]
As against the chessboard method, however, the
moving about of smooth counters, we have the
method of poetry, which corresponds to—no, not to
reality, but to *the way we really experience it*, the
way we think it when we aren't ordering and smooth-
ing our thoughts to impress someone else, or our
least honest selves. Here is Hulme honestly thinking
to himself:

> Dancing to express the organization of cinders,
> finally emancipated (cf. bird).
> I sat before a stage and saw a little girl with her
> head thrown back, and a smile. I knew her, for she
> was the daughter of John of Elton.
> But she smiled, and her feet were not like feet,
> but. . . . . [sic]
> Though I knew her body.
> All these sudden insights (*e.g.* the great analogy of
> a woman compared to the world in Brussels)—all of
> these start a line, which seems about to unite the
> whole world logically. But the line stops. There is no
> unity. All logic and life are made up of tangled ends
> like that.
> Always think of the fringe and of the cold walks,
> of the lines that lead nowhere. [*Speculations*, 235]

Such reflections are Hulmean pre-poetry. Hence his
distinction between prose and verse: verse lets things
lead nowhere; "It is not a counter language, but a
visual concrete one. It is a compromise for a lan-

---

[5] *Speculations*, 230.

guage of intuition which would hand over sensations
bodily." It is physical, primitive, and sketchy; and
as Mr. Davie at this point cunningly shows, it has
by this account no use for syntax, which corresponds
for Hulme to the licit and preordained moves of
chess. Having gotten a firm grip on Hulme, Mr.
Davie then so places a fulcrum that he can uproot
with one heave everything in the present-day poetic
landscape: "I get the impression that Hulme's views
about the nature of poetical language are the ideas
most generally current, almost the standard ideas,
among poets and their readers today . . ." (p. 13;
and cf. 102).

The short answer is, that whatever Hulme's vogue
he can be jettisoned without embarrassment. His
ideas, with their postulation of an opaque universe
handled one way by "reasoners and mechanists" and
another way by poets, are those of Shelley stripped
of the *Defence's* jittery eloquence. If his critical
repute is high, it is because most critics still live in
1820. Of course his admirers have been claiming for
thirty years that Imagism, Vorticism, Pound, Eliot,
Lewis, modern poetry, the modern mind, are just
applied Hulme (". . . through Pound particularly,"
writes Mr. Hynes, ". . . Hulme's theories became
current, and changed the face of English poetry");
but the inventors of modern letters have declined to
endorse such claims. He is a stimulating writer, especially in the aphoristic writings he didn't publish,
notably the "Cinders" section of *Speculations* and
the "Notes on Language and Style" in the newer
collection: so heterogenous you can always find

something you nearly agree with. His death was a loss to England: he had a persistent howitzer of a mind which ranged itself by preference on otiose nuisances; he differed from the ordinary journalist in his ability to apprehend the subtlest distinctions, and from the scrupulous philosopher in his tendency to become obsessed by them once apprehended. The survivors of his age remember him with evident affection. There is no reason to belittle him. But his views aren't sufficiently representative of significant poetic practice to have taken up, for instance, so much of Mr. Davie's attention, and it is generally by confounding the actual practice of the twentieth-century inventors with some Hulmean extreme that Mr. Davie is misled.

Bending the rays of light, Hulme's proximity exerts an Einsteinian deformation on Mr. Davie's treatment of Fenollosa, whose seminal value ("the only English document of our time fit to rank with Sidney's *Apologie,* and the Preface to *Lyrical Ballads,* and Shelley's *Defence,* the great poetic manifestoes of the past") he is admirably equipped to register. Thus he notes that Fenollosa is "as insistent as Hulme that poetry should get close to 'things,'" then supposes that the way to get at the Fenollosan essence of "things" is to differentiate his view of "things" from Hulme's; which is like defining dogs, in a discussion bedeviled with pigs, by asserting that they are anyway not porcine. Fenollosa, he states, "realized as Hulme did not that 'things' were bundles of energies, always on the move, transmitting or receiving currents of force." True, but off center;

though it is fair to add that Fenollosa himself, re-
futing blindly a Hulmean view of the universe,
thought it was central. We needn't subscribe to a
buzzing vitalism to make use of Fenollosa, only to
a pervading intelligibility. What Fenollosa does is
install us once again in a universe where intelligibility does not need to be imposed by the mind:
Pope's universe and Chaucer's, as well as Shakespeare's. Such a universe, as Mr. Davie is aware,
restores the possibility of syntax to poetry; it also
makes its use optional. The moment intelligible
things approach one another, "webs of force" spring
into being. Mr. Davie is compelled to argue that on
Fenollosa's own showing "the Chinese sentence . . .
does not just put things together, it moves from one
to another, knitting webs of force." Hence Fenollosa's preference for transitive verbs seems essential,
and it is a mistake to claim his authority for a poetic
of juxtapositions; hence also a syntax indifferent to
transitive verbs falls somehow outside Fenollosa's
sphere. But Mr. Davie is compelled to argue in this
way because he apparently supposes that the poetic
microcosm is the *statement,* a linking of opacities
which diction and tone, both attributes of the author, not the subject, render pregnant. But the statement can be regarded as a special case, useful whenever the "transfer of force" in question has a name:
"John *threw* the ball." What a ship does to the waves
has no name; so writing "The ship plows the waves"
we operate by analogy from the plow's operation on
the ground, juxtaposing two intelligibles. Formally
this sentence has a verb; but the verb is meaningless

without the whole of the analogy. And by extension of this principle, Dr. Williams can write "By the road to the contagious hospital . . ."—a poem about a nameless process which is wholly real though only felt as a potentiality, not a sum or sequence of actions occurring, subject-verb-object, before one's eyes—and do it with perfect lucidity with no formal verb for the first fifteen lines. For the poetic microcosm isn't the statement but the Aristotelian *action,* the process by which the poem gets from its own first word to its own last word, sometimes a syntactic process, sometimes not. This action, because it occurs in arrangements of words, is an intellectual action, traced as the mind moves through the poem; and it can be called *mimesis* because it parallels the similar movements of apprehension performed by a mind moving among intelligible things and situations, knitting webs of intelligibles. It was the possibility that the mind could so move, that Pope's Great Anarch negated. That possibility once negated, syntax, as Mr. Davie sees and brilliantly shows, is meaningless except as a binder for the stimuli of more or less subtle stock responses. But it does not follow that on every occasion when formal syntax is absent we have what Yeats described as "mere works of an heroic sincerity, the man, his active faculties in suspense, one finger beating time to a bell sounding and echoing in the depths of his own mind."

13. Supreme in Her Abnormality

THE ACHIEVEMENT OF MARIANNE MOORE'S VERSION
of La Fontaine is to have brought over a number
of the 241 poems virtually intact, and (by dint of
persevering with the least tractable) to have discovered the principles of a badly needed idiom,
urbane without slickness and brisk without impre-
cision. Since Chaucer's fell into disuse, English
verse, constantly allured by the sonorous and cata-
chrestic, hasn't had a reliable *natural* idiom that can
imitate the speech of civilized men and still handle
deftly subjects more complex than the ones whose
emotions pertain, like Wordsworth's, to hypnotic obviousness; hence nothing existed for a La Fontaine
to be translated into. Pope's ease (as distinguished
from his wit) is slippery, treacherous even in his
own hands; Dryden's directness clangs on iron
stilts; and the "naturalness" of various minor
eighteenth-century compoundings—tinctured by ballads and diluted by preoccupations with nerveless
diction—offers no equivalent at all for La Fontaine's
hard neatness. Miss Moore's best work demonstrates
that a specialization of one language may be the
best possible parallel for the simplicities of another;
the very artlessness with which she can employ a
Latinate diction without sounding as though she had
read Vergil ("Clemency may be our best resource"
for *"Plus fait douceur que violence"*) helps to keep
her least natural locutions in touch with speech.

Her artlessness isn't at all like La Fontaine's trans-
parency; it resembles the "unconscious fastidious-

189

ness" which she once illustrated by adducing "childish . . . determination to make a pup eat his meat from the plate." [1] Her air of plunging without premeditation into tortuousness which she subdues *ambulando* is sometimes annoying, but it confers virtue too, complicating the plain sense enough to fend off *simplesse*. La Fontaine's curiously *pastoral* urbanity (not the least like Pope's), his devaluing of lions and busy kings, his citation of self-sufficient foxes or asses wise too late, and his implicit appeal to the wisdom of a Greek slave who perceived a wealth of analogies between the courtly world and the animal kingdom because he stood outside both of them, present the translator with problems perhaps greater than those posed by his intricate rhythms and rhymes. Previous translators, assuming that the transparent sense will look after itself, have been misled into foisting on their author a world of simple follies from which one can detach oneself by an act as facile as walking out of the zoo, in order to live by a few *simpliste* maxims. His situations are postulated with misleading ease:

> *Maître corbeau, sur un arbre perché,*
> *Tenait en son bec un fromage;*
> *Maître renard, par l'odeur alléché,*
> *Lui tint à peu près ce langage:*

A crow with some cheese, and a fox attracted by the smell; nothing more casual (assuming that foxes like cheese). The fox has a few conventional phrases:

---

[1] "Critics and Connoisseurs," in Marianne Moore's *Collected Poems.*

"*Hé bonjour, Monsieur du Corbeau.*
  Que vous êtes joli! que vous me semblez beau!
    Sans mentir, si votre ramage
    Se rapporte à votre plumage,
  Vous êtes le phénix des hôtes de ces bois."

Perceiving, however, that the French neatness would make for empty English, Miss Moore with incomparable deftness complicates the diction very considerably:

On his airy perch among the branches
  Master Crow was holding cheese in his beak.
Master Fox, whose pose suggested fragrances,
  Said in language which of course I cannot speak,
  "Aha, superb Sir Ebony, well met.
How black! who else boasts your metallic jet!
  If your warbling were unique,
  Rest assured, as you are sleek,
One would say that our wood had hatched nightingales."

The "airy perch," the pose suggesting fragrances, "Sir Ebony," the "metallic jet," the "warbling," the sleekness and the nightingales we owe to Miss Moore; La Fontaine by contrast sketches his situation with a few swift platitudes. What has happened, however, is not simply the interposition of a more crinkly language; the tone, and so our relationship to the fable, is newly complicated. "*A peu près ce langage*" is one of La Fontaine's negligent gestures of paraphrase; he wasn't there at the time (as he frequently tells us in other fables), but feels it safe from general knowledge of flatterers to assume that the sense was about as follows. Miss

Moore's deliciously practical "language which of course I cannot speak" effects at a stroke, however, the complete separation of this incident from its human analogies: this is fox- and crow-talk. Hence the "Sir Ebony," the "metallic jet" and the rest of the specificities; hence too the pervading *strangeness* of idiom, which she isn't at all at pains to mitigate. In the authoress of "The Jerboa" and "The Pangolin" this strangeness may be idiosyncrasy, but here idiosyncrasy is as good as principle.[2] La Fontaine's crow, responding to the fox's flattery, *"pour montrer sa belle voix, ouvre un large bec."* He reminds us of a man. But in Miss Moore's version,

> All aglow, Master Crow tried to run a few scales,
> Risking trills and intervals,
> Dropping the prize as his huge beak sang false.

Exquisitely absurd, because he is unambiguously a crow; and his corvine ungainliness gives the twentieth-century fable an edge the seventeenth-century ones acquire, in a different language, by different and more insinuating means.

[2] Mr. Eliot made the fundamental observation about her diction in 1923: ". . . a peculiar and brilliant and rather satirical use of what is not, as material, an 'aristocratic' language at all, but simply the curious jargon produced in America by universal university education. . . . Miss Moore works this uneasy language of stereotypes—as of a whole people playing uncomfortably at clenches and clevelandisms—with impeccable skill into her pattern. She uses words like 'fractional,' 'vertical,' 'infinitesimal,' 'astringently'; phrases like 'excessive popularity,' 'a liability rather than an asset,' 'mask of profundity,' 'vestibule of experience,' 'diminished vitality,' 'arrested prosperity'." In America this jargon forms part of popular speech; Mr. Eliot was illustrating the principle that "fine art is the *refinement*, not the antithesis, of popular art."

That a Marianne Moore crow even in a translation should be unmistakably a crow, not a symbol,
is what we should expect from the use to which
she puts the celebrated animals in her poems. Her
characteristic beast is the only thing of its kind,
prized for its uniqueness ("an aye-aye is not/an
angwan-tíbo, potto, or loris" [3]); her "zebras, supreme
in their abnormality," and "elephants with their fog-
coloured skin" don't impress us as members of the
animal kingdom but as grotesque individualities;
while the indubitably human cat in the same poem[4]
who speaks the astringent moral isn't "people" but
a well-remembered person. When she uses an elephant to voice her characteristic theme in "Melanc-
thon":

Openly, yes,
with the naturalness
    of the hippopotamus or the alligator
    when it climbs out on the bank to experience the

sun, I do these
things which I do, which please
    no one but myself . . .

it isn't the elephant's abstract ponderosity that recommends it to her as a persona: rather, the gesture
it performs by existing at all

                        (for the
patina of circumstance can but enrich what was
there to begin with)

[3] "Four Quartz Crystal Clocks."
[4] "The Monkeys."

allies itself with her own temperamental taut self-sufficiency, mutating primness into resilience.

The uncompromising inhabitants of Miss Moore's zoo, cross-bred with the citizens of the urbane La Fontaine's hierarchic animal kingdom, lend to an enterprise endangered by obviousness a jaunty manner of speaking that always arrests and often wholly entrances the modern reader:

> A mite of a rat was mocking an elephant
> As it moved slowly by, majestically aslant,
> > Valued from antiquity,
> > Towering in draped solemnity
> > While bearing along in majesty
> > A queen of the Levant—
> With her dog, her cat, and sycophant,
> Her parakeet, monkey, anything she might want—
> > On their way to relics they wished to see. . . .

Every word has its presence, and the tone is inimitable. Some of the beginnings (less often the endings) are less happy:

> When warm spring winds make the grass green
> And animals break from winter captivity,
> A certain wolf, like other creatures grown lean,
> > Was looking about for what food there might be.
> As said, a wolf, after a winter that had been hard
> Came on a horse turned out to grass. . . .

This isn't the way to begin this story, though it is a desperate attempt to include all the words that are in the French. La Fontaine, however, arranges them differently; he begins with the wolf (*"Un certain loup dans la saison/Que les tièdes zéphyrs ont*

l'herbe rajeunie . . .") and the *"Un loup, dis-je"*
five lines later is accompanied by a discreet cough
as he realizes that he has been drawn into digressive
poetizing about the spring. Miss Moore, on the other
hand, began with the spring, then got around to the
wolf, and looks excessively awkward when two lines
later she has to pretend that she is remembering
with a start a subject only just introduced. Given
her opening, omission of the "As said, a wolf" clause
would make infinitely better sense; it is probably a
sound rule in translating to omit what won't function in your new poem. Whether her native stub-
bornness interfered, or a failure to comprehend La
Fontaine's delicate gesture involved itself with a
determination to render his faults word for word as
well as his beauties, there is no guessing. There is a
third possibility. From an exceedingly odd foreword
to the volume we learn of a condition—presumably
the publishers'—"that Professor Harry Levin examine the work to ensure a sound equivalent to the
French";[5] further that after Mr. Levin's "scholastic
intensities of supervision" Mr. Monroe Engel of the
Viking Press "ameliorated . . . persisting ungainli-
nesses"; finally that "as consulting editor at the Press
Malcolm Cowley pronounced certain portions of the
text 'rather far from the French'; he has contributed
lines in addition to pedagogy." With such a committee at work, one may trust that every word of
the French has gotten represented somewhere; it

[5] Though no one's vigilance prevented *"Le fantôme brillant
attire une alouette"* from getting rendered by ". . . allured by his
bright mirroring *of her* a lark" (p. 131). Surely it was the sun's
reflection, not her own, that attracted her?

is perhaps surprising that Miss Moore was able to
get away with inserting "Aha, superb Sir Ebony."

It is only her habitual nonchalance that prompts
inquiry into Miss Moore's poetic lapses; their mag-
nitude is seldom sufficient to damage even single
poems, and the enterprise as a whole succeeds aston-
ishingly. As often as not they occur where oddness
of expression (for the sake of tone) complicates the
sense beyond easy decipherment:

> Where in spring find the flowers gardens bore,
> Like Flora's own in bloom at his door?

seems an unnecessarily tortuous way of saying that
Flora's choicest gifts grew in this man's garden.
When Miss Moore gets preoccupied (understand-
ably) with tucking all the words into the given
rhythms and rhyme schemes she frequently produces what may be the neatest solution to this particular crossword puzzle, but is not the best way of
conveying the subject at hand in English.

It is often, however, the best way of creating a
climate of mind, not heretofore available in English,
in which the wit of the Fables can thrive. All convincing translation remains miraculous, but the normal excellence of this one is surprisingly sustained:
the work of a deliberate and indefatigable intelligence, which earns its reward when the translator's
special diction, personal and by existing literary
standards impure, re-creates the French aplomb with
an absoluteness no careful reader is going to ascribe
to luck. The fable, already cited, about the rat mock-

ing the elephant illustrates this order of triumph as
well as any. Here is the rest of it:

> But the rat was not one whom mere weight could
>   daunt
> And asked why observers should praise mere size.
> "Who cares what space an object occupies?"
> He said. "Size does not make a thing significant!
> All crowding near an elephant? Why must I worship
>   him?
> Servile to brute force at which mere tots might faint?
> Should persons such as I admire his heavy limb?
>   I pander to an elephant!"
>
> About to prolong his soliloquy
> When the cat broke from captivity
> And instantly proved what her victim would grant:
> That a rat is not an elephant.

14. At the Hawk's Well

I: A Parable

THE OLD MAN WAS ASLEEP WHEN THE WATER BUB-
bled; the young man, his blood entranced with a
dance, was pursuing the Guardian of the Well when
the water bubbled. Some years after Yeats' death,
a Scholar came to the Hawk's Well. The Dance of
the Guardian bored him, and he began to turn over
his index cards. When he put them down he noticed
a sheen on the stones. "It is lacquer," he said, "clev-
erly applied with a brush. I wonder how she did
that without my seeing her." He put one of the
stones into his pocket for chemical analysis. Then
he noticed that some of the leaves were wet. "The
details are marvelously attended to here," he said.
"If those were lacquered, they would be brittle. It
must be done with tiny glass tubes, by capillary
action, and the water must come from little vials
hidden amid these sticks." He then gathered up all
the leaves and sticks from the dried bed of the well,
took them home with him in a cardboard box, and
in due time wrote a book.

II: Sticks and Leaves

The 900-page selection of Yeats' *Letters*—"those
which can, in the widest sense, be considered auto-
biographical"—manifests all the disabilities of a
compendium. It is a book to read in, not to read.
Like the *Encyclopaedia Britannica*, it contains a va-

riety of matter and itself adds up to nothing new, though numerous sums can be extracted from it. It is also, through no fault of the editor's, shockingly incomplete. The letters to Ezra Pound were inaccessible in Rapallo; letters to James Joyce were entoiled in buyer's and seller's red tape; letters to George Moore were destroyed by the recipient; letters to Maude Gonne destroyed by the Irish Civil War; letters to William Sharp ("Fiona Macleod") destroyed unexamined, under instructions, by his widow's executor; letters to Bernard Shaw are concealed in a mass of documents in the hands of the Public Trustee, not yet sorted; and "some letters to Lionel Johnson were lent by Miss Johnson to a gentleman who was writing a book on that poet, and have not been heard of since."

Such perforce omissions are especially irritating, not so much because we are deprived of the kick of listening in on the intimacies of giants, as because until late in his life the interest of what Yeats is saying in a letter depends to an unexpected degree on the person to whom he is saying it. Unlike Mr. Pound, whom his published letters reveal to have functioned with the same voltage whatever ear trumpet he was connected with, Yeats was exceedingly sensitive to the interests and receptivity of the correspondent. If in conversation, as Olivia Shakespeare is reported to have remarked, he was "conscious only of what he's saying at the moment, except *sometimes* the person he's saying it to," in letter writing he was, until about the age of fifty, all compliance. Thus on neighboring pages we find him

writing easy gossip to Katherine Tynan, deferential
second thoughts to an editor:

> Thank you very much for the cheque. What you say
> about the style of the article is I think true. And one
> of the ballads is certainly morbid (the woman about
> whom it is, is now in the Sligo madhouse or was there
> some while since). However I do not think the Howth
> one morbid, though now in thinking it over I quite
> agree with you that neither are suitable for a news-
> paper. . . . [38]

—and heavily Briticized irony in a public complaint
about misprints:

> Dear Sir, I write to correct a mistake. The curious
> poem in your issue of the 19th inst. was not by me,
> but by the compositor, who is evidently an imitator of
> Browning. I congratulate him on the exquisite tact
> with which he has caught some of the confusion of his
> master. I take an interest in the matter, having myself
> a poem of the same name as yet unpublished. Yours
> faithfully, W. B. Yeats. [55]

Within this early prose style, leisurely without distinction, one observes a constant shifting of center,
a complaisant mutation of what seems too amor-
phous to be called personality, while a mind active
at intervals, like a chameleon's tongue, comes at unexpected moments into view. The early letters are
mostly taken up with small talk and the practical
details of making a hack's living:

> I told you about the man who came and asked me to
> do literary notes for the *Manchester Courier*. They
> give me very little trouble and are fairly profitable.

I got £7 for an article in *Leisure Hour* and have had two in *Scots Observer* and I sent off another. The *Scots Observer* pays well, about £1 a column. These matters have made the *Countess* [*Cathleen*] fare but badly. . . . I shall have a day at the *Countess* tomorrow. . . . [122]

He even wrote, for money, verses to illustrations supplied by the Tract Society, for publication in the *Girls' Own Paper:*

> . . . The sunlight flickering on the pews,
>   The sunlight in the air,
> The flies that dance in threes and twos,
>   They seem to join her prayer. . . .

This sample he sent, good-naturedly, to Miss Tynan, to show her, he explained, how orthodox he could be. "You see how proud of myself I have been for being so businesslike. I have been making amends to myself by doing little else than planting sunflowers and marigolds all afternoon." But by the end of the letter he had lost confidence in the efficacy of his genial poise; there is an anxious postscript: "Do not be disgusted at these trite verses for the Tract Society. I shall never do any more, I think." [122]

That isn't the Byzantine Yeats; but midway in the same letter we come across this classic paragraph:

> What poor delusiveness is all this "higher education of women." Men have set up a great dull mill called examinations, to destroy the imagination. Why should women go through it, circumstance does not drive *them?* They come out with no repose, no peacefulness, their minds no longer quiet gardens full of se-

cluded paths and umbrage-circled nooks, but loud as
chaffering market-places. Mrs. Todhunter is a great
trouble mostly. She has been through the mill and
has got the noisiest mind I know. She is always deny-
ing something. . . . [123]

It is like crossing a sudden loop in time. Yeats might
have written that at sixty; he wrote it at twenty-
four. And there are many such loops. By careful selection one might compile from the first third of the
book (1887–1900) all the elements of developed
Yeatsism: for instance—

Yet this I know: I am no idle poetaster. My life has
been in my poems. To make them I have broken my
life in a mortar. . . . I have brayed in it youth and
fellowship, peace and worldly hopes. I have seen
others enjoying, while I stood alone with myself—
commenting, commenting,—a mere dead mirror on
which things reflect themselves. I have buried my
youth and raised over it a cairn—of clouds. [84]

—not from the decade of *The Tower,* not from the
year of "The Wild Swans at Coole" and "Men Improve with the Years," but from the months just preceding the publication of *The Wanderings of Oisin*
(aetat. 23). The matrix for his famous confronta-
tions of impotent wisdom and uncomprehending
passion is this more fundamental antithesis between
those who participate and the artist whose soul reflects.

What portion in the world can the artist have
Who has awakened from the common dream
But dissipation and despair?

—in 1915 a more trenchant expression, but not a newly discovered theme. Time, in the conventional scheme posited by Yeats criticism, has received credit for bringing him many things which were part of his initial kit.

What happened with time was not so much that the essentials were augmented, as that the inessentials were evaporated. The unpurged images of day recede. The small talk fades from the letters, or is transmuted into accomplished anecdotage; the concern for practical detail is turned away from his own affairs, away from fascination with the Robinson Crusoe mechanics of getting a writer's living, and directed outward on programs of ameliorative public action: the Irish Literary Movement, the Abbey Theatre, work to be done because it needed doing. Finally the personality attains the dimensions, and the confidence, to engulf both gossip and business. The letters of the last ten years are, unlike all the rest, continuously exciting. Nothing seems trivial, and as the time shortens the pace mounts:

> . . . One reason why these propagandists hate us is that we have ease and power. Your tum ti-ta-tum is merely the dance music of the ages. They crawl and roll and wallow. You say that we must not hate. You are right, but we may, and sometimes must, be indignant and speak it. Hate is a kind of "passive suffering," but indignation is a kind of joy. "When I am told that somebody is my brother Protestant," said Swift, "I remember that the rat is a fellow creature"; that seems to me a joyous saying. We that are joyous need not be afraid to denounce. . . . You say we

must love, yes, but love is not pity. It does not desire
to change its object. It is a form of the eternal contemplation of what is. When I take a woman in my
arms I do not want to change her. If I saw her in
rags I would get her better clothes that I might resume my contemplation. But these Communists put
their heads in the rags and smother. [876]

Three weeks before his death he is writing,

I know for certain that my time will not be long. . . .
I am happy, and I think full of energy, of an energy
I had despaired of. It seems to me that I have found
what I wanted. When I try to put all into a phrase I
say, "Man can embody truth but he cannot know it."
I must embody it in the completion of my life. The
abstract is not life and everywhere draws out its con-
tradictions. You can refute Hegel but not the Saint
or the Song of Sixpence. . . . [922]

III: Unpurged Images

There is nothing essentially new here. The reader
will already be familiar with the outlines of this development from diffident youth to outrageous passionate sage. It has been for some years the theme
of the standard books about Yeats, which, bending
to the temptations of the subject, have gotten themselves written out of a division of interest in which
poetry—the part of himself Yeats designedly gave
to the public—is treated chiefly as a body of evidence throwing light on the personal integration of
an old man now many years dead. He wanted the
integration so as to be more wholly a poet—"Man

can embody truth but he cannot know it"—but one is led to suppose that it had some independent importance. Dr. Jeffares' book is called *W. B. Yeats, Man and Poet;* it ends, "He had made himself a great poet." Mr. Ellman's first book is called *Yeats: The Man and the Masks;* in its summary chapter we read how "with great courage and will, he tried to become the hero of whom he had dreamed. . . . His amazing achievement was to succeed partially. . . . He looked the poet, and he lived the poet." Even Miss Koch, who pretends (*W. B. Yeats: The Tragic Phase*) to guide us through the last poems by the unaided light of the poems themselves, in fact does nothing of the kind. Her initial premise is but the orthodox one inverted: "In old age, Yeats became a great poet but he was more than conscious that he had not become a great man." She dilates on the Steinach operation, fusses with interim drafts, and boxes the bibliographic compass in—of all places —her discussion of that cryptic but admirably direct poem "The Statues."

It is arguable that Yeats would be better read if less were accessible that he didn't mean the reader of his poetry to see. One advantage of having the *Letters* to plow through is that one can learn in an evening how the principle of obfuscation operates. We find him thanking Sarah Purser for her "charming embroidered book cover" (235), or anxiously writing Lady Gregory about his forgotten trouser stretcher (543), or requesting Olivia Shakespeare to send him from a bird shop a bundle of nesting material "to help my canaries who are nest-making but

with sheep's wool and green moss which they dis-
like" (680), and observe, in the contexts, a progres-
sive tightening. It is an effort for him (1894) to seem
at ease about the book cover, but it is part of the
serene bardic role (1922) to be occupied in the
Tower with his canaries. The random social gestures, we note with satisfaction, are becoming the
very repertoire of the self-dramatizing style. But
there are hundreds of paragraphs that won't fit into
this comfortable progression, and these contain the
very things that Yeats is intent on *telling* his corre-
spondents, in a constant obsession with stating with
exactness something of importance:

It is not inspiration that exhausts one, but art. [87]

The best argumentative and learned book is like a
mechanical invention and when it ceases to contain
the newest improvements becomes, like most things,
not worth an old song. [246]

I hold as Blake would have held also, that the intellect must do its utmost "before inspiration is possible."
It clears the rubbish from the mouth of the sybil's
cave but it is not the sybil. [262]

I do not understand what you mean when you dis-
tinguish between the word that gives your idea and
the more beautiful word. [343]

The subjects which people think suitable for drama
get fewer every day. [361]

Drama for them consists in a tension of wills excited
by commonplace impulses, especially by those impulses that are the driving force of rather common na-

tures. . . . The commonplace will, that is, the will of
the successful business man, the business will, is the
root of the whole thing. Indeed when I see the realistic
play of our time, even Ibsen and Sudermann, much
more when I see the plays of their imitators, I find
that blessed business will keeping the stage most of
the time. What would such writers or their stage man-
agers do with the mockery king of snow? Or with
Lear upon his heath? [441]

One thing I am now quite sure of is that all the finest
poetry comes logically out of the fundamental action,
and that the error of late periods like this is to believe
that some things are inherently poetical, and to try to
pull them on to the scene at every moment. [460]

These are all early; the date of the latest of them is
1904. Their range and point need no comment. They
exhibit none of the dreaminess we have been trained
to expect from the Yeats of that period. Nor, really,
does the context from which they are excerpted,
much of it a tissue of shrewd maneuvers for earning
necessary money or arranging sympathetic reviews.
What developed wasn't the grip of his mind, though
it came to grip more and more things; what developed was the art: specifically, the art of putting
things more and more arrestingly, and setting the
matters that interested him in closer, more electrifying relationship with one another. This is a technical
development; what makes it look like a development
of personality is our proneness to forget that we are
not after all in touch with a *person*, but with written
words.

The reader of the early letters, then, confronted

by so many things pointing in so many directions,
soon grows inured to their penetrative force and
starts listening to the Yeatsian voice, which grows,
plainly, more assured. In the same way, it is natural
to assume that that is the outline of Yeats' poetic
development too—the personality ramifying, consolidating itself, assuming control; hence that what
his published books are "about" is the effort to fabri-
cate a durable self. This is an especially natural
assumption for the reader of the *Letters* because of
the color it acquires from whatever he remembers
of whatever books about Yeats he may have read:
Mr. Henn's, Mr. Jeffares', Mr. Ellman's. Each of
these writers, one may surmise, has fallen victim to
the experience of reading through a great deal of
material which Yeats did not intend for the public
eye; this is exactly the position of a reader of the
Letters. His ostensible subjects, when he writes for
himself alone or for friends, are so miscellaneous
that one ignores them and attends to the constant
element, the style; and what the developing style
does—so runs the account—is to parallel, as one
mushroom does another, the fostered growth of the
famous personality. Q.E.D.

Hence the Yeatsian critical tradition: an industry
erected on the premise that the coherence of the
poetic oeuvre not only reflects supinely some coherence lying outside the volumes of poetry themselves, but cannot even be said with confidence to
exist until that external center has been located, de-
limited, and surveyed. The usual procedure is to

play down his activities as too miscellaneous to keep track of, and offer, as fulcrum, *A Vision,* of which Yeats wrote in a letter of 1931,

> The young men I write for may not read my *Vision*— they may care too much for poetry—but they will be pleased that it exists. Even my simplest poems will be the better for it. . . . I have constructed a myth, but then one can believe in a myth—one only assents to philosophy. [781]

He was sanguine if he thought that the books about him would be one day written by these young men who cared much for poetry. Instead of addressing themselves to the poems, a brief generation of critics assaulted the doors of that Gothic fortress, *A Vision,* or scrutinizing its interior by periscope reported that it was full of bats. Worse followed: an immense limbo, consisting of the poet's diaries, notebooks, drafts, and unpublished mss., was opened to certified explorers after his death, and the heady possibility that the clues to what Yeats had been making lay in his lumber room, or in the chips from his workbench, overwhelmed everyone who has so far reported. It is doubtful if what a major writer actually published has ever been so little trusted.

What you can reconstruct from such materials is the poet's biography, or one level of it; the current postulate of Yeats criticism is that the poems depend from the life, not so much the public life as the inner life, the diary life, and are explicated one by one in the light of their author's private obsessions and self-communings:

Caught in that sensual music, all neglect
Monuments of unaging intellect.

One hears at great length what Yeats' notebooks
contained on the subject of Byzantium ("Idea for a
poem . . ." etc.), and receives assurance, from a
letter to Lady Gregory on the death of Mabel
Beardsley, that Yeats didn't invent the rouged
cheeks or the trousered dolls. It grows harder and
harder for the tradition to preserve him as a major
poet, except by an act of assertion, or by transposing
to the verse the impressiveness of the persona of the
last decade. Gradually, in the texture of critical emphasis, the poems whose strings lead back to some
inner crisis are allowed to supplant all the rest
(which, when clues turn up, get explicated as puzzles), and no poem is allowed, as Yeats intended, to
explicate its neighbor in the cunningly arranged volumes.

IV: The Water

Yeats, to be sure, had his mind all his life on more
things than the technique of verse. It is fashionable,
however, to apologize for the sort of intellectual interests displayed by a man of his admitted intelligence, while conceding that they did keep his poetry
going: as though their function had been to redupli-
cate the images presented by a sensibility inherently
as limited as a dentist's mirror. No attempt seems
commonly made to gauge the extent to which he
may have held them half in jest. To determine and
weigh his tone is frequently difficult; in *A Vision*

and the *Autobiographies* the significant humor is a concomitant of weight and tension, like the sheen at the brink of a massive waterfall. The public Yeats, executing the Dance of the Guardian of the Well, had another kind of humor besides, which consisted in pretending that there was no waterfall at all, only a few intermittent bubblings among the sticks. It was the kind that appeared when he spun outrageous anecdotes like the one about George Moore and the three Miss Beams (*Autobiography,* p. 270), and while this humor hasn't usually been missed by his readers, it has tended to obscure the existence of the former kind, since people are supposed to have only one way of being funny. Yet the tone in which the symbolic Moon is adduced, in a remark (*Autobiography,* p. 202) about an amorous friend —"For him 'the visible world existed' as he was fond of quoting, and I suspect him of a Moon that had entered its fourth quarter"—isn't as solemn as expositors of the System would lead us to expect.

For assessing the implications of this tone, and hence of the System, the volume containing his correspondence with T. Sturge Moore is of peculiar value, partly because Moore was neither the Public nor a revered lady, so that Yeats didn't feel it incumbent to generate any of his bardic personae. He could even smile at them—

I . . . walk about in the sun feeling very old and dignified, and look forward to some weeks of the gardens of the Alcazar, dropping crumbs to some equally old and dignified goldfish. [115]

"I liked him best alone," Moore wrote; "then the provocative truculence of his talk often gave place to seductive delicacy." It was the presence of *others*, less intimate, such as the reading public, that called out the sometimes impenetrable provocativeness. Moore seems to have been a man in whose presence no public man was tempted to ride a patent high horse: we even hear of his holding casual conversation about God with Wyndham Lewis. Certainly the Yeats who appears in his presence, even in the thick of philosophical discussion, is the most relaxed Yeats we encounter anywhere:

> You say Bertrand Russell says that Kant smashed his own philosophy by his doctrine of practical reason. So indeed he does say, and what more can you expect from a man who has been entirely bald during the whole course of his life. . . . [124]

Russell's symbolic baldness is a recurring joke; if it had appeared in *A Vision* some biographer would have noted it as an example of Yeats' solemn mysticism. "I am reading that baldpate daily," he writes in another letter (115); three sentences later he remarks of Wyndham Lewis, "What an entangled Absalom!" This game of arranging his current interests into whimsical systems keeps peeping through his side of the correspondence; it was not out of solemnity that he kept pegging argument after argument for his own brand of idealism to a phantom called "Ruskin's cat." This cat (which no one else could see, and which Ruskin threw out of the window claiming it was a demon) was adduced by

Yeats in a letter of 1926; he recurs and recurs in the correspondence for twenty months. He is just absurd enough to key Yeats' tone—one paragraph cites the fact that he "does not seem to have kittens"—yet the arguments through which he prowls are logically serious.

Yeats wields his logic ironically, aware that he is flashing what his own premises would force him to regard as a tin sword. He never tires of denouncing "the rat-catchers and cockle-pickers who would deny us the right to draw conclusions from those experiences common to all men before they have caught the last rat and picked the last cockle." Sturge Moore (whose brother was a philosopher) kept replying courteously and persuasively (the philosophical phase of the correspondence lasted some six years, while Yeats was preoccupied with *A Vision*), without ever quite grasping the scope of Yeats' central intuition—that the data the mind is to take into account can't be selected by a majority vote. The worldful of people who did not see Ruskin's cat didn't worry him in the slightest. The botanist who has seen an agapanthus or a night-blooming cereus can't be expected to base his classifications on the experience of fifty million Higginses who have seen nothing but daisies and buttercups. "Provocative truculence" perhaps determined the examples Yeats chose to underwrite, but the principle is sound. The least escapable form of tyranny restricts by tireless suggestion the things we are at liberty to think about. Like Blake, Yeats was aware that a middle-class tyranny of this order had been in force since

1690. Wyndham Lewis' *Time and Western Man,*
the fullest account of this racket, has of course itself
been proscribed by the forces it anatomizes; the
public has not been allowed to hear of Lewis, though
it knows all about the expression-aesthetic of Croce,
of whom Yeats remarked that he knew how the bird
got out of the egg but had no notion how it got in
(113). In the course of the Sturge Moore correspondence we discover Yeats reading Lewis' last
chapters "again and again." "Henceforth I need not
say splenetic things for all is said."

There is still room for a book on Yeats which neither affords breathless peeps into "his brown calf
1893 Order notebook bearing a rose cross on the
cover and marked PRIVATE," nor numbers every
stone of the great System and its outbuildings for
future identification, like an Irish castle knocked
down for shipment to America, and then heaps
them into piquant effects, like Bouvard and Pécuchet's landscaped Garden, nor rehandles the standard plot in which an earnest young man who did
not know how to do what he wished forged a self
that could do anything it wished at all; but examines
what he had to say.

15. The Devil and Wyndham Lewis

Nous sommes
La triste opacité de nos spectres futurs.

IN *The Human Age,* WYNDHAM LEWIS ENTERS, AND
fills with his inimitable voice, very lofty mansions
indeed, challenging, without swank or irrelevance,
comparison with Swift and Milton. That it is surely
the only book in English that brings to mind these
two great writers simultaneously is a measure of
Lewis' authenticity; no one concocting a novelty
would cross-breed such ill-matched giants. Lewis,
the least literary of writers, doesn't reshuffle styles,
he discovers the unique and natural tone of what he
has to say; any likeness to past stylists is a by-
product. What Lewis has to say is, *first,* that mankind must, as a working hypothesis, be considered
as an agglomeration of hopeless brutes, preserved
for consideration by the presence of a very few men
of intelligence, and by the exertions of these men
maintained above a void; *second,* that this hypothesis, though wrong, must not be replaced by anything
less austere, more sentimental, or merely self-flatter-
ing, but modified by a context of inexplicable grandeur ("God *values* man: that is the important thing
to remember"). One might have expected to be able
to state this second theme more precisely had Lewis
lived to complete the final part, *The Trial of Man;*
positing and then eroding the first theme is the busi-

ness of Parts II and III, *Monstre Gai* and *Malign Fiesta*. Lewis did complete a revision of Part I, *The Childermass*, which served to bring certain disparate details—Pullman's religion, for instance, or the number of World Wars—into accord with the parts published twenty-seven years later, but hardly perfected a junction between that showpiece of Vorticism and the maturer narrative. There is a discrepancy of style, readily illustrated; it incarnates a radical discrepancy of conception. By 1955, Lewis was no longer, in the smallest degree, showing off, nor was his imagination any longer dominated by the now faded phenomena of the decade that bungled its chance to remake the world. In *The Childermass* (1928) he was bucking not only a massive political and philosophical trend, but the most impressively staffed and glitteringly publicized literary movement in two hundred years: the age of Joyce, Stein, Lawrence, Hemingway, the Paris expatriates, the literary Freudians, and the Bloomsbury set. One of his intentions was, singlehanded, to outdo them in brilliance. Another was to incarnate in a ruthless and permanent mask that particular grimace of the Zeitgeist which in "the twenties" came to apotheosis. These two intentions somewhat interfered with one another.

> The age demanded an image
> Of its accelerated grimace

—and was discouraged by a surface of inchmeal pyrotechnics from learning that it had been accorded *The Childermass* and its memorable Bailiff.

In thin clockwork cadence the exhausted splash of the
waves is a sound that is a cold ribbon just existing in
the massive heat. The delicate surf falls with the abrupt
clash of glass, section by section. [7]

Virginia Woolf, we concede, couldn't have written
that; unfortunately such a surface is so arresting that
it is difficult to see past it. Everything, for 322 pages,
is in a documentary present tense. The minutest
flashback is rigorously excluded, even from details
of syntax. The long sentences are compound, not
complex: they evade time (on principle) by eschewing the normal gesture of Western syntax, the holding of one thing in the mind for the duration which
another thing requires to modify it. Lewis (1928)
does not write, "Each time the ass brayed, the man
who was holding it stiffened and straightened up."
He writes: "One holds by the bridle an ass, which
trumpets with sedate hystéria. Electrified at each
brazen blare, its attendant stiffens. He is shaken out
of an attitude to which on each occasion he returns, throwing him into a gaunt runaway perspective. . . ." (13) There are three more lines of this;
when you lift events out of time, instead of rendering them as processes, you can dilate on them for-
ever; the great difficulty in organizing such writing
is to get to the next idea; it always presents itself
(when you do at length admit it) abruptly, a new
card from the deck. The determined reader gets the
hang of the book by discerning and connecting passages in which the doctrinaire objectivity of presentation locks, somehow, with the theme. This account

of the locale, for instance, induces malaise, like the mise en scène of the newspapers:

> The scene is steadily redistributed, vamped from position to position intermittently at its boundaries. It revolves upon itself in a slow material maelstrom. . . . Never before have there been so many objects of uncertain credentials or origin: as it grows more intricate Pullman whisks them forward, peering into the sky for lost stars twirling about as he has to face two ways at once, on the *qui vive* for the new setting, fearing above all reflections, on the look-out for optical traps, lynx-eyed for threatening ambushes of anomalous times behind the orderly furniture of Space, or hidden in objects to confute the solid last moment. . . . [35]

We have read enough about the postwar breakup of a settled order—or at any rate read enough commentaries on *The Waste Land*—not to find this phantasmagoric landscape baffling. It is dominated by the walls of a Magnetic City, supposed to be Heaven, which everyone wants to get into. Vast troops of people who have died out of life on earth are assembling in the plains to await interrogation and possible admission. They recall very little of the past, find the small shocks of the new life—especially its costumes—outrageous until gotten used to, and settle down to await a millennium which seems interminably postponed by noisy public discussions. "The ice is broken," the doll-like Satters reflects on his new state. "Fresh bearings have to be taken. New worlds for old—all is in the melting pot" (5). These are the clichés of the twenties; gradually it dawns on us that what the souls at this Feast of the

Innocents have been catapulted into is the ante-
chamber of the Marx-Lawrence-*Transition*-Bertrand
Russell-*Daily Mirror* heaven, and that the "peristal-
tic process" by which they have been extruded on
this plain, feeling "as natural . . . thanks to the efficient nature of . . . the process of psychic mum-
mification they have undergone, as though it were
their *natural life* that they were still enjoying," was
simply the highly salvationist alchemy of the Great
War. The Bailiff, at whose daily court proceedings
for admission to the City are supposed to be carried
on, is a protean Mr. Punch, a shameless entertainer,
a vulgarizer of useful ideas, and (possessing no personal center distinguishable from the congeries of
effects he produces) a tireless mimic. His official
status is ambiguous, but his artistic use is clear: he
is the incarnate Zeitgeist, the irresponsible clownish
will behind the linked political, philosophical, and
aesthetic programs of the 1920s. He can mimic Lawrence, Joyce, or Stein, delude like Bergson, pontifi-
cate like the BBC, or coruscate with the purposeful
breeziness of a newspaper pundit. The Lewis who
created this figure is one of the great virtuoso per-
formers of literature, convincing us by sheer vitality
and technical resourcefulness that the Bailiff, for all
his shoddiness, is a focus of energy, of mythological
proportions, the incarnate implacable frivolity, in
fact, that makes the quotidian world go round. He
so fastens on the magnetized reader's imagination,
and so fills it, that when Miss Stein rhapsodizes
about Tender Buttons, or Professor Whitehead in-
vokes his magical flux, or pages of glossy advertise-

ments exude the good fellowship of abstract business, we grow accustomed to reflecting that it is simply an aspect of the Bailiff that is performing.

There seems to be no precedent for the creation of a satiric figure whose reality so obliterates that of the milieu out of which he is drawn. A Volpone, by contrast, isn't an age, or an omnipresent force, but simply a permanent human type among other types. One reason why the Bailiff has no predecessors is that there has been no previous need for such a creation. Swift, for instance, dealt with material of sufficient structure to be brought within the confines of such a communal image as Lilliput. He created mock commonwealths. It was one of Lewis' key insights, that one could do nothing with such a time as his own but personify it. Its phenomena aren't rationally interrelated, they merely cohere, with the restless radiance of a Bergsonian "person." "Our period is like a person, in short," Lewis wrote in the first number of *The Enemy*, "just as we are less and less like one; the secret of its being is technically expressed in terms of 'mass-psychology'."

To this gay monster, "what every creature ought to understand is that he is never worth a fraction of the trouble we take with him here" (221). His Heaven, a miscellaneous clutter of façades like a Paris art movement—"the upper stages of wicker towers; helmet-like hoods of tinted stucco; tamarisks; the smaragdine and olive of tropical vegetations; tinselled banners; gigantic grey-green and speckled cones, rising like truncated eggs from a system of profuse nests; and a florid zoological symbolism . . ." (7)—this place is, he explains confidentially, "in the truest sense an asylum, and our patients are our children" (224). The sensational milieu over which he presides makes no sense; it isn't the coherent product of some man's will, like the Caliph's Design of Lewis' 1919 parable, nor the fulfillment of an orderly document like Jefferson's Constitution, but an assemblage of time-serving whims, "built in a bare thinking cube innocent of the compass, a microcosm indifferent to physical position, nowhere in nothing" (222). It is a vulgar sensational corruption of what might have been expected to arise in the clearing left by the War. Lewis had written, in 1921, of a new epoch in which "creatures of a new state of human life, as different from Nineteenth Century England, say, as the Renaissance was from the Middle Ages" might move "forward, and away from the sealed and obstructed past."

> A phenomenon we meet, and are bound to meet for some time, is the existence of a sort of No Man's Land atmosphere. The dead never rise up, and men will not return to the Past, whatever else they may do. But as yet there is Nothing, or rather the corpse of the past age, and the sprinkling of children of the new. There is no mature authority, outside of creative and active individual man, to support the new and delicate forces bursting forth everywhere today.
>
> [Editorial in *The Tyro*, No. 1]

Instead there had burst forth—it is true, in a No Man's Land—the Sitwells, Miss Stein, Bergson, Behaviorism, a hundred inanities devoid of focal interest but symptomatic of a dismally cheery freudo-marxist collectivism, the frivolous annihilation of all that traditionally won't herd. "What are your intentions as regards the mass of men, wicked or charitable, old mole?" a Lewisian spokesman twits the Bailiff. "You know, you sugary ruffian, of what quality is your *charita!* Heaven preserve us from—your Heaven!" (153).

Amid the great debate between this figure and the Bailiff *The Childermass* breaks off, possibly in part because, in order to go on, Lewis needed to know more about the inside of that celebrated Heaven. It is facile to say that he at length got on with the work after the Magnetic City had finally materialized itself around him for detailed inspection as Mr. Attlee's Welfare State; facile because, though *Monstre Gai* draws heavily on the writer's experiences in postwar Britain, he has raised those experiences from the plane of ebullient documentation at which he presents them in *Rotting Hill* (1951) to a dimension of fantasy whose function is to make the near-Sartrean absurdity of life in the Bailiff's bailiwick crushingly real. An image of this nauseous reality occurs early in the new book; from "a bare thinking cube . . . nowhere in nothing" the protagonists of *The Childermass* are translated into "a cheerless twentieth century side-street," uncompromisingly physical, which epitomizes what lies behind the cyclopean battlements:

Meanwhile, the bodies of both Satters and Pullman were subject to internal disturbances of some violence. . . . Then a sensation, originating in the bladder, gave

him a clue: for neither the bladder nor intestines had
played any part in his life in the camp. He had not
made water since his death on earth. Satters whispered, hoarse and urgent, "I must find a urinal!"

Like the personnel of a circus parading a mediter-
ranean city, the Bailiff's big drums, thudding like artil-
lery, wheeled into a grandiose boulevard.

"Is this Heaven?" Pullman at last blankly inquired
of the air. It reminded him of Barcelona. This, like the
Rembla, was a tree-lined avenue with huge pavements,
across which cafes thrust hundreds of tables and chairs,
to the edge of the gutter. . . . [11]

The novel necessities of the body ("'I say, I just
can't wait any longer!' He was stamping about, with
his hands in his trousers pockets") and the idiocies
of the café-lounging populace (for whom, with a
pension adequate to keep them at the café all day
and indulge their love of pink hats, hand-painted
ties, and strident socks, it *is* without qualification
Heaven) receive sufficient stress in the first thirty
pages of *Monstre Gai* to posit a new kind of world,
which is in fact a new angle of vision on this present
world. Their fidelity in sustaining this unique vision
would alone entitle these books to rank among
Lewis' principal artistic achievements. Here is Pullman's response to what would be in an ordinary
piece of fiction a commonplace enough experience,
a glimpse into a vacantly exhilarated crowd:

> . . . Lastly came three, who had not the vigour to
> think about a sock. Their mouths hung open beneath
> stupidly smiling eyes, their skins like vellum, their
> teeth like a mummy's; they encouraged one another

to laugh—for if you cannot think you can always laugh—at the stars. They seemed to believe that these were bubbles of light, and that they might at any moment burst. Pullman would have said that they were showing off for the benefit of the strangers, but they seemed too absorbed in themselves to be doing that: their eyes, also, looked aloof and demented. . . .

"Vacuous as London is," Pullman observed, "it does not manufacture a citizenry so mentally void as you do."

Their guide received this with a laugh so harsh and troubled that Satters was visited with an icy touch of goose-flesh, and Pullman glanced sideways inquiringly. Were these skeletons in somebody's cupboard?—Was Mannock responsible for this lunacy? Mannock's voice was as uneasy as his laugh had been, and all he said was, "We are not all like that." [18]

Lewis can not only make mere commonplace idiocy chilling ("Everything to do with human life is, was, and always will be a little terrifying"), he can render casual hostilities with imperishable directness:

"Pulley, I say, these people give me goose-flesh. I feel I am walking among dead people, Pulley, all of them cracking jokes."

"So you are," Pullman told him. "Can you smell them?" . . .

"Ugh, ugh, Pulley!" How sad they look, don't they? When they make a crack their faces break up into a hundred tiny little wrinkles."

There was a croak in their ear, "You two stop whispering. We don't allow that. All cards on the table."

Pullman half-turned round, and said, "My friend is so young that is why we whisper. We won't any more."

"I don't mind," shrugged the mask—and it was so terribly like a mask that Pullman felt that that was what in fact it might be. This one had a monocle, and he fluttered his hands. "I am a newcomer myself."

"I don't think you are, buddy," Pullman blew at him through his beard.

"I think you're a horrid old man." There was a nasty look in the eye of the mask. "Go away . . . and have a good wash. You are filthy both of you. You stink."

Pullman drew Satters away, towards one of the shops. . . . [44]

This isn't Swiftian: there is no rictus. When the Legions of Hell visit their thunders on the City, Lewis portrays with equal impartiality the victims ("Beneath him Mannock lay trembling on the floor, but it was an automatic rattle of his flesh, not one at which his consciousness assisted. He adhered to the floor like a piece of paper, a gasp stifled and stuck, his mouth as round as a penny-piece. Satters' head adhered to Pullman's body at about the level of the hip, like an unsightly wen of dough texture. He was quite motionless. It was a stricken group") and the violence (. . . three or four mammoth voices on high, crashing out the alphabets of Heaven and of the Pit. The nasal tongues of giant viragos at one time conducted a screaming argument among the clouds, which, if translated, was totally absurd. . . . The giant sounds shrank to a hubbub of monkeys, and a psittacine screaming. As abruptly as it had begun this chaotic orgasm ended . . .").

Behind that crisis lies a London air raid; behind the street throng lies a London street; behind the men who laughed at the stars lies, say, a vignette of Boat Race Night. It is with surprise, long after finishing the book, that one so reflects; within the book the phantasmagoria imposes its own reality, capacious enough to handle, without change of manner, an encounter between giant angels:

> With the little garments of a mere six-footer hanging from them in loops and wisps, two vast nudities rose into the air and disappeared over the roofs. But they made their exit buttocks uppermost. . . . Hell's messenger protruded against the azure sky an anchovy-coloured balloon. But this was immediately succeeded by an upsurge of pink limbs, of enormous size, climbing up on top of the darker element; and that is how they actually vanished behind the roofs, a picture in pink, wine-brown and azure, the last things seen being three or four violently agitated feet, pink feet and brown feet, the stiff tumbling spikes of twenty toes signalling the agitation beneath. [110]

What Lewis has succeeded in doing is to engulf the reader, for the first time, with the clinical aloofness from which his books have always been written, so that one is no longer aware of the showman's personality. The absurdity seems not a way of seeing the material but intrinsic with the material. This inane city, one reflects, is one Wyndham Lewis has long inhabited. It is Tarr's Paris, or Victor Stamp's London, with the whimsical sensations of the old Lewis style withdrawn.

Not that James Pullman, the protagonist and observer, is Wyndham Lewis; though he was in life the greatest writer of his time (the encomium comes from the Bailiff) he shares with Lewis only the familiar penchant for eloquent analysis, and the indifference to sensual blandishments. Like René Harding in *Self Condemned*—whose fate, an imprisoned spectator in Hell, with no Dante's return ticket, is oddly parallel—Pullman repudiates improprieties not to his taste with a vehemence that affords a clue to the corruption beneath his detachment. His plight images that of the intelligent man in a world which seems to offer him nothing but a variety of ways of selling himself. In one of the most hair-raising scenes in the book he dismisses a valet who attempts to augment the luxuries of the womanless City by pathic seduction:

> Pullman glared drearily at Sentoryen. "My imagination is defective," he replied. "It would be no use trying to believe that you were a glamorous screen star. Apart from the question of certain outstanding anatomical details, you have not the necessary lovely husky voice."
>
> The young man sprang up and began pacing up and down.
>
> "Very well, very well. You will go to seed sexually! Just because I have not got . . . oh fou-ee! . . . a great apparatus teeming with germs, chock full of dangers . . . of which a somewhat milder form of leprosy is not the worst—just because I have not got the famous female stink you scorn my proposal!" He flung himself into a bandy-legged attitude, with a transformation of his face into the mask of a repulsive zany, by developing a sparkling squint and pouting his lips out in an obscene smile—snatching a cyclamen from a vase within easy reach, and sticking it in his thick

hair, the stalk finding a foothold behind his ear, acquired the flowery symbol of the female.

"Like that, would you love . . . me more!" he cried.

Pullman continued to stare at this performance—hostilely however.

"Can you find nothing disgusting to do," he jeered, "to provide yourself with the authentic female whiff?" [187]

Yet when the Bailiff attempts to recruit him as an ally in the power struggle that ferments behind the façade of the City, Pullman's "impassible calm . . . which hid an implacable refusal to be deceived" (177) is undermined by the Bailiff's elementary flattery of literary vanity. Offered life in the comfort to which he has always believed himself entitled, in an apartment whose living room or sitting room, in addition to "everything a human being can want, either for sitting or living," contains brand new copies of two of his own best books, Pullman sinks into "the silken billows of a sumptuous settee," exclaiming, "This is authentic! This, beyond the shadow of a peradventure, is Heaven."

What unites Pullman to the Bailiff, Pullman tells himself, is simply the Bailiff's willingness to support "the literary god, James Pullman by name." He reassures himself that he has made no compromise. "Pullman claimed full independence; would be quite capable of criticizing this all-powerful magistrate, and would take sides with him under no circumstances. His tenancy of 400 would in no way change that." Thus Pullman rationalizing; but what really unites them is their shared distaste for the human aggregate. Pullman feels set above it as a man of intelligence, the Bailiff as a man of power, a supernatural transposition, Pullman comes to realize, of "gangster-wealth at its most irresponsible." Later he has a bad half-hour reflecting that he is repeating the pattern of his life on earth:

> It was made clear to you that the role which had been yours on earth was essentially diabolic. To your confusion, your faithfulness to your earthly part in this play led you into the strangest supernatural company. . . . as in my own case, you would find yourself involved with a powerful demon, whereas on Earth he would merely be dear old so-and-so, a rich patron of the arts, or a go-ahead publisher. [263, 265]

Truncating these morose reflections, however, he elects anew for the Bailiff, as "the supernatural agent, paradoxical as that might seem, most favourable to man" (267). So when the Bailiff's Palace is destroyed by supernatural invaders, who come provoked by this plausible rogue's villainies and peculations, Pullman and his side-kick Satters accompany the gay monster on a flight through space to his city of origin, which men know as Hell.

Hell, the Bailiff has been explaining, is much maligned by childish tales. By comparison with Third City, it is an intellectual center. His own father, the Bailiff recalls, having been sent there through a misunderstanding, married and "followed the calling of most of its inhabitants . . ."

> "Which is what?" Pullman interrupted.
> "Oh, nothing much, psychology mostly . . ."

"A city given up to psychology? That is exceptionally unusual, is it not?"

"I have always rather felt that myself, Pullman. . . ."

Not long after his arrival as a tourist trapped in Hell, Pullman learns more about this "psychology" from the Bailiff's elderly mother, a sepulchral crone who partakes with her guest in one of the most electrifying luncheon dialogues in English fiction. Her late husband, it seems, was supervisor of Dis.

"What, Madam, is Dis?" Pullman inquired.

"Oh yes, it is where people are punished for their sins. . . . There are no people in this city other than those doing Dis work. There are only Us and the Sinners—and you are not Us. See? . . ."

"Ah!" declared Pullman. "Ah!"

"What do you mean, Ah?" the old lady demanded.

"Oh, I meant *Hum.*"

The old lady burst into shrieks of antinomic merriment. "*Oh you!*" she howled. "If you were a Sinner, and I were your guardian, I would tickle your pretty feet, and draw out your banter." . . . [324]

When Pullman remonstrates with the Bailiff—

"It is hardly the charming little burg you described,"

the Bailiff's rejoinder is final:

"Have you seen the fires of Hell so far? Is this street not a normal street in a modern city?"

Pullman was silent. [323]

The astonishing achievement of *Malign Fiesta*—surely Lewis' most continuously powerful piece of

writing, not excepting the second half of *Self Condemned*—is this representation of a Hell deprived
of romance, continuous with civic normality and
quiet. In one respect he surpasses Milton and even
Dante: he contrives an Inferno of overwhelming
power while making no attempt to be picturesque,
or evocative, or to intimidate. He is not interested,
like Dante, in the gradations of sin and punishment;
sin, in fact—this is one way of characterizing his intensely tragic art—was never a subject of much
interest to Mr. Lewis. So it is on the technology of
Hell that he concentrates, and he has in this sphere
the advantage over Dante of writing in a century
that has so mechanized death and suffering that it
can organize human brutality with managerial calm.
A burning heretic was a strident admonition to the
faithful, a set piece of fiery secular rhetoric; in Bel-
sen, from which Lewis has drawn numerous hints—
as he has also from the assembly-line methods of
hospitals and slaughterhouses—human annihilation
was organized as a problem in waste disposal, to be
carried out by Yahoos whose animal sadism entered
into the calculations of planners who did not necessarily share it. All Lewis' polemic accounts of what
scientific detachment may mask come to fruition in
the account of Pullman's guided tour through the
House of Dis ("'His eyes will have been burnt out
of his head,' Hachilah said, 'and his lips must have
dropped into the fire. I believe I saw the skin dropping'"). The Lord Sammael (Lewis' Satan) maintains specially bred beasts, part man, part goat,
whose faces bear "a goatish grimace of ineffable self-

satisfied lubricity," for woman Sinners to be flung to. He describes the sounds with which they rend their prey with a biologist's detachment "I have a recording of it, a number of discs. If you like, I will let you hear it") but actually to deliver a victim to their mercies he regards as an ordeal.

> "You must regard me as an out-and-out brute," and the lord of Hell made a self-amused grimace. "I really am much less of a brute than I appear. Those animals fill me with horror, they cause me such inexpressible disgust that it is as much as I can do to go near them. But that is physical and visible, nasal and visual; and the Women-Sinners disgust me even more. I realize that that is a little obsession. But what can you expect of an angel!" . . . [377]

Sammael's hatred of man is nearly metaphysical ("that small scale, short lived imitation, Man, was nothing short of a scandal"); so, oddly enough, is his more melodramatic attitude to woman, by whom he is affected "as some people are affected by cats." When he calls her "that nastiest innovation of my colleague 'God the Father'—the nursery, the procreative side of Man," he voices not a deflected sexual development but an Angel's aesthetic distaste for the messiness of procreation. "What he most looked like was an American of high managerial class, Indian blood, perhaps, accounting for an invincible severity." He is a tireless moralist, but he barely distinguishes the Sins. Though sexual activity disgusts him more than anything, and though some of God's code of sin he considers fatuous, he is willing to take any misbehavior as confirming his estimate of the "nasty little animals" sent him for punishment. "On principle, I approve of punishing Man just for being Man: but I do not enjoy playing the *bourreau.*" He is an intelligent being and a fascinating Puritan; a considerable artistic improvement on Milton's curled Antony and a good deal less susceptible of Byronic vulgarization.

In part, of course, he is the satiric impulse carried to an insane extreme; did not Lewis argue, in *Men Without Art* (1934), that satire is a metaphysical, not a moral, criticism of Man? "An animal in every respect upon the same footing as a rat or an elephant, I imagine you would agree—man, except for what the behaviourist terms his word-habit, is that and no more, except for his paradoxical 'reason'." Aware of this paradox, the reason itself—so ran Lewis' argument—"the god in us," explodes with laughter. The satirist, however, confronted by Man, *does something.* And so does the Lord Sammael. Sammael stands aloof from human affairs, from beer and skittles and fornication. He is not the Devil of romance, who occupies himself endlessly with entangling man in wily snares. He is a punisher merely; one cannot imagine him inducing Eve to take an apple. That would have been the work of the Bailiff, a *vulgar* devil, who is also *The Diabolical Principle* of Lewis' 1931 polemic against the mongrelization of European art, and *The Demon of Progress in the Arts* excoriated in his 1954 assault on "the dead hand of the new" and its "'daring' extremes which end in an insane zero." In both these polemic books Lewis is attacking activities with

which his own are often confused; on the first page
of *The Demon of Progress in the Arts* he points out
that he was England's first abstract painter. So folklore—this is Sammael's account—confuses the inter-
fering Bailiff with the Lord Sammael, who stands
apart from men's actions and annihilates whatever
men are delivered into his demesne. *Malign Fiesta*
is Lewis' explicit separation between Wyndham
Lewis the artist and such a figure. Lewis has habit-
ually, as a satirist's strategy, dramatized the assumption that only one's self is real, and he has been able
to make that seem a necessary assumption for con-
ducting an equilibrized life. Toward the close of
Malign Fiesta, however, Pullman is shocked into
reflection:

> God *values* man: that is the important thing to remem-
> ber. It is this valuing that is so extraordinary . . . The
> only value for Sammael is solipsistic. I, Pullman, am
> acting in a valueless vacuum called Sammael. [528]

This is one of the bridges into *The Trial of Man*; we
should have expected to read more about the grounds
of this valuing.

Lewis' extraordinary success in rendering convincingly the angelic mentality should be attributed
to the fact that in forty years' practice he never
sought to master the conventional novelist's way of
rendering human beings. His unintelligent characters, the Kreislers and Dan Boleyns, he always presented externally and comically, as though making a
virtue of a certain bafflement at how intelligent fiction can manage with people who incarnate them-

selves in trivialities. The comical schoolboy Satters is dragged through *The Human Age* at Pullman's heels in token acknowledgment of such a dimension of existence. His intelligent characters aren't ordinary men who in addition make bright conversation, like Aldous Huxley figures; they operate out of their analytic intelligence, with a disconcerting directness to which new readers commonly have great difficulty refocusing the expectations they bring to a book labeled "fiction." These men, whether half-mad like René Harding, or detached like Tarr, or untalented but tenacious like Victor Stamp, all belong to the camp of genius, a human type in which Lewis is fiction's only specialist. The Lord Sammael belongs to this class of figures, and is presented by similar techniques; his actions and his superbly functional eloquence, not his mannerisms, occupy the writer's attention. James Pullman is such another; and he and Sammael come to a fatally intimate understanding. Before *Malign Fiesta* is over, Sammael is employing Pullman as his Machiavellian adviser (the angelic intelligence isn't tortuous, and needs to consult an expert in that human specialty) in a scheme to diversify the angelic perfection with a human admixture, by wedding the dark angels to female sinners. The Angels have been living a Hollywood existence in Frank Lloyd Wright houses, undeviatingly perfect but for the most part stupid. Perfection, it seems, implies an exclusivity of function which leaves no room for the self-knowledge which in Lewisian terms is the ground of intelligence, and so intelligence is as rare among angels as among men.

The Cowboy, the Aristocrat, the great Athlete, the
Ace airman; each in his way is a perfect being, but
completely stupid. . . . Now to be a real angel, and,
just on the same principle, to be God, you must be entirely stupid. We are compelled deeply to admire such
perfections. And it is in no way to take away from the
splendid pre-eminence of God—in no way to diminish
one's awe of His might—if one said one did not desire
to *be* God, or to be an angel. . . . Only what is intelligent really interests me. Perfection repels me: it is
(it must be) so colossally stupid. Here—in Third City
—we are frail, puny, short-lived, ridiculous, *but* we
are superior, preferable to the Immortals with which
we come in contact. [165]

Thus Pullman theorizing in the comparative aloofness of the Magnetic City. Perfection also bores
Sammael, so Pullman finds himself, like a number of
previous manifestations of Wyndham Lewis, "brood-
ing up another world," fertile in shoddy expedients
for consolidating a Human Age in Hell's Angeltown,
complete with girls, false noses, squirting flowers,
water polo, the gimcrack machinery of an infernal
Festival of Britain sufficient (but for the stupidity of
the angels, and the absorption of Pullman in techni-
calities) to bring all things human into eternal dis-
repute. The Malign Fiesta is a perfect orgy of human
silliness. Pullman, more Bailiff-like than ever, is once
more repeating the pattern of his life on earth, once
more placing his intelligence at the disposal of the
regnant focus of power; and there is nothing more
terrifying in the book than the sudden intimation,
arriving from Heaven that he has sold his soul to

the veritable Devil and is being narrowly watched. *Malign Fiesta* ends, as did *Monstre Gai*, with the destruction of his current patron's palace; Heaven, enraged at this corruption of the Divine, moves in, and at the climax of the effortless bombardment "an ocean of light seemed to have settled down around the lair of the Lord Sammael—who, Pullman thought, would use that telephone no more" (566).

In the last sentences Pullman is being carried off by two of God's angels, to assist at the Trial where human triviality and human value were to be brought into confrontation in a heavenly forum stage-managed by the man who, more than any other novelist of the twentieth century, devoted his incomparably lively intelligence to these uncompromisingly fundamental themes.

Addendum—The Trial of Man

Since the last book of the tetralogy remained unwritten when Wyndham Lewis died in March 1957, the available clues to his intention seem worth putting on record. The original plan extended to three books only, and the first version of *Malign Fiesta*, a radio script commissioned by the BBC, closes with the annihilation of Pullman by an enormous foot. Accidentally stepped on by an angel, one of the Lord Sammael's mustering host, he underwent the gratuitous violent death which terminates all other Wyndham Lewis novels.

Subsequently Lewis began to envisage a fourth phase for Pullman's extra-terrestial career. In the

published text of *Malign Fiesta* the "enormous san-
dalled foot, the size of a German farm-cart," crashes
down instead on Satters' cherished peony, a miracu-
lously beautiful plant "from the Far-East of the Earth.
There physical beauty was understood. The European believed he had evolved spiritual beauty of a
high order—but did the spiritual product ever come
up to this physical perfection?" Though the spiritual
is corruptible, as Pullman and the dark angels have
demonstrated, the physical (the province of the
artist who was for fifty years belligerently concerned
with the *outside* of things) is capable of unam-
biguous perfection. It is this that the dark angel mon-
strously destroys: "The glass case and the peony
vanished beneath this awful tread, and when the
angel's foot rose and swept onward there was nothing left but a crushed handful of glass and a meaningless mash of vegetation."

Pullman, on the other hand, the corrupted spirit, is
carried off forcibly to Heaven: knowing "that he
should never have assisted at the humanization of
the Divine—because he was now in the divine element."

In a letter of August 29, 1955, Lewis amplifies this
theme:

> *The Human Age* is the title at present of what I
> have done, but I am proposing to write a further book
> which will necessitate an alteration of the overall title.
> You will notice that *Malign Fiesta* significantly ends
> with two White Angels carrying off Pullman. He finds
> himself, in the final book, in the Celestial Camp. This
> is very much to his satisfaction.

Monstre Gai shows him entrapped by the Bailiff, in whose power he reluctantly remains. There is a passage in that book in which he analyses his dilemma (it occurs in the covered walk along the side of Tenth Piazza). The Bailiff is, of course, not Divine. Then the same situation is repeated in *Malign Fiesta,* only even more tragically, and the figure in that case is Divine, though Diabolic.

In the last book of all the hero, Pullman, is at last in Divine Society. He favours the Divine. I favour the Divine. There is a gigantic debate, in which Sammael's purpose to combine the Human and the Angelic is discussed, the Celestial spokesman naturally attacking Sammael's big idea.

He repeated that Pullman was a most unwilling adjutant of the Lord Sammael in his denaturing of the Angelic. "In order to save his life Pullman gives it his support. But Pullman is, of course, an adherent of the Divine, not of the Diabolic."

Two months later Lewis had finished the manuscript of *The Red Priest,* a novel about a more-than-life-size tortured servant of the Divine whose relations with Russia are less reluctant than those of Pullman with Sammael. Father Augustine Card sees England in the 1950s metamorphosing into something like Sammael's severe domain. "England is not on the way to being a second Sweden, with the beautiful houses of working men, whose rooms glow with the inside of forest trees—not that, but a sort of Methodist's model of Russia." That being the case, the Red Priest defines his alliance with the diabolic. "I know where power is, and power is where

I must be. It is no longer a matter of waving a red
flag with a schoolboy fierceness, but the necessity of
getting as near as possible to a vodka-tippling diplo-
mat—near enough to the Black Throne to get a little
straight news from the other side of Nowhere."
Lewis was winding up his intellectual affairs; though
the execution falters badly, the intention of this
flawed and hasty book was to ally the themes of his
political works with the uncompromising eschatology
of *The Human Age*. Father Card's communism has
no comic dimension; it has nothing in common with
the sententious machine-tending of Percy Hard-
caster in *The Revenge for Love*. His own aberrations,
consonant with the dilemma of Cartesian Man, doom
him to "blast his way across space and time"; he
commits two murders, one unintentional, and dies,
amid newspaper sensationalism, on the Polar ice-cap,
amid "the absolute loneliness he desired," at the
hands of a maddened Eskimo.

A year later Lewis was completing a second interim novel, *Twentieth Century Palette*, the chronicle
of an artist, the metaphysical man-out-of-his-element,
doubly displaced in modern England. His thoughts
were now wholly taken up with the still unwritten
Trial of Man. Its theme, he said during a conversation in November 1956, was to be Pullman's gradual
acclimatization to the Celestial environment; that
was where he was to be at last at home, the first
Wyndham Lewis character to achieve a meaningful
destiny. The great Trial was to be an episode merely;
the focus was to be on Pullman. Whether God would
make a personal appearance he had not decided; he

rather thought not, being disinclined to repeat Milton's mistake. The tragedy of Europe, he asserted, was its loss of a common religion; he spoke of his mother, a Catholic who had ceased to practice her religion, and of his own growing interest in the Catholic faith. His interest in his earlier books had much faded. It was for the *Human Age* tetralogy that he expected to be remembered. Two more weeks would see *Twentieth Century Palette* finished; he then proposed to take up the theme of James Pullman and God.

But he had already entered his final illness; so *The Red Priest* remains his last word on the subject of presumptuous man. Father Card's hubris on the ice-cap—"As to the ultimate Eskimo he would whisper in the ear of this diminutive savage that he was terribly wrong—that there was no God but God. And this enormous man would return to civilized life with the dark soul of this little savage in his pocket" —Father Card's hubris had its fated resolution; he strangled the ultimate Eskimo instead, for trying to steal his wallet, and was butchered by his victim's companions. He was for Lewis the ultimate case of human intoxication with absolutes from which man was meant to be shielded. It was such a dilemma as his that was to be resolved by the Trial of Man, and by Pullman's assimilation into the Divine. "He is for the Divine. I am for the Divine."

16. Inside the Featherbed[1]

DESPITE HIS HABITUAL DOODLING WITH OTHER MEN'S idioms ("The menace and caress of wave that breaks on water; for does not a menace caress? does not a caress menace?"—p. 204) in the hope that something critically significant will occur, Mr. Blackmur has achieved institutional status among the company, not inconsiderable in numbers, for whom "words alone are certain good." He can pursue and isolate any subtlety provided it is sufficiently encased in language. His virtues are clearest in the very early essay on Cummings, where Cummings' way of turning terms into flat absolutes—"flower" isn't a flower but a cant term for anything the poet happens to hold in esteem—is subtly anatomized into twenty-four pages of scrupulous sentences in which we never lose confidence. And he is excellent—disregarding the pinnulate writing—on Emily Dickinson and Wallace Stevens, and pretty good on Hart Crane and Marianne Moore, all of them poets whose effects depend chiefly on closed systems of words interacting. On such subjects he is even unexpectedly epigrammatic: Marianne Moore's exiguous rhyme schemes are "part of the poem's weather"; one of Cummings' phrases has "a great suggestion of precision about it—like men going off to war." Mr. Blackmur achieves divinations of this kind by inspecting the entrails of his own formulations: the least irritating case of his habitual procedure, which is to find

---

[1] R. P. Blackmur, *Language as Gesture.*

out what he means by exploring the words in which
he is trying to say it.

> Coleridge defined meter as the motion of meaning,
> and accepting that we must also for our present pur-
> pose turn it around and say that motion is the meter
> of meaning. That is, if meter as motion brings mean-
> ing to gesture, then motion as meter moors gesture
> to meaning. . . . [20]

The impulse behind these alliterative jingles betrays
him into compulsive repetition of quotations that
catch his fancy. The phrase "In the gloom the gold
gathers the light against it" occurs five times in a
seven-page note on Pound. Two lines of Eliot irrupt
three times, one line of Yeats five times, and the title
phrase six times, each time portentously, in the intolerably kittenish *Lord Tennyson's Scissors*. Whole
paragraphs elsewhere are collages of half-relevant
quotations. It also causes him frequently to break
loose from the subject altogether to jingle phrases:

> Again, in an older phrase, it is in the context of habit-
> ual analogy that we take upon us the mystery of
> things and become God's spies. Lear himself is a
> multiple analogy—both in pattern and in image—of
> the boredom, the horror, and the glory; and the ripe-
> ness (which is all) is the ripeness of each phase as it
> drifts, or crosses the gap, into the other place. [208]

This isn't pseudo-reasoning but pseudo-wisdom; toy-
ing so idly with three quotations, it makes large gestures of being utterly free in the possession of their
contents. Mr. Blackmur isn't really claiming all that,

but his words claim it, having escaped from his control. It is as a sort of thwarted poetry, in fact, that much of his prose claims attention.

For better or worse, the Word is all. "When a word is used in a poem," Mr. Blackmur thinks, "it should be the sum of all its appropriate history made concrete and particular in the individual context; and in poetry all words act *as if* they were so used, because *the only kind of meaning poetry can have* [my italics] requires that all its words resume their full life: the full life being modified and made unique by the *qualifications* the words perform upon one another in the poem" (323). This is an excellent statement of one of Mr. Blackmur's two guiding principles—the other being that all the visible parts of a poem are conventional forms, which serve to liberate and make public what would otherwise be merely personal intentions. He harvests his insight in showing us how Stevens' words remain words and so viable, Cummings' become ideas and so opaque, while Emily Dickinson's oscillate between meaning and indicative notation. But "the only kind of meaning poetry can have. . . ." It is the kind of meaning Wallace Stevens has: "His great labour has been to allow the reality of what he felt personally to pass into the superior impersonal reality of words." It is, one may grant, the kind of meaning Yeats has too, but the formula is treacherous: it doesn't discourage the critic from coming at Yeats' meaning the wrong way. Seeking to justify his 1935 designation of Yeats as "our one indubitable major poet," Mr. Blackmur has been driven to positing inspired "ad-libbing," a sort of magnificent bluff, between the terms that bear weight. Several applauding reviewers have been grateful for this reduction—anything you don't understand can be written off as ad-libbing—but the Yeatsian Hydra won't behead that easily. In the passage from "Under Ben Bulben" which contains the lines,

> Michael Angelo left a proof
> On the Sistine Chapel roof,
> Where but half-awakened Adam
> Can disturb globe-trotting Madam
> Till her bowels are in heat,
> Proof that there's a purpose set
> Before the secret working mind:
> Profane perfection of mankind,

Mr. Blackmur settles like a wasp on the concluding line, puzzles for half a page with the dictionary meanings of "profane" (a *big* dictionary—he calls it "that place of saltatory heuristics"—is one of his fetishes), wonders whether it may be "alternately both verb and adjective," fools for a paragraph more with the combination "profane perfection," hallucinates himself into deciding that "the relatedness between profane and perfection becomes almost a matter of sensation," and finally asks the reader to believe that "all except the lines quoted separately" —the last three—"could have as well been different, most of all could have been their own opposites without injury to the meaning which is under the lines." Yeats, however, demands that we think of what the words are talking about. It never strikes Mr. Blackmur that the meaning of "profane" is controlled, via its etymology, by the cited depiction of a kinesthetically sexual male figure on a Chapel roof. Michelangelo's "secret working mind" pursued a purpose at variance with the Pope's.

There is worse than this. Of the line of Greek in the first poem of *Hugh Selwyn Mauberley* we are told,

> The line about the gods is in Greek script because the syntax of the poem demands it; the substance, perhaps, is in the fact that it is in Greek. In English the lovely rhyme of Τροίη and *leeway* would have been impossible; but that is not the only loss that would have been incurred. In English, "Be the gods known to thee which are lawful in Troy," could never have been "caught in the unstopped ear" (the next line) at least not without considerable circumlocution. . . . [128]

The line, ἴδμεν γάρ τοι πάνθ' ὅς ἐνὶ Τροίη, is in Greek script because it is quoted from the *Odyssey* (XII: 189), and is in fact the gist of the song the Sirens sang. And it means "For we know all the things that in Troy. . . ." Where the "gods" of Mr. Blackmur's gloss came from one cannot guess, unless "*toi panth'*" reminded his language-ridden eye of "pantheon." One expects a critic to be handier with a crib than that. Mr. Stanley Hyman in his critical peep-show *The Armed Vision* credited Mr. Blackmur with "among other things translating a Capaneus line Pound quoted in the Greek"; he was praising the thoroughness with which Blackmur did his homework. One can't hold Mr. Blackmur responsible for his admirer's precipitance—including, unless we are in turn misreading Mr. Hyman, the delicious inven-

tion of a Greek poet named Capaneus—but the confusion does illustrate how difficult it is for a glib
reader, and often for a cautious one, to be sure just
what Mr. Blackmur is saying. No one's attention,
for that matter, seems to have been caught by the
original *gaffe* in the twenty years since it was first
published.

There are critics whose exegesis is sounder. Mr.
Blackmur was most nearly illuminating when, in the
early thirties, he was still trying to define the mode of
operation of various poets who didn't require exegesis
so much as delicate commentary on their verbal
procedures. Even then the appearance of a whole
ramifying poetic was appearance merely; attentive
rereading discloses not branches interpenetrating a
space previously empty, but prose with a sort of
close springy life, like moss. And now in the forties
and fifties, now that he has begun to feel he knows
where he is, his linguistic playfulness has run wild.
Now, without discomfort, he can deal in loose trumpery counterfeits of the profundities of the poets
themselves:

> The painter puts into his portraits the crossed gesture
> of knowledge and mystery, of the intolerably familiar
> and the impossibly alien, which we see in the looking-
> glass. That is why in great portraits we see ourselves.
> [8]

Now more than ever his hair-trigger pen, tickled by
some homonym or cadence, is free to twitch out dozens of words at a spurt: the page-long fiddle with
"respond" and "sponsor" (415); or "he [Stevens]

darlings the syllables of his ideas: it is the stroke of
Platonism on prosody that produces Euphues, wit
with a secret, ornament on beauty" (436); or the
record incantation on a line of *The Dry Salvages:*

> Here is the salt of death and of truth and of savor, the
> salt in our souls of that which is not ours, moving
> there. The salt is on the wild and thorny rose grap-
> pling in the granite at the sea's edge, grappling and
> in bloom, almost ever-blooming; and it is the rose
> which was before, and may yet be after, the rose of
> the Court of Love, or the rose of the Virgin. It is the
> rose out of the garden which includes the rose in the
> garden. There is in Eliot's line (alien but known to our
> line that we read) also all the roses that have been in
> his life, as in the next line is all the fog. . . .

Mr. Blackmur's admirers refer guardedly to his "difficulty." It would be pleasant to discern a trace of
irony in Mr. John Crowe Ransom's description of the
book as "the official classic, in exegesis of the poetry
of an age," or in Mr. Blackmur's own quotation from
T. E. Lawrence, that the effort of writing is "like
trying to fight a featherbed."

17. Alice in Empsonland

IN 1930 WILLIAM EMPSON PUBLISHED A BOOK OF CRIT-
icism which had the unique distinction of reducing
the passivity before poetry of hundreds of readers
without imposing—or proposing—a single critical
judgment of any salience. *Seven Types of Ambiguity*
neither altered the genealogy of sensibility, like
Eliot's advocacy of the Metaphysicals, nor renovated
the criteria of technique, like Pound's studies of Renaissance translators, nor suspended familiar works
from new terminological pegs, like Eliot's "serious
farce" (Marlowe), "objective correlative" (Hamlet),
or "intellect at the tips of the senses" (Marvell).
About the only section one is likely to be able to
paraphrase some weeks after reading is a digression
on Shakespeare commentators; the rest of the book
hangs in the mind like the ghost of a brilliant evening's talk, inspiriting because what was discussed is
supposed to be undiscussable.

The author was twenty-four. At twenty-nine he
published a collection of striking poems, and another
book cantering the circuit of five whole works rang-
ing from a Shakespeare sonnet (discussion inconclu-
sive) to *Alice in Wonderland* (analysis excellent).
That was in 1935. The subsequent sixteen years were
spent in gestating, amid less showy activities, *The
Structure of Complex Words,* in intention a systematic treatise, a work meant to issue in a theory of
language abstractly defensible, a landmark of speculative linguistics, applicable in numerous critical
and pedagogical situations beyond those tackled in

exemplification by the ingenious author. Parts of it are of interest to many sorts of specialists. Critics may pick up one or two terms, lexicographers some excellent stimulus, annotators various insights, semanticists some controversial bones to gnaw. It is difficult to say who wants the whole of it. The book is disappointing, and its disappointingness illuminates, as could no third success, the principles behind Mr. Empson's influential career. The lamp by which he hunted for a generalized theory of ambiguity illuminated everything to which he held it; the theory, now found, proves to be rather phosphorescent than enlightening.

Despite the symbolic notation or the tone of the opening pages, the organization of *Complex Words* isn't particularly rigorous. The uniform and conscientiously arid terminology merely gives the appearance of holding together what are in effect disjunct critical essays written over fifteen years (two of them, "Timon's Dog" and "Honest in Othello," appeared in a pamphlet published that long before, and we discover on the very last page that "some way of separating out the emotions, implications, personal suggestions and suchlike in our complex words, seeing how they are related, how a learner might pick them up more easily" was engaging the author's attention in 1935). On the other hand the essays, unlike those in *Some Versions of Pastoral,* aren't particularly engaging apart from the theory whose usefulness they are meant to illustrate. It is not that they are spoiled by the theory; the theory remains the most interesting part of the book. There is no sign that the chapters in question—on the *Essay on Criticism, The Prelude, Paradise Lost,* and four Shakespeare plays—might have been interesting if they had been written differently. What has happened is that Mr. Empson's old exploratory zest in the face of poems and plays has evaporated because he has discovered a short cut to the answers he sought. He no longer, necktie flying, paces off triangles; he has worked out a table of sines.

What he has actually done is tidy up the concept of Ambiguity, the very vagueness of which lent picaresque zest to the early book. It is characteristic of a new evasiveness about the scope he claims that only in a footnote on p. 103 do we learn that he knows it is old ground that is being ordered, rather than new ground that is being broken. The old ground was canvassed early in the first chapter of *Ambiguity:*

> Thus a word may have several distinct meanings; several meanings connected with one another; several meanings which need one another to complete their meaning; or several meanings which unite together so that the word means one relation or one process.

A poem calls these components of its complex words into explicit play; what Mr. Empson was doing in *Ambiguity* and *Pastoral* was tracing out the lines of interaction in a passage one at a time:

> . . . the words of the poet will, as a rule, be more justly words, what they represent will be more effec-

tively a unit in the mind, than the more numerous words with which I shall imitate their meaning so as to show how it is conveyed.

For old-style paraphrase, that *bête noir*, the "prose sense," which assumes that words are atoms, he substituted multiple paraphrase, a sort of hedonistic calculus, the assumption behind which is that the word-atom can be split into smaller particles, or that the effect of a piece of verse is like the synthetic colors in a magazine reproduction, resolvable into dots of varying sizes but standard hues. The analyst takes the "effect" for granted; he is interested in showing us how it arises. The technique is not one for arriving at evaluations, nor for enforcing evaluations once arrived at. It simply locks poet, poem, language, and reader inside a "communicative situation" and explores the intricacies of that. Suggestively, Mr. Empson's analogy for the fact that the good reader can get the effect without doing the analysis is "the way some people can do anagrams at a shot, and feel sure the letters all fit."

In *Complex Words*, therefore, we get an atomic theory of language, with symbols for the components of the atom. Words carry Emotions, and Doctrines. Emotions in words are on the whole perfectly analyzable, whether or not they are in life; the opponent in the preliminary pages is the man who cries, "This is inexplicable because it is Pure Emotion," just as in the first book it was the man who attributed the effect of poetry to prose sense plus "Pure Sound." Taking A for the Sense under discussion, the emotive components are: A/1, its main "implication" or "association" or "connotation"; (A), a sense held at the back of the mind, so that A (B) means the sense A secretly bolstered by the sense B; —A, a sense deliberately excluded in a given usage; A+, the sense made "warmer and fuller"; A—, the sense made more astringent; A£1, the first Mood of sense A (a mood conveys the speaker's relation to an audience or context); 'A,' the mood conveyed by quotes: either "What *I* call A but *they* don't," or "What *they* call A but *I* don't"; A?, the sense used of oneself under cover of using it of someone else, more commonly —A?: "I am not like that"; and finally A!1, the primary Emotion associated with sense A when all the above have been eliminated: thus the first emotion for sense 1 of *honest* ("not lying") is 1!1, approval.

Doctrines are conveyed in words mainly by what Mr. Empson calls Equations; an Equation ties two senses together and implies that they have an intrinsic connection (A = B). The equations go into four classes: I: Context-meaning implies dictionary-meaning; II: Major sense implies connotation (A = A/1); III: Head-meaning implies context meaning; IV: Neither meaning can be regarded as dominant. The meaning that does the implying in the first three classes tends to be (1) more obvious; (2) less emotive; (3) narrower in range, than the one that gets implied.

These are Mr. Empson's "little bits of machinery"; I list them for the convenience of students, since it is laborious to dig them out of the chat in the first eighty pages. The first thing one notes about them, when illustrations of their use begin to occur, is that witty paraphrase, of the sort in which *Ambiguity* abounded, does their job much better. Referring to the brief table of meanings and implications for Pope's "wit" on p. 86, one can work out that one use of the word, 3b+ = 1a − .1£1, assembles the following parts: Poet or artist (3), acting as judge (b), and on that account admired (+), implies (=) a bright social talker (1) mocking (a) and so giving rise to satirical amusement (−) but still to be valued as one values such talkers (1£1). The Empsonian paraphrase elucidates this use of the word "wit" like a shot: "Even in authoritative writers one must expect a certain puppyishness." It is hard to see what is gained by the symbolic terminology here, except a rhetorical assurance that the components of this complex usage of the word are few and enumerable.

The second thing one notes is that in the chapters on specific works of art all that the machinery can do is done on the first few pages. The spectrum of a key word—"honest" in *Othello*, "fool" in *Lear*, "dog" in *Timon*, "sense" in *The Prelude*—is displayed, in part by logical analysis, in part by combing the N.E.D. (which receives repeated sententious homage as "the great work"), in part by etymology, and the results are put into symbolic notation. This lexicographic feat once performed—and no one is going to underrate its impressiveness, in a case like "honest" or "sense"—the various uses of the word are extracted from the text in hand and each is shown to correspond to something in the schema. This will seem like a parody to anyone who has worked through one of these chapters, but it is what the chapters amount to, with the parenthetic insights trimmed off. Mr. Empson tells us all he can in his first deployment of the word; the rest reads like a laborious attempt to convince himself—and us— that the machinery of notation is indeed adequate.

If the chapters are dull, it is because the method is wrong for discussing poetry. Long poems deploy a far more complex weight than Mr. Empson appears to suppose. They can't really be reduced to the intricacies of their key words—it is a little like discussing an automobile solely in terms of the weight borne by its ball-bearings. As a way of showing off the analytic machinery, however, the method succeeds quite well; the machinery is usually adequate, for the words he picks. These are rather blank words, frequently, like Pope's "wit," great puzzles, which derive most of their body from context and tone. Mr. Empson's symbols depend on his supposition that a complex meaning can be resolved into linked senses plus a blend of attitudes and intentions. A/1, (A), and —A are *senses* advanced, reserved, and suppressed. A+ and A— are Ricardian *feelings* (speaker's attitude to topic). A£1, 'A,' A?, and A!1 are Ricardian *tones* (speaker's attitude to audience). These latter are ingeniously sorted out; but the sense of "sense" goes virtually uninvestigated. Mr. Empson conceives "sense" mathematically. A sense is like a number, atomic and drastically invariable. A word doesn't pull an image into the matrix of discourse. It posits a sense, to be lit obliquely by attitudes. Naturally, the poetic image gives him trouble, as it always has; but he is cannier than he was in *Am-*

biguity, and plays down the trouble by careful
choice of cases. Of all the words Mr. Empson discusses, the only ones which carry an image are "fool"
in *Lear,* which was troublesome enough to yield a
rather flat chapter, and "dog" in *Timon,* where the
perspective is forced by a preliminary chapter transforming "dog" from an animal into an epithet packed
with complex and shifting attitudes. When Timon
says to Alcibiades, "I do wish thou wert a dog,"
Mr. Empson doesn't talk about dogs but about the
"logical puzzle" of railing against mankind. He can
live with an image if it is really a gesture. If it is not
that, it must be a Ricardian "vehicle" for saying
something else, and is so discussed under "Metaphor" (Ch. 18).

To the extent to which poetry concerns itself with
the concrete fact, then, Mr. Empson's machinery appears to lose hold of it. He provides notation by
which one could discuss a good deal of Pound's
Propertius and *Mauberley,* for instance, where there
is endless play with speech-contexts ("logopoeia");
but one suspects that the word "dead" in *The Waste
Land* would give trouble, the word "city" a great
deal more, and the "broken Coriolanus" near the end
of the poem would wreck the machinery entirely.
The feelings in "dead" and "city" are carefully
neutralized by Eliot's usage, and the senses are too
profound for atomization; only a real city or actual
death can contain them.

It is perhaps not an accident, then, that Mr. Empson's most enlightening performance is with Pope's
"wit"; in the eighteenth century (the century of ra-

tional lexicography, which kept prose sense under control) a social matrix—what the speaker was doing with a word against a background of social usages and implications—was predominant enough to give such analysis a main handle. Similarly, when he is surveying the history of a word like "honest" or "dog" or "sense," it is around the eighteenth century that the grip of his machinery on buried implications is most impressive. One of the finest insights in the book concerns the anthropocentric structure such words assumed with the Restoration. A dog becomes a fellow creature, not a lower animal; the word carries Johnson's attitude to Savage, not Antonio's to Shylock.

Behind this suppressed assumption that words are more the property of speakers than of things, one hears the voice of Humpty Dumpty saying, "When I use a word it means what I want it to—neither more nor less." Mr. Empson's charm has always depended on a sort of Alice-persona: the cool-headed quizzer of semantic monsters, seeking to adequate his understanding to the verdicts of his taste. He comes to poetry with an air of being surrounded by plangent irrationalities which can be shown to be quite orderly at bottom; a characteristic key word in his earlier books was "absurd." In fact, as he explains in the present book, "What Humpty Dumpty gives is not the 'connotations' but the 'central meaning' and then the reason for the 'connotation'; 'That'll do very well,' says Alice, who had the feeling already, as a person of taste, and only wanted the plain sense to fit in." They have to fit in, they have to be shown to be orderly, because the inexplicable has terrors. The motive behind such criticism as is contained in *Seven Types of Ambiguity* is not the enlightenment of the reader but the satisfaction of the author: "The object of life, after all," he tells us late in *Ambiguity*, "is not to understand things, but to maintain one's defences and equilibrium and live as well as one can; it is not only maiden aunts who are placed like this." Hence his usefulness to the sort of academic who does not want poetry to disturb him or change him. Hence the absence of intellectual gymnastics in his second volume of poetry (1940). An equilibrium has been discovered; it consists in contemplating the way your peripheral emotions get entangled with the absurd.

Hence, too, his very curious tastes, and tone, and blindnesses. His real focus of interest has always been Alice's nineteenth century. It is surely no accident that his finest piece of sustained writing is his exegesis of *Alice*. Like Lewis Carroll, he maintains a mathematical self (he started in mathematics at Cambridge) which is always trying to tidy up the decayed fish carried into the kitchen by the "sensitive" self. The analytic machinery is a Carrollean invention, too complex for the uses to which it is suited, like the "Nyctograph" Carroll invented for taking notes in the dark, and tried, naïvely, to put on sale. We are told in the preface to the revised *Ambiguity* that one of the motives of composition was a desire to get Swinburnean plangencies into stereoscopic focus with rediscovered Wit. Nothing, for Mr. Empson, has happened in poetry since the nineteenth century, except rounder and defter examples of the same thing. Eliot is the only contemporary poet he has tackled, and then only Eliot reverberating amid Victorian submarine darkness: the dressing-table scene in *The Waste Land,* the leaning creatures in "Whispers of Immortality." He finds *Finnegans Wake* "a gigantic corpse," essentially because you can't tell, in a Joycean compound, which of the meanings is primary: this is the howl of the machine striking granite. He is unexpectedly old-fashioned, again, in finding "very little for anybody to add to A. C. Bradley's magnificent analysis" of *Othello,* except a few alterations of proportion, and he spends pages rationalizing the character of Iago. We must pretend that these are real people; we cannot afford to be cut loose in a universe of poetry, *lo spettatore nel centro del quadro.* We are aware, however, that it is a pretense; the play is "really" a group of effects hinging on how people at a given point in history would take the meaning of a tricky word like "honest": "The character is only made plausible by puns on one word . . . all the elements of the character are represented in the range of meanings of 'honest,' and (what is more important) the confusion of moral theory in the audience . . . was symbolised or echoed in a high degree by the confusion of the word."

That he pushes discussion of a complex poetic work back into a discussion of writer-audience relations is, though it has a specious validity for drama, fundamentally indicative of Mr. Empson's attitude to poetry in general. His own early poems are full of images derived from exploration of interstellar space, "That network without fish, that mere / Extended idleness, those pointless places." Language is a kind of heliographic signaling, a faint and desperate attempt to stretch filaments from monad to monad. Style is narcissistic, like Alice's poise; a kind of pathetic elegance in manipulating the inconsequential; it is as if a cockroach should wave his feelers with an air.

> His gleaming bubble between void and void,
> Tribe-membrane, that by mutual tension stands,
> Earth's surface film, is at a breath destroyed.

Hence "All styles can come down to noise," and language is a collection of devices whereby we are perpetually well deceived.

> All these huge dreams by which men long live well
> Are magic-lanterned on the smoke of hell;
> This then is real, I have implied,
> A painted, small, transparent slide.

Literary criticism switches its attention to and fro between slide and projected image. The slide is a lie and the image an illusion; but critic and reader can conspire with the brave writer to "Feign then what's by a decent tact believed":

> Imagine, then, by miracle, with me,
> (Ambiguous gifts, as what gods give must be)
> What could not possibly be there,
> And learn a style from a despair.

So it is with words like "quite" and "honest" that Mr. Empson succeeds most impressively; the special flavors of these words ("Quite a nice time"; "Really, that is scarcely honest") are part of the machinery by which maiden aunts bear up; they are flourishes with the sword of the human creature, his back to the wall, antagonized by a shadow. The colloquial examples he coins always have a Victorian governessy flavor; innocent bits of language, in that circumlocutory period, got loaded with unexpected amounts of nervous force. When you are making up your world as you go along there is no safeguard against ingenious exegesis of the null (such as a whole page on a bad distich from a 1913 Cambridge anthology), or against subtleties about pronunciation (*God* "begins at the back of your throat, a profound sound, with which you are intimately connected—'ich'—, and then stretches right across to a point above the teeth, from back to front, from low to high, with a maximum of extension and exaltation"). And the Ricardian tenor-vehicle treatment of metaphor comes in patly because words are a way of saying something else, not of placing an intelligible structure of analogies on the page; at bottom nothing is really intelligible anyway, although almost anything turns out to be explicable.

It is no dispraise to Mr. Empson's ingenuity, energy, and industry to find something in their quality consonant with the poems and passages on which he employs them best; low-pressure entertainments like *The Beggar's Opera,* whose strength consists in a jaunty flexibility of tone; or flyweight acrobats of pathos like Hood; or the more colloquial parts of Pope and Chaucer, continuous with the spectrum of urbane chat; or (in works less conducive to composure) the moments when a character is sententiously weighing his wit against the will of a mistress or his littleness against a universe of murk or tragic machinery or fate; and the point of the analysis is to show how the tumult of language reflects the way the speaker is placed.

The infectious zest of *Ambiguity* was like that of a boy taking watches apart, but it was at least related to a sense of the wonders of watches. Mr. Empson has always taken poetry seriously, though like Alice confronted by vanishing cats he has always maintained in its presence a disconcerting composure; since poetry like everything else was to his supple Carrollean intelligence a trick we conspire to believe in. It is melancholy that in a book from which much of the enthusiasm has retired he is Alice no longer; he has accommodated himself at length to his own image of the Victorian scientist, who was "believed to have discovered a new kind of Roman virtue," and whom the public could always surprise, as Alice did the White Knight, obliviously head down in his suit of armor, hung with bellows and beehives, "patiently labouring at his absurd but fruitful conceptions."

18. Ezra Pound and the Light of France

I

POUND'S CONVICTION THAT FROM 1830 TO ABOUT 1910 virtually all technical growth in the art of writing took place in France, and his consequent forcing of Stendhal, Flaubert, Laforgue, Rimbaud, and Corbière on the attention of people who imagined that writing had reached an apex in Keats, has obscured the nature—not the fact—of his debt to the French tradition. It is natural to look for the antecedents of a modern among the near-moderns, natural to forget that the poet can stand to the past in a relation other than that of twig to trunk, that one of his most significant creative acts may be his choice of material to learn from.

One becomes obsessed by chronology in scholarly absorption with minor works; the second-rate is precisely that which demands for its elucidation a knowledge of the style of the period. All literatures pass their time developing what was done yesterday, modifying one "period" style into another. Once in a while this process, the concern of the literary historian, gets interrupted when someone rediscovers a classic as contemporary matter. Pound's whole critical sense is built on his perception that there are works that break free from "period," and qualities of mind that endure and can recur. Homer is a contemporary; he can be picked up and read as such. Much of Conrad is already old-fashioned.

263

Villon has been so rediscovered a number of times. The fact that Swinburne put him into Swinburnics shows that Swinburne was able to feel at home with him, just as Pope's Homer shows that Pope was capable of reading Homer not as a Greek but as an Augustan. Pope learned a great deal from Homer. His "original" work improves as he works at the translation. The *Dunciad* would have been impossible without it.

Pound too has learned from such masterworks, but his work also exhibits learning of a less often recognized kind: learning from the whole quality of mind displayed by a nation or an age, a quality not always located in single works. His problem, in 1910 or shortly thereafter, was to break free from Rossetti, "the nineties," and the opalescent word. His realization that the France of the Enlightenment afforded the condition for such a break was a creative discovery. It has, in retrospect, the air of inevitability, as creative acts always have. If Pound's Enlightenment, with its stress on Bayle, Voltaire, a few historians, and the antecedents of Revolutionary America, is not precisely that of the eighteenth-century specialist, that is because of the sharp selection and re-emphasis incident to solving a poetic problem located two centuries later.

II

One doesn't "learn" by acquiring other people's tricks with language. Pound made the distinction in a 1913 letter to Harriet Monroe:

. . . there are few enough people who know anything beyond Verlaine and Baudelaire—neither of whom is the least use—pedagogically, I mean. They beget imitation and one can learn nothing from them. Whereas Gautier and de Gourmont carry forward the art itself, and the only way one can imitate them is by making more profound your knowledge of the very marrow of art.

This juxtaposition of two poets with detachable mannerisms and two poets who "carry forward the art itself" defines the criterion by which Pound has always picked masters. It should be considered along with another formulation: "I revere good sense much more than originality."

The carrying forward of the art itself can be performed only in a climate of "good sense." An artist's mannerisms are excrescences of his personality or his period; the Verlaine or Baudelaire whose very center is a mannerism of the sensibility is, however genuine, the most dangerous of models. You can learn nothing from Verlaine except how to be Verlaine. James Joyce learned from him, because he wanted to become, partly, a Verlaine; it was the best way of installing himself in the central sensibility of a Dublin not unlike Verlaine's Paris. Joyce was to devote a patient lifetime to illuminating his subject from within. That wasn't the way Pound wanted to work. The nineteenth century into which he was born was merely his countersubject; his subject—the subject of the *Cantos*—is the light of the intelligence itself: *il ben dell' intelletto*. It was the "good sense" of the eighteenth century that drew him.

That is why he concluded a hugely admiring 1918 essay on Henry James by juxtaposing Remy de Gourmont. "On no occasion would any man of my generation have broached an intimate idea to H.J., or to Thomas Hardy, O.M., or, years since, to Swinburne, or even to Mr. Yeats with any feeling that the said idea was likely to be received, grasped, comprehended. . . . You could, on the other hand, have said to Gourmont anything that came into your head; you could have sent him anything you had written with a reasonable assurance that he would have known what you were driving at." James' interests stopped with the world in which he was placed:

> He has left his scene and his characters, unalterable as the little paper flowers permanently visible inside the lumpy glass paperweights. He was a great man of letters, a great artist in portrayal; he was concerned with mental temperaments, circumvolvulous social pressures, the clash of contending conventions, as Hogarth with the cut of contemporary coats.

De Gourmont, on the other hand, "an artist of the nude," "differentiates his characters by the modus of their sensibility, not by sub-degrees of their state of civilization."

> He was intensely aware of the differences of emotional timbre; and as a man's message is precisely his *façon de voir,* his modality of apperception, this particular awareness was his "message.". . . Emotions, to Henry James, were more or less things that other people had and that one didn't go into; at any rate not in drawing-rooms.

The appeal of de Gourmont to Pound's imagination is a critical fact, independent of what the mid-twentieth-century reader may or may not find in de Gourmont. In Pound's mind de Gourmont confronted Henry James, Henry James gravely recording with infinite tact and subtlety the externals of a civilization that had become obsessed with externals, Henry James carrying on in his own way the work of Flaubert. Henry James and Flaubert immersed themselves in the externals of nineteenth-century civilization and underwent its limitations in order to do what could be done toward rendering it intelligible. The nineteenth century was a perfect case of a time in which "period" followed "period," and very little work broke loose into self-sufficiency:

> . . . a limitless darkness: there was the counter-reformation, still extant in the English printer; there was the restoration of the Inquisition by the Catholic Roman Church, holy and apostolic, in the year of grace 1824; there was the Mephistopheles period, morals of the opera left over from the Spanish seventeenth century plays of *capa y espada;* Don Juan for subject-matter, etc.; there was the period of English Christian bigotry, Sam Smiles, exhibition of 1851 ("Centennial of 1876"), machine-made building "ornament"; there was the Emerson-Tennysonian plus optimism period; there was the "aesthetic" era during which people "wrought" as the impeccable Beerbohm has noted; there was the period of funny symboliste trappings, "sin," satanism, rosy cross, heavy lilies, Jersey Lilies, etc.,
>   "Ch' hanno perduto il ben dell' intelletto";

all these periods had mislaid the light of the eighteenth century. . . .

III

"The light of the eighteenth century" wasn't that of Dante, "the radiant world where one thought cuts through another with a clean edge, a world of moving energies . . . the glass under water, the form that seems a form seen in a mirror." It was a light of the less passionate intelligence, characterized by prose that stuck close to meaning. The Enlightenment was capable of discovering Confucius and not considering him quaint, as Butcher and Lang were to consider Homer Biblical. It valued the mind, was sufficiently skeptical of the passions to undercut adolescent excess, and had an appetite for facts.

European litterati
having heard that the Chinese rites honour Kung-fu-tseu
and offer sacrifice to the Heaven etc/
and that their ceremonies are grounded in reason
now beg to know their true meaning and in particular
the meaning of terms for example Material
Heaven and Changti meaning? its ruler?
Does the manes of Confucius
accept the grain, fruit, silk, incense offered
        and does he enter his cartouche?
The European church wallahs wonder if this can be
        reconciled.   [Canto LX]

There is irony in Pound's use of this document, but its author (A.D. 1699) hadn't a tourist's concern with the externals of Chinese ritual to the exclusion of respectful curiosity about its rationale. Nor were the writers of that era occupied with the words on the page to the exclusion of the light held in the mind.

England had no Enlightenment; it had the Royal Society and an Augustan Age. It underwent Queen Anne and the Georges while France was preparing the civic ideas that informed Jefferson's mind. To Pound, Milton seemed in the realm of language a cause of this duncery, in other realms a symptom. The mind wasn't functioning when Milton wrote

> . . . the setting sun
> Descended . . . (!)

and his language is entoiled in sonorities, opacities, inversions, allusions, merely linguistic accidentals not controlled by the thing seen in the mind:

> Sporting the Lion rampd, and in his paw
> Dandl'd the Kid; . . . th' unwieldy Elephant
> To make them mirth us'd all his might, & wreathd
> His Lithe Proboscis. . . .

Nineteenth-century poetry had the ill-fortune to branch forth just at this point of decay. To bypass this withering branch altogether and build a new English speech as though in an eighteenth century without Milton behind it was Pound's crucial enterprise. That was what he undertook in his *Lustra* volume (1915). *Lustra*'s roots are in Martial's Rome, via France. It abounds in classical themes and analogies, but its classicizing is purged of Renaissance magniloquence and Miltonic-Victorian sonority. The characteristic *Lustra* poems would translate readily into French, and have the air of having been translated out of it. The French eighteenth century is behind this scrap from the Greek Anthology:

> Woman? Oh, woman is a consummate rage,
>   but dead, or asleep, she pleases.
> Take her. She has two excellent seasons.

This expanded epigram, "Phyllidula and the Spoils of Gouvernet," appears in a brief sequence headed "Impressions of François-Marie Arouet (de Voltaire)":

Where, Lady, are the days
When you could go out in a hired hansom
Without footmen and equipments?
And dine in a soggy, cheap restaurant?
Phyllidula now, with your powdered Swiss footman
Clanking the door shut,
        and lying;
And carpets from Savonnier, and from Persia,
And your new service at dinner,
And plates from Germain,
And cabinets and chests from Martin (almost lacquer),
And your white vases from Japan,
And the lustre of diamonds,
Etcetera, etcetera, and etcetera?

Phyllidula is getting overwhelmed by opaque *things;* the Enlightenment could often accept expensive elegance in a playful spirit, and it sustained intellects which could perform an ironic dissociation between James's civilization and de Gourmont's. Furthermore, Voltaire's name may remind us, the Enlightenment connotes a strong civic sense; the man of letters had a conception of his own public

utility which bourgeois England never encouraged
and the nineteenth century utterly lost. Pope had it;
he got it from France. Voltaire "at WORK, shovel-
ling out the garbage, the Bourbons, the really filthy
decayed state of French social thought" is emulated
in the epigraph to *Lustra*:

> DEFINITION: LUSTRUM: an offering for the sins
> of the whole people, made by the censors at the expira-
> tion of their five years of office. . . .

In Canto XIII,

> Kung raised his cane against Yuan Jang,
>   Yuan Jang being his elder,
> For Yuan Jang sat by the roadside pretending to
>   be receiving wisdom.
> And Kung said
>   "You old fool, come out of it,
> Get up and do something useful."

The next words—

>   And Kung said,
>   "Respect a child's faculties
>   "From the moment it inhales the clear air,
>   "But a man of fifty who knows nothing
>   Is worthy of no respect"

—chime with the Encyclopaedia and with Rousseau.
Indeed, the Kung of Canto XIII is coming to us via
the French tradition, as he came first to Europe. The
Canto is an eighteenth-century rather than a Chinese
pastiche; the diction is elegant, supple, ironic—

> And even I can remember
> A day when the historians left blanks in their writings,

I mean for things they didn't know,
But that time seems to be passing. . . .

The words and tone of this Canto lean heavily on Pauthier's, whose vision of Confucius as a great gentleman can be glimpsed from a charming phrase marginally conserved by Pound in his 1950 version of the *Analects*: *"ses manières étaient douces et persuasives! Que son air était affable et prévenant!"*

Not only Confucius but the whole civilization of China, the China from which Pound derives his ethical positives, came to the West via France. The Enlightenment was able to transmit this knowledge because it was in sympathy with it. ("The only religious teacher who didn't claim to be divinely inspired," said Voltaire of Kung.) The missionaries of the early 1700s found an emperor to their taste:

                              Set up board of translators
Verbiest, mathematics
Pereira professor of music, a treatise in chinese and
    manchu
    . . . revised by the emperor as to questions of style
A digest of philosophy (manchu) and current
Reports on the mémoires des académies
des sciences de Paris.
Quinine, a laboratory set up in the palace.
He ordered 'em to prepare a total anatomy, et
qu'ils veillèrent à la pureté du langage
et qu'on n'employât que des termes propres
                    (Namely CH'ing Ming)   [Canto LX]

In fact the *Histoire Générale de la Chine*[1] from

---

[1] *Histoire Générale de la Chine, ou Annales de cet Empire,* traduites du Tong-Kien-Kang-Mou, par le feu père Joseph Anne-Marie de Moyriac de Mailla, Paris, 1777–83, 12 vols.

which Cantos LII–LXI are drawn is so far from mere
antiquarianism, its author is so absorbed in the
cogency of what he is setting down, that Pound can
blend bits of the French into his English text without a jar. One can imagine the eighteenth-century
reality on which père Moyriac had his eye as he set
down the words Pound renders in Canto LIV:

and the country was run by Yang Siun
while the emperor amused himself in his park
   had a light car made, harnessed to sheep
The sheep chose which picnic he went to,
ended his days as a gourmet. Said Tching, tartar:
   Are not all of his protégés flatterers?
   How can his country keep peace?
And the prince Imperial went into the cabaret business
   and read Lao Tse.

It is the laconic common sense of the great Emperors that emerges most memorably from the chronicle; one can see why the Enlightenment displayed
a connoisseurship of their sayings, and why the publication by subscription of the *Histoire* was a public
event.

If the Chinese material of *The Pisan Cantos* displays less urbanity of surface, and a sense of *mys-
terium* the Enlightenment was incapable of transmitting—

in the light of light is the *virtù*
"sunt lumina" said Erigena Scotus
   as of Shun on Mt Taishan

—still this new vision, attained by contact with the
Chinese text without French mediation, never slides

into the mere rapturously poetic; the solid eighteenth-century criterion of social relevance remains:

> and in the hall of the forebears
>   as from the beginning of wonders
> the paraclete that was present in Yao, the precision
> in Shun the compassionate
> in Yu the guider of waters.

IV

A paradigm of the ability to savor wisdom in particular sayings and actions, to conduct a life of the
mind that could work through circumstance without
entanglement therein, was what Pound found in the
France of the eighteenth century. He didn't, need-
less to say, find there an ideal civilization; but he
found a standpoint in sympathy with the modern
world, yet outside the nineteenth century, and a
prose language unclotted with merely decorative
rhetoric. On this language he was able to base a
verse without Milton and a prose without Pater. It
was about 1915, the year of the *Lustra* volume, when
he had discovered the eighteenth century, that he
was able to begin meditating the *Cantos*. The first
thirty Cantos build toward the America that was
rooted in Leopoldine Tuscany and Enlightened
France; one of the most dramatic structural breaks
in the poem is the irruption, with Canto XXXI, of
Jeffersonian prose into Renaissance rhetoric.

"The light of the eighteenth century," however,
gave him something more than a language of elegant
urbanity. It revealed to him the clue to history that
organizes the *Cantos*, the principle toward which he

had been reaching when he first noted the nature of the contrast between James and de Gourmont, "the little paper flowers permanently visible inside the lumpy glass paperweights" and "characters differentiated by their modus of sensibility." A pseudo-civilization, as Voltaire saw, supervenes when a Phyllidula surrounds herself with

> cabinets and chests from Martin (almost lacquer)
> And your white vases from Japan,
> And the lustre of diamonds,
> Etcetera, etcetera, and etcetera.

It was such a "civilization" that Henry James took for granted. Its tokens are *things*, "clutter, the bane of men moving"; its touchstone is the multiplication of things.

> With our eyes on the new gothic residence, with our
> eyes on Palladio, with a desire for seignieurial
> splendours
> (AGALMA, haberdashery, clocks, ormoulu, brocatelli,
> tapestries, unreadable volumes bound in tree-calf,
> half-morocco, morocco, tooled edges, green ribbons,
> flaps, farthingales, fichus, cuties, shorties, pinkies
> et cetera
>   Out of which things seeking an exit
>   [Canto XL]

The exit is into a Carthaginian voyage, a duplicate of Odysseus' expiation of the sack of Troy.

The nineteenth century with its multiplied bric-a-brac Pound came to regard as something more than a tract of time uncongenial to his temperament. It acquired a rationale; it was "the age of usury" par excellence. Usury in Pound's poetry means the assumption that money is wealth, that the coin in the hand (or, in letters, the word on the page) is the supreme reality, that gold breeds; that crops and herds are mere economic abstractions, that human beings are "labour," that natural increase, the breeding of sheep, the fruition of grain, are the secondary, not the primary, manifestations of economic power. It means inability to see through the symbol to the reality, to see through the tool to its use, to see through conveniences and elegance to civilized living, *il ben dell' intelletto.*

It was by way of the Enlightenment's respect for common-sense facts that Pound arrived at his diagnosis of history. The familiar Enlightenment epigrams, like *"En pareil cas, il n'y a que le premier pas qui coûte,"* exemplify something more than "wit": their principle is the ability of reason to see through facts to their essential dynamics. The effect is witty because this penetration is unexpectedly juxtaposed with the données; it is shocking or blasphemous only *per accidens.* Canto LIV contains the anecdote of the minister Lou-kia and the know-nothing Emperor. The minister (B.C. 202) wanted the seminal books restored;

to whom KAO: I conquered the empire on horseback.
to whom Lou: Can you govern it in that manner?

This isn't a wisecrack but a mind unimpeded by military swagger perceiving the nature of government. It isn't snobbish; it doesn't imply that the empire could have been conquered from a library.

Pound's analogous act of penetration was his choice of gold as a controlling symbol. The nineteenth century chose the machine. Incapable of seeing that the object of work is production of "goods that are needed and wanted," its poets and rhetoricians characteristically saw the machine only as a monster that put people out of work. The counter-symbol to the machine was Wordsworthian "nature" and Ruskin's handicraft economy. By 1910 the tradition of decorous English verse had undergone forty mutations of landscape-painting and was virtually bankrupt. This, it seemed to Pound from his vantage-point outside the nineteenth century, was because the perception underlying the original choice of symbols, machine vs. nature, was sentimental. It wasn't a perception of what machines are for or what labour is for. Poetry depends on the mind, though it isn't written by calculation. Even derivative poetry stands when it derives from someone's use of the mind. The eighteenth-century minds that dissociated elegant surroundings from civilization aided Pound in his dissociation between gold as a metal with certain uses,

> (None learneth to weave gold in her pattern)
> [Canto XLV]

gold as ornament implying Rembrandtian darkness circumvolvent

> (In the gloom the gold
> Gathers the light about it) [Canto XVII]

gold as a mere token of opulence

(And his wife that would touch food but with forks
Sed aureis forculis, that is
                with small golden prongs
Bringing in, thus, the vice of luxuria)   [Canto XXVI]

gold as a rhetorical epithet

(The whole fortune of
MacNarpen and Company is founded
Upon Palgrave's Golden Treasury)   [Canto XXII]

and hence gold as the norm of wealth, used against
reason to back credit the true basis of which is

                the abundance of nature
with the whole folk behind it.   [Canto LII]

The nineteenth century could not see beyond gold;
could not carry its sense of language beyond Tennyson's aureate word, its economic thought beyond
wages and the gold standard, its architectural sense
beyond ornamentation, or its sense of civilization
beyond elegant manners amid parlor bric-a-brac: the
paper flowers in the glass paperweights of the scru-
pulously observant Henry James.

That is the meaning of Pound's usury-axis; he continues to insist that literal usury coexists with this
state of mind, but it is on the mind, not the mere
economic arrangements, that his poetic focus rests.
The mental climate in which he was able to achieve
this focus and so bring his work out of cultured dilet-
tantism is the greatest of his debts to France. It is
royally paid in the gold of the eighty-first Canto, a
gold of the mind, refined by mental passion ("the
rest is dross"), unstealable, beyond counterfeit, a

heritage which no government can confiscate, no booby receive, and no heir squander:

> What thou lovest well remains,
>   the rest is dross
> What thou lov'st well shall not be reft from thee
> What thou lov'st well is thy true heritage
> Whose world, or mine or theirs
>   or is it of none?
> First came the seen, then thus the palpable
> Elysium, though it were in the halls of hell,
> What thou lovest well is thy true heritage. . . .

This final poetry is no longer close to French. It is rooted in English idiom; it would, one imagines, defy a translator. Between the Renaissance and the twentieth century it was France that kept in being the mental world in which such work could be conceived. Via *Lustra* and much later work prolonging the tone of *Lustra*, Pound so formed his mind as to be able triumphantly to conceive it.

19. Under the Larches of Paradise

R*ock-drill,* POUND'S FIRST POST-PISAN SEQUENCE, opens with a Canto that defies the elocutionist; it is written for the printed page, as it were for stone tablets. The hundred or so ideograms sound more richly to the eye than to the ear (even when their pronunciation is indicated), and evidently concentrate the meaning rather than decorate it. The metric, furthermore, has acquired some wholly new component, possibly from the Chinese Odes with which the author has been much occupied in recent years:

> Y Yin sent the young king into seclusion
> by T'ang Tomb to think things over. . . .

—this isn't one of the Greek meters salted with an abnormal proportion of long syllables; its nature rather is to isolate *each* of the words so that we have not primarily "lines" diversified with a pattern of stresses but a succession of unshakeable terms. The Greek meters, for that matter, developed in a language abounding in particles, modifiers, syntactic bric-a-brac: they presume that only every third word or so is of overwhelming importance:

> When the HOUNDS of SPRING are
> on WINTER'S TRACES

—five inessential (though not unnecessary) words out of nine. How much these metrical traditions

have perverted the agglutinative nature of English
it is vain to inquire, though Dr. Williams has no
doubt an opinion. For one reason or another, at any
rate, writers of English verse haven't much tried
doing without nonfunctioning syllables. For the
gnomic convention of Canto 85, however, an attempt
to make English profit by the Chinese indifference
to syntactic apparatus is highly relevant:

> no mere epitome without organization

—such a line isn't prose but a metric sophisticated
on new principles, the grammar-school notion of a
"foot" abandoned, greater deliberateness before the
caesura poised against greater suaveness after it, and
no word present solely for grammar's sake. So with

> Awareness restful & fake is fatiguing.

—which does not end with three dactyls; the words
space out. It is worth exhibiting these devices in a
passage of some length:

> . . . in rites not flame-headed.
>   "Up to then, I just hadn't caught on."
>   chung
>   wang
>   hsien
>   said KAO TSOUNG
> Imperator. Sicut vinum ac mustum
>   brew up this directio, tchéu,
> fermentum et germina,
>   study with the mind of a grandson
>   and watch the time like a hawk
>   taó tsi

```
½ research        and    ½ Techne
½ observation,            ½ Techne
½ training,               ½ Techne
            Tch'eng T'ang for guide.
```

That one gets things done by working ("not serendipity") and writes—or should—at the prompting of
something to be said ("Sagetrieb") are among the
themes of the Canto; it is his wrestling with a subject that keeps Mr. Pound athletic.

So the great work draws toward its close, with
undiminished élan:

> that the body of light come forth
> > from the body of fire
> And that your eyes come to the surface
> > from the deep wherein they were sunken,
> Reina—for 300 years,
> > and now sunken
> That your eyes come forth from their caves
> > & light then
> > > as the holly leaf . . .

There can be no doubt that the author of *Rock-Drill*
is at the height of his powers; in those majestic, assured rhythms inheres a new elation proper to the
region the poem has now entered. The old themes
are recapitulated with new power; the aphorisms
vibrate on the target—

> Awareness restful & fake is fatiguing.

*   *   *

> study with the mind of a grandson
> and watch the time like a hawk

*   *   *

The pusillanimous
wanting all men cut down to worm-size.

Beginning with Canto 90, some forty pages of un-
faltering lyric brilliance initiate us into the realm of
"the values that endure like the sea," a hundred
startling motifs arrayed like fireflies around a the-
ological armature.

Their coherence is easily indicated from the passage first quoted. The reader of the *Cantos* has encountered Aphrodite's eyes many times—

Your eyen two wol sleye me sodenly
[Canto 81]

—and been told of their immersion in the accidental
postures of matter—

all that Sandro knew, and Jacopo
and that Velásquez never suspected
lost in the brown meat of Rembrandt
and the raw meat of Rubens and Jordaens . . .
[Canto 80]

The beauty inheres in the "meat," but the meat oc-
cludes our sight:

"This alone, leather and bones between you and τὸ πᾶν"

When the body of light comes forth from the body
of fire, the permanent disengages itself with finality
from the casual: not, since it remains a *body* of
light, by some academic extraction of essences, but
by a process akin to revelation, prepared by Love.

Love, gone as lightning,
enduring 5000 years.

The new Cantos abound in such phrases, holding in
tension the transient and the inextinguishable, and
always having something to do with Light. That the
light-philosophers, Erigena, Avicenna, Richard St.
Victor, inhabit Pound's pantheon we have known
since the Pisan sequence; but there the ideograph
for "the sun's cord unspotted" did duty as synec-
doche for a process of irradiation now brilliantly
displayed. So we are told how

> The waves rise, and the waves fall
> But you are like the moon-light:
> >   Always there!

Light endures, and the sea endures; but the visible
part of the sea is a turmoil. Elsewhere the enduring
substantial luminousness, the crystal sphere, enters
this context—

> & from fire to crystal
> via the body of light . . .

Or again,

> Crystal waves weaving together toward the gt/healing
> Light *compenetrans* of the spirits
> The Princess Ra-Set has climbed
> >   to the great knees of stone,
> She enters protection,
> >   the great cloud is about her,
> She has entered the protection of crystal
> >   convien che si mova
> >   la mente, amando

The crystal links itself with a recurring phrase,

> The light there almost solid,

and late in the last Canto of the sequence the whole
complex is joined with a now permanent sea:

> That the crystal wave mount to flood-surge . . .
> The light there almost solid.

This is a permanence that contains and requires all
orderly movement, not an arrest nor, we are explicitly told, a stasis; and in the Poundian Paradiso
all movement is both orderly and free.

The precision of natural renewal has replaced the
cut stone of the early Cantos:

> The clover enduring,
>   basalt crumbled with time.
> "Are they the same leaves?"
>   that was an intelligent question.

For one of the purposes of the poem, they are the
same leaves; since the form persists, a mode of intelligence informing, as Agassiz would have said, the
vegetable order. The visible is a signature of the
invisible, notarized by, for instance, a seventeenth-
century Neoplatonist, "Secretary of Nature, J. Hey-
don."

>   "We have", said Mencius, "but phenomena."
> monumenta. In nature are signatures
>   needing no verbal tradition,
> oak leaf never plane leaf. John Heydon.

Such motifs reach far back into the *Cantos*, the
large-scale structure of which becomes more clear
and massive as we get more and more of it. From
the very beginning of his career, Pound's work has
been polarized by two implicit themes: the hero in

rebellious exile, and the emergence of order from chaos: respectively, the story of Odysseus, and the story of Aphrodite born from the sea. The Odysseus figure specifies and generalizes all Pound's wandering or proscribed or forgotten or embattled heroes: the troubadours, Dante and Ovid the exiled poets, Fenollosa and Dolmetsch ignored by specialists, Frobenius with limitless curiosity traveling through Africa, Agassiz dumped by the evolutionists, Douglas and Gesell, Sigismundo, Mussolini: every one the object at some time of a campaign of vilification, or a conspiracy of silence. Aphrodite we glimpse whenever the work breaks through into lyric, or forms half-congeal in the waves, or eyes pierce the mist, or some flux of events locks into an intelligible pattern. Because she comes from the sea, Pound welcomes into his epic the look of chaos, for the sake of its potentialities of order; "points define a periphery"; the entire work is a seeming flux amid which Odysseus voyages and out of which, at the very least, a tone, a shape, a personality emerges. Out of the endless interaction of these two myths comes the scenario of the *Cantos*. Canto 1 gives us Odysseus visiting the dead; Canto 2, Aphrodite's sea, with forms in it, and a metamorphosis that uses the mutability of matter to suggest the permanence of the intelligible species. The Pisan Cantos commence with a formal reprise: paralleling Canto 1, Canto 74 abounds in references to a beached Odysseus, while paralleling Canto 2, Canto 75 presents via Jannequin's bird-music a sequence of metamorphoses in which the form of a natural beauty—like the signature of the oak leaves—persists indestructible.

The Rock-Drill sequence in turn opens with a reprise of the structure of the China-Adams sequence, Cantos 52–71. In the first Rock-Drill Canto, 85, we are given the parallel with 52–61, the moral essentials of Chinese history, blended, through Cantos 86 and 87, into contemporary analogies and contrasts. In the second Rock-Drill section, Cantos 88 and 89, we have the American application, the struggle of Jackson and Senator Benton against the usurious Bank of the United States: a structural parallel with 62–71 (Adams as Chinese Emperor), and a thematic explication of 37 (the Bank War). Near the end of *Rock-Drill*, Odysseus and the girl from the waves reappear, transfigured. Odysseus, transposed to a plane of sensibility where cunning and heroics are irrelevant, moves through the latter part of Canto 94 as Apollonius of Tyana, who slaughtered no beast, wandered through India, Egypt, and Asia Minor teaching and learning, held parley with the shade of Achilles without having to visit Hades and feed it blood, and (like Pound) was laid under indictment in the capital of the world. As for the figure out of the flux, she is this time the sea-nymph Leucothea, who rescued Odysseus when his raft was overwhelmed (*Odyssey* V: 333) and with her magical veil ("my bikini is worth yr/raft") enabled him to reach Phaeacia. She has a greater sense of utility than one can read in the eyes of Botticelli's Aphrodite; she is also, we are reminded several times, *Kadmou thugater*, daughter of Cadmus who invented the alphabet, and bears analogy to the poetry of the *Cantos*, no vendable objet d'art but a force serviceable to storm-tossed author and reader alike.

The *Cantos* generally rise into independence of their sources, but page references at three points in *Rock-Drill* direct our attention explicitly to three books laid under systematic contribution: Couvreur's *Chou King*, from which the ideograms come; Benton's *Thirty Years' View*, for the account of American government; and Philostratus' *Life of Apollonius*, the record of the least fanatical and most percipient of sages. The first is moral, the second historical and practical, the third spiritual.[1]

After salvaging a few introductory phrases, Pound generally starts his systematic dealings with a source book about a third of the way in. The references to the *Chou King* or History Classic begin in the fourth chapter of Part III with the teachings of the minister Y Yin, and utilize all the rest of the book in order. Pound echoes all of Couvreur's apparatus: Chinese text, transliterations, French version, Latin version, footnotes identifying and dating Emperors, so borrowing from this plenitude of scholarly reverberation a sense of copiousness to furnish the brief space

[1] The *Thirty Years' View* hasn't been reprinted for nearly a century, though the Benton volume in the Square Dollar Series contains much of the relevant material. The Chinese references are to the History Classic, *Chou King*, edited by S. Couvreur, S.J., printed in China; my page references are to the 4th edition, 1934. The Coneybeare translation of Philostratus' *Life of Apollonius of Tyana* is in the Loeb series.

allotted in the poem. "Birds and terrapin lived under Hia," is the first item in his systematic summary:

> beast and fish held their order
> Neither flood nor flame falling in excess"

We are on page 114 of Couvreur; immediately a column of Chinese sounds, "i moua pou gning," lures us to the source book, where we find "and no one not contented." The Bill of Rights passage refers us to page 131 of Couvreur: "If one person lacks freedom to do good, the ruler will have one auxiliary the less, and his work will be incomplete." Throughout Canto 85 the reduplicated ideograms reiterate an active *senso morale;* the handsome "ling" with which the volume opens—

> Our dynasty came in because of a great sensibility

—is defined in Mathews' dictionary (No. 4071) as "the spirit of a being which acts upon others," with the sub-entry "intelligent," but in Couvreur's glossary as "Intelligent; bon; âme d'un défunt"; while in the *Chou King* text it is repeatedly used to denote the Emperor's "feel of the people." Pound's word, "sensibility," gradually irradiates its context with all these meanings.[2] The "hsien form" at the bottom of the first page (Mathews 2671) has a heart in the upper right corner and moving legs beneath: virtue is active. The "luminous eye" on page 89 also has

[2] His mode of generalizing and compressing may be gauged from the fact that the opening line of the Canto is based on a verse which Couvreur (p. 285) renders thus: "Les empereurs de notre maison de Tcheou (Wenn Wang et Ou wang), à cause de leur grande bonté, furent chargés d'exécuter l'oeuvre du roi du ciel." "Our dynasty came in because of a great sensibility."

legs; and the presence of legs explains why *chen* (a designation of virtue, p. 61) is "beyond ataraxia," the Greek word for freedom from passion.

Tê on pages 6 and 8 (Mathews 6162) has the prefix denoting action (man in two positions) and the "heart" component at its base. Mathews defines it as "practice of truth and acquisition thereof in the heart." The chronicle of its involvement with the themes of the *Cantos* is characteristic of Pound's intentions. On pages 5–6 we read:

Perspicax qui excolit se ipsum,
Their writings wither because they have no curiosity,
This "leader", gouged pumpkin
       that they hoist on a pole,
But if you will follow this process

. . . here the *tê* sign occurs, its form suggesting a forward motion of which the pumpkin-procession is a ghastly parody. On page 8, the ideogram recurs in connection with the function of the genuine leader:

Not serendipity
    but to spread
      tê thru the people.

These two passages distill the context of the salient occurrence of *tê* in the *Chou King* (p. 123), where Couvreur has, "Qui excolit se ipsum et vera virtute concordat sum subditis, est perspicax rex," alternatively, "Un prince intelligent se perfectionne lui-même, et pratique la virtue sincèrement avec ses sujets." But Pound isn't quite through with the ideogram; much later he recalls it in a context of natural history (p. 34):

> As the water-bug casts a flower on stone
> > nel botro
> One interaction. Tê   interaction. A shadow?

—the interaction between heaven, prince, and people paralleled by that between the descent of light, the refractive processes of dented water, and the substantiality of the water-bug, which results in a radiant unforeseeable entity, the spectral flower on the stone. This metaphysical image effects a blending of the moral ambience of the *tê* ideogram with the motifs of the Paradiso proper in the latter half of the book.

Such a process of moral circulation, starting with the ruler's "sensibility" and effecting the dissemination of "*tê* thru the people," is once more tied tightly to the Paradiso sequence on the first page of Canto 90:

> Templum aedificans, not yet marble,
> > "Amphion!"
> And from the San Ku
> > to the room in Poitiers where one can stand
> > > casting no shadow,
> That is Sagetrieb,
> > > that is tradition.
> Builders had kept the proportion,
> > did Jacques de Molay
> > > know these proportions?
> and was Erigena ours? . . .

The San Ku (the ideograms mean "Three Alone") was a council of three established by Tch'eng Wang

in the Tcheou dynasty, inferior but not subordinate
to the grand preceptor, grand master, and grand
guardian. (The quasi-masonic terminology suggests
one link with Jacques de Molay.) Their function
was to "étendre partout la réforme, s'appliquant
avec respect à faire briller l'action du ciel et de la
terre" (Couvreur, p. 333). "Faire briller" reaches
forward to Erigena with his "omnia quae sunt lumina sunt," and out to the irradiated room in Poi-
tiers, or the temple, not marble, which Amphion is
to build with music. Nor is this a nest of bright associations, but the profile of a forward drive in time:
"Sagetrieb," etymologically word-drive, the urge to
say something, denominates a tradition backed by
energy, thrust forward and sustaining the builders
who "kept the proportion."

Benton maintained this tradition; his speeches in
the Senate, as recorded in his *Thirty Years' View*,
are steadily urgent and steadily enlightening, with
neither quality sacrificed to the other. His great
speech of February 1831 against the renewal of the
Bank's charter loses none of its momentum or precision in Pound's summary on pages 46–47; its ordonnance is attested to by the fact that Pound is
mainly using the head-phrases of Benton's paragraphs:

> . . . Such
> a bank tends to subjugate government;
> It tends to collusions,
> to borrow 50 and pay back one hundred,
> It tends to create public DEBT.

1694: Loan One Million 200,000
         Interest 80,000, Expenses 4.
GERM, nucleus, and is now 900 Million.
It tends to beget and prolong useless wars;
    aggravate inequalities; make and break fortunes. . . .

There was a time when the Senate could expect and
would listen to serious arguments whose eloquence
survives a century and has the utmost contemporary
relevance. Benton provides Pound with a powerful
summary of the Jackson-Van Buren Cantos, as well
as with a measuring-rod for the contemporary presi-
dent who would listen to nothing:

> "Don't write me any more things to tell him
>   (scripsit Woodward, W. E.)
> "on these occasions
>   HE
>   talks." (End quote)

This great block of material shores up the lyric
Paradiso which commences with Canto 90 and in
turn sustains the narrative of Apollonius of Tyana
(Canto 94).

The Apollonius sequence rhymes with the voyage
of Odysseus to the underworld in Canto 1 and the
Carthaginian voyage down the west coast of Africa
in Canto 40; except that, whereas Odysseus did
magical rites to compel the shades, and the Cartha-
ginians went as tourists after marvels, "seeking an
exit" from a commercial civilization from which they
didn't really dissociate themselves (their heroism
was a buccaneer's virtue, and they brought back

the skins of three "folk hairy and savage/whom our Lixtae said were Gorillas"), Apollonius journeyed into India and Egypt to parley peaceably with sages. He taught, and was taught, "that the universe is alive, ἔρωτά ἴσχει" ("possessed by a love that knits it together"), and Pound records the Greek of his fine leave-taking of the Indian host who conducted him back out of the interior: "You have presented me with the sea; farewell." On the next page comes the explicit parallel with Canto 1, "And then went down to the ship":

> ἐπὶ τὴν ναῦν ἑσπέρας ἦζη
>   embarking at sunset
> That he passed the night on the mound of Achilles
> "master of tempest and fire"
>   & he set up Palamedes[3]
> an image that I, Philostratus, saw
>   and a shrine that will hold ten people drinking.

We then hear in Apollonius' own words how the great shade appeared to him, and faded away:

> "It was not by ditch-digging and sheep's-guts . . .
>   "in Aeolis close to Methymna"
> in the summer lightning, close upon cock-crow.

Whereupon, to unite this interview with his Paradiso rather than with Odysseus' Underworld, Pound interpolates:

> So that walking here under the larches of Paradise
> the stream was exceedingly clear
>   & almost level its margin

[3] This memorial to a forgotten hero of the Trojan war parallels Odysseus' stele to Elpenor, "man of no fortune and with a name to come."

Though "Man is under Fortuna," Apollonius moves exempt from calamity:

> for the doers of holiness
> γῆν μεν πᾶσαν ἀσφαλή[4]
> they may ship or swim, being secure.

He is the personification of the moral precept on the second page of the book:

> Not led of lusting, not of contriving
>   but is as the grass and tree
> eccellenza
>   not led of lusting,
>   not of the worm, contriving

He also was interviewed by Vespasian, and spoke of the rightness of the latter's intention to seize absolute power, in the circumstances that then obtained (this is the V: 35 which Pound notes is worth attention); but, being no doctrinaire monarchist, indeed, "not particular about theoretical organizations," he later sent Vespasian a letter of rebuke when the latter, enslaving the Hellenes, "did not show good sense in Greece."

Like the *Chou King* and the *Thirty Years' View*, the Philostratus *Life of Apollonius* is worth reading. Long proscribed by the Christians, it is one more of the neglected books to which the *Cantos* have drawn attention. Primary sources are always the richest. Pound has looked into the 1901 *Apollonius of Tyana* of his old acquaintance G. R. S. Mead, and used just two details, the accentuation of Týana and the romantic fact that the Empress Julia Domna who

---

[4] "The whole earth affords secure ground."

commissioned Philostratus' work was the "daughter
of a sun priest in Babylon," but otherwise he has
stuck to Philostratus' text, mainly Books III–V, ex-
tracting nuggets like Apollonius' refutation of the
Greek maxim that "one penny begets another," or
the etymology of "Red Sea," or the tigers that wor-
ship the sun. In Canto 91 we find one anticipa-
tory glimpse from Book VIII-3; when Apollonius
went on trial before Domitian he was told he must
enter the court with nothing on him, meaning no
books or papers; and he replied with whimsical composure, "Is this a bath-house? Or a Court House?"
Pound's reference to this incident is folded around
a line from the *Odyssey* (V: 332) about the winds
playing shuttlecock with the hero's raft, and accompanied by a reminder that the sea-nymph made
Odysseus cast off the garments Calypso had given
him: "get rid of parapernalia."

"We think because we do not know"; all is para-
phernalia that does not at length float easily in the
mind; the mind at length having encompassed without strain what is necessary may dream of coming
to "that High City."

> "Ghosts dip in the crystal,
>   adorned"
> That the tone change from elegy
>   "Et Jehanne"
>   (the Lorraine girl)
> A lost kind of experience?
>   scarcely,
> O Queen Cytherea,
>   che 'l terzo ciel movete.

Index

Coleman Dowell Series

The Coleman Dowell series is made possible through a generous contribution by an anonymous donor. This endowed contribution allows Dalkey Archive Press to publish one book a year in this series.

Born in Kentucky in 1925, Coleman Dowell moved to New York in 1950 to work in theater and television as a playwright and composer/lyricist, but by age forty he turned to writing fiction. His works include *One of the Children is Crying* (1968), *Mrs. October Was Here* (1974), *Island People* (1976), *Too Much Flesh and Jabez* (1977), and *White on Black on White* (1983). After his death in 1985, *The Houses of Children: Collected Stories* was published in 1987, and his memoir about his theatrical years, *A Star-Bright Lie*, was published in 1993.

Since his death, a number of his books have been reissued in the United States, as well as translated for publication in other countries.